Pica Roman Type in Elizabethan England

Pica Roman Type in Elizabethan England

W. CRAIG FERGUSON

Scolar Press

First published in Great Britain in 1989 by
SCOLAR PRESS
Gower Publishing Company Limited
Gower House, Croft Road
Aldershot GU11 3HR

Gower Publishing Company
Old Post Road
Brookfield
Vermont 05036
USA

British Library Cataloguing in Publication Data
Ferguson, W. Craig
Pica Roman type in Elizabethan England.
1. Latin alphabet. Typefaces, 1558–1603
I. Title
686.2′17′09
ISBN 0–85967–718–4

Preface

Scholars have been too quick to abandon their efforts to identify the types used by Elizabethan printers. The differences among letter forms do exist, and do sort themselves out into recognizable patterns by which families of types can be identified and, within the families, individual founts and their owners singled out. The most widely used type face was roman, which during the second half of the sixteenth century replaced black letter as the standard face in English books. The most widely used size of type was pica or, in technical terms, twelve point, of which twenty lines measure about 82mm. or three-and-a-quarter inches. A sensible starting point seemed to be the early 1550s when punch-cutters first came to this country, and as a point at which to end 1610 was chosen, for soon after that date the shops were flooded with new Dutch faces which give an entirely different appearance to later seventeenth-century printing. It is the aim of this study to show the reader how the types of this one common size and face are differentiated, and then to show how this knowledge may be used to pursue the solutions to a number of problems facing the student of Elizabethan texts.

This study has engaged my attention for well over a decade, and during that time I have consulted various people. In particular, I have received valuable help from David Foxon, the late Harry Carter, and Nicolas Barker. I am grateful to Queen's University at Kingston for providing research funds in the early stages of the work, and to the Social Sciences and Humanities Research Council of Canada for giving me a Leave Fellowship in 1978 and 1979. During that year I worked from the Shakespeare Institute, University of Birmingham, and am greatly indebted to Dr T. P. Matheson, the Acting Director, to Dr Susan Brock, the Librarian, and to the Fellows, for placing the resources of the Institute at my disposal.

W.C.F.

Contents

Introduction

I. THE MANUFACTURING PROCESS

There have been many books written about the processes used by early founders, but it may not be out of place to recapitulate what is known. Type was manufactured in three stages. The designer, who was also a punch-cutter, having settled on the shapes and size of his letters, carved his design for each character, exact in every detail, backwards and in relief on the end of a steel rod, the size and shape of a small pencil. This was called the 'punch'. The next stage was the making of the matrix, and this may or may not have been done by the same person. In this operation the punch was carefully hammered into a flat rectangle of copper, so that the impression of the letter, now right way round, and called, for fairly obvious reasons, a 'strike', was made in the metal. Copper was chosen because it is malleable, expands very little when heated, and can withstand high temperatures. One technical problem encountered here was that the copper bulged under the pressure from the hammering, and it was the work of a rare craftsman to file the matrices down to where they were wanted: a delicate process called 'justifying'. The punch had to be centred exactly, impressed just the right depth into the copper, and the matrix just the right size to fit the vertical opening of the mould.

Now that the matrices, one for each character to make up the fount (small letters, capitals, numbers, accented letters, punctuation, etc.), had been made and justified, they could be sold as a set or kept, depending on who was to carry out the third step, the actual casting of the letters. It was here that Gutenburg's elementary but fundamental contribution came in, for it was he who invented an adjustable mould in which to cast the type. The mould, basically, consisted of two L-shaped sliding frames of metal which could be set at different widths, depending upon the width of the letter to be cast. The height of the opening was fixed; only the width could vary. It was necessary that different moulds be used for the different sizes of type. We know, for example, that Henry Bynneman had seventeen moulds. It was normal that matrices and moulds to fit them were made and sold together.

A matrix was fixed to the bottom of the mould by a spring, and the sides of the mould were adjusted to give just the right amount of space to the sides of the matrix so that the finished letters would be the proper distance from each other when finally set and printed. With the matrix in place in the mould, the next step was the pouring of the molten type-metal into the mould, which was then immediately shaken so that all crevices of the matrix were filled with the molten metal. After the metal had been allowed a few seconds to solidify, the mould was opened and the casting was turned out. The caster now had an oblong piece of metal, which had the letter in relief and mirror image on one end of it. At the other end of the shaft was a tapered piece of metal called the 'tang', which was excess metal to be broken off and reused. The piece of type, or 'sort', as a single piece was called, was carefully planed down so that it was a standard height. All the sorts had to be exactly the same height ('height to paper' it was called); for if a sort were too short, it would not make any impression on the paper, and if it were too high, it would bite too deeply into the paper and interfere with the letters beside it.

When enough sorts of each character to allow the printer to set up several pages of type without running out of any particular letter had been cast, one had a 'fount'. Obviously there would be more vowels needed in a fount than letters such as 'x' or 'z', and a ratio was hit upon which allowed for convenience. The ratio varied with the language, of course, and English posed the particular difficulty for continental founders that it required 'k' and 'w', an interesting difficulty which was overcome in time, as we shall see.

2. DISTINGUISHING THE FOUNTS

LARGER LOWER COUNTER

DOT LEFT | DOT CENTRE | DOT HIGH

Founts of type differ in their design; this is obvious. However, just how do they differ? And how may one distinguish the different designs at the level of individual letters? Some letters offer more scope for design differences than others, of course. There is not much scope for design in, say, the letter 'l', although there is some. The problem of distinguishing designs is more difficult as one moves down to smaller sizes, where varieties of design are almost invisible to the naked eye, or are blurred by inking. As we are dealing with pica, these problems are present; but there are several design characteristics which can be readily distinguished with the naked eye even at these smaller sizes, and it is on these that this study will concentrate.

The letter 'g' is found in sixteenth-century pica to be of two basic designs. In one design the upper and lower counters[1] are the same size, while in the other the lower counter is larger than the upper.

The designs of the letter 'i' are differentiated by the position of the dot, which is found in one of four positions – either left or, more rarely, right of the stem, or, if directly above it, either close to the stem or as high up as the ascender line, which is the line to which the tallest letters reach. These positions in any particular case may be either the result of conscious design, certainly that is so with the centred dot, or a result of the use of a step-punch, as is more likely with the off-centred dot. All founts had in them vowels with accents over them; but with the letter 'i' there was a complicating factor in that the accent replaced the dot. Therefore, in order to avoid having to make two 'i' punches, one with a dot the other with an accent, one could make a punch for the stem of the letter only, and leave the space for the accent or dot blank, cutting away the shank of the punch so that a small step-punch, containing accent or dot, could be inserted and tightly bound into place. That being done there would be room for some lateral movement, and the dot could be tied in either centred or ever so slightly off to one side or the other. In one set of founts of French origin the positioning of the dot to the left was a regular feature.

1. The technical terms are those of Philip Gaskell in his 'A Nomenclature for the Letter-Forms of Roman Type', *The Library*, vol. XXIX, no. 1, March, 1974. A counter is simply the hole found in the middle of certain letters.

The letters ‘k’ and ‘x’ may be considered together, as they seem to be related in design. The diagonals of the ‘k’ can be positioned at different angles to the stem, and thus will stick out a greater or lesser distance from the stem, depending upon the angle. Let the terms ‘condensed’ and ‘expanded’ mark these variations. The ‘x’ likewise can be condensed or expanded, depending upon the angle at which the diagonals cross. One normally finds that both the ‘k’ and ‘x’ within a fount were similar in design. The ‘z’ too follows the same pattern, but as this is an ‘unnecessary letter’ it is too seldom found to be useful in identification.

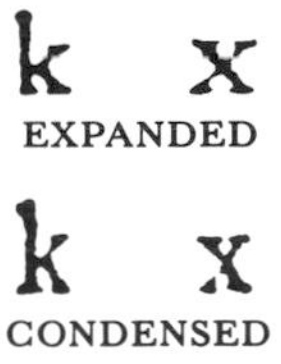

The ‘o’ can be distinguished by the axis of the counter, which can lean in either direction, or be vertical. In any particular instance, the position of the axis may be not so much a design characteristic as a result of the way the punch was held when the matrix was struck. Of course, if it is a design characteristic, left or right slants required different punches.

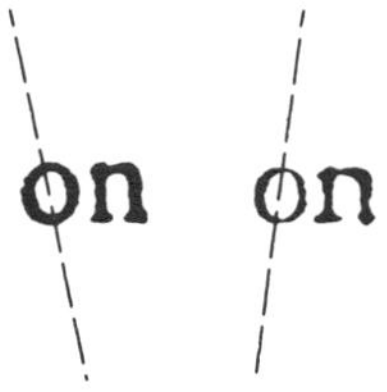

The letters ‘bdpq’ in each face form a family of their own, and are distinguished as a family by the conscious design differences among the members. In fact, it is the evidence of these letters which is often of the greatest importance in distinguishing founts. The important thing to notice is the relative size of the counter of each of these letters. They can be all the same size, or each letter can have a larger or smaller counter than one, two or all of the others. One fount, for example, had small counters for the ‘d’ and ‘p’, a larger one for the ‘b’, and an even larger counter for the ‘q’. Another fount had the ‘p’ the largest. And so on through different combinations which mark the founts as distinct.

The ‘s’ in one set of founts was slanted to the right almost invariably. This could have been caused by the striking of the matrix on an angle, but is much more likely to have been a conscious, built-in design factor.

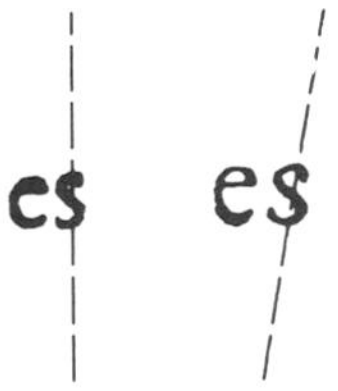

The ‘v’ can differ in the angle of the diagonals, giving either a condensed or an expanded letter. This is the letter, curiously, which is sometimes found to have been too small for the fount, not quite reaching the full distance between base and mean lines. The problem was caused by failure to allow for an optical effect.

The ‘w’ is the most interesting letter of all, as it is peculiarly English and probably had to be manufactured specially for the English market. Ordinarily one could do without the letter, making do with two ‘v’s, and this was what was done in the early years. John Day tried to solve the problem in 1559 by using

a 'w' which he happened to have in a fount of larger letters. It was an ill-fitting letter, in which the second and third diagonals crossed half-way up, so that the letter had four points instead of the normal three. Needless to say, it was replaced when a better letter came onto the market. The next 'w' to appear was a very wide letter in which the second diagonal meets the third half-way up, but then terminates instead of crossing. It is found in the work of Reyner Wolfe, and Isaac suggests that he obtained it in Frankfurt.

The first 'w' to find general acceptance, designated here as 'w–1', appeared first in the work of Richard Jugge, in 1566. This was an awkward, very heavy letter, with the second and third stems meeting at the mean line. The left and right serifs were pronounced, and were heavier than the serifs found on any other letter in Jugge's fount. This was a letter created to 'make do' and did not fit the design of the remainder of the fount. It was discarded within a decade.

The second form of the letter to be generally accepted ('w–2') was introduced in 1564 when Reyner Wolfe replaced his first letter. John Day took it up in 1567, and the letter became popular.

The form of 'w' which looks the most normal to our eyes is here designated 'w–3'. It fitted the founts in which it was used, and came into the country in 1576, when Hugh Jackson obtained it. Over the years there were variations in the pattern, with a shallow letter appearing in the 1590s, followed later in the same decade by a slightly condensed variant. Both would have required separate punches.

The 'y' can vary in the angle of the diagonals and also in the point at which the diagonals meet. The most common forms of the letter have the diagonals, at either wide or narrow angle, meeting at the base line, although there are one or two which meet either slightly below or slightly above it.

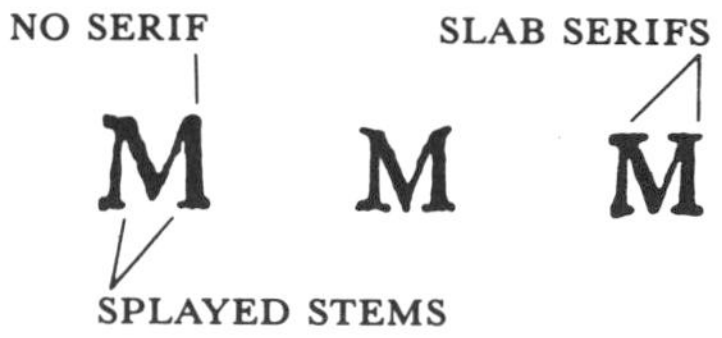

Generally speaking, then, founts in small sizes may be distinguished by the treatment of counters and diagonals. The treatment of diagonals is crucial in determining the width of many letters, and of the general set of the fount, for the curved letters are generally designed to complement the width of the other letters.

So far, nothing has been said about capital letters. One problem about using capitals for identification is the infrequency of their use, while another is that they may not have been provided along with the lower-case letters. In one design the capitals rise to the full height of the fount, measured by the height of the ascenders of the lower-case letters, while in others the capitals are just a shade shorter. The most easily recognized and frequently used capital letter is the 'M', which is found in three forms. One form is slightly splayed and lacks the upper-right serif. Both the other forms have vertical stems and possess the upper-right serif, but their serifs are different: one has normal serifs and is a slightly smaller letter than the splayed 'M', while the third has very heavy serifs extending on both sides of the stems.

3. THE PICA ROMAN FACES IN ELIZABETHAN ENGLAND

There were three major and five minor pica roman type faces used in Elizabethan England. Their histories will be told elsewhere in this book, but at this point the faces may be named and described. The first and most popular face is based on a French original which appeared in the work of the Lyon printer Jean de Tournes in the 1540s. I do not know who designed this type, and therefore cannot designate it using its designer's name. For convenience I will call it the 'Lyon' face, after the city in which it probably originated. The most obvious general characteristic of Lyon is a generally wide set to the letters, caused by the angles of the diagonals. With this goes a pronounced difference in the size of the 'g' counters, with the lower counter being considerably larger than the upper. Only in this design does one find this singular 'g'.

There are actually two different designs to Lyon, together with a variation, making a total of three members of this family. The general set of the letters is the same in all three, and the 'g' remains constant. The basic distinctions are in the 'bdpq' counters, and the letters 'i', 'k' and 'o'. The earlier design, designated as 'Lyon (a)', lacked a 'k' until late in the sixteenth century, and then used a condensed design which does not fit in well with the rest of the fount, as can be seen most readily by comparing it with the expanded 'x'. It also lacked a 'w' until quite late, when a standard 'w–3' was used. The 'i' dot is always centred, and the 'o' is unusual in having its axis tilted to the right. The counter of the 'p' is smaller than that of the other three letters in the 'bdpq' group, and does not quite touch the base line. The 'd' and 'q' counters are slightly larger and of equal size, while the 'b' counter is the largest of the four. The 'M' is the splayed variety found in all Lyon founts, and the 'O' is distinctive in that it matches the lower-case letter in having its axis tilted to the right.

The 'Lyon (b)' design is very similar, except for the

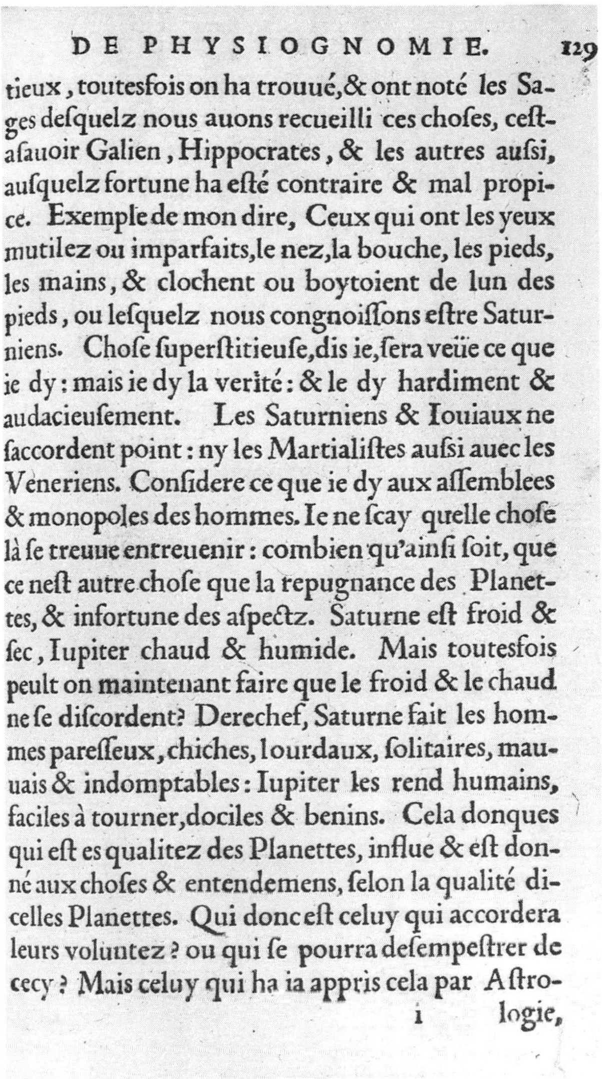
DE PHYSIOGNOMIE. 129
tieux, toutesfois on ha trouué,& ont noté les Sages deſquelz nous auons recueilli ces choſes, ceſt-aſauoir Galien, Hippocrates, & les autres auſsi, auſquelz fortune ha eſté contraire & mal propice. Exemple de mon dire, Ceux qui ont les yeux mutilez ou imparfaits,le nez,la bouche, les pieds, les mains, & clochent ou boytoient de lun des pieds, ou leſquelz nous congnoiſſons eſtre Saturniens. Choſe ſuperſtitieuſe,dis ie,ſera veüe ce que ie dy: mais ie dy la verité: & le dy hardiment & audacieuſement. Les Saturniens & Iouiaux ne ſaccordent point: ny les Martialiſtes auſsi auec les Veneriens. Conſidere ce que ie dy aux aſſemblees & monopoles des hommes. Ie ne ſcay quelle choſe là ſe treuue entreuenir: combien qu'ainſi ſoit, que ce neſt autre choſe que la repugnance des Planettes, & infortune des aſpectz. Saturne eſt froid & ſec, Iupiter chaud & humide. Mais toutesfois peult on maintenant faire que le froid & le chaud ne ſe diſcordent? Derechef, Saturne fait les hommes pareſſeux, chiches, lourdaux, ſolitaires, mauuais & indomptables: Iupiter les rend humains, faciles à tourner,dociles & benins. Cela donques qui eſt es qualitez des Planettes, influe & eſt donné aux choſes & entendemens, ſelon la qualité dicelles Planettes. Qui donc eſt celuy qui accordera leurs voluntez? ou qui ſe pourra deſempeſtrer de cecy? Mais celuy qui ha ia appris cela par Aſtro-
i logie,

JEAN DE TOURNES, Lyon 1549. Joannes de Indagine, *Chiromance et physiognomie*. By courtesy of the Wellcome Trustees.

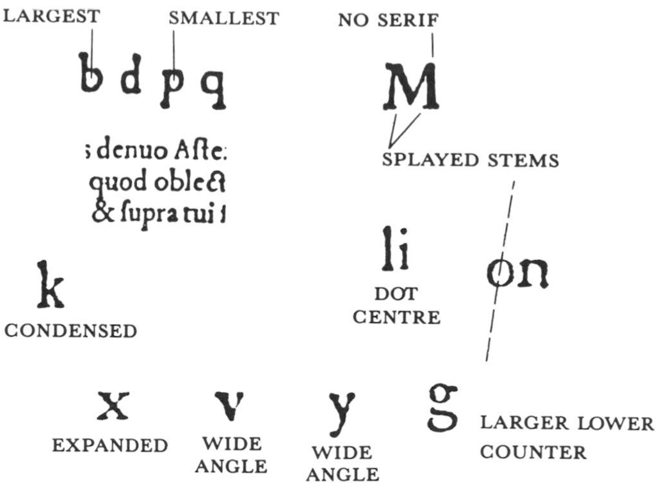

Lyon (a)

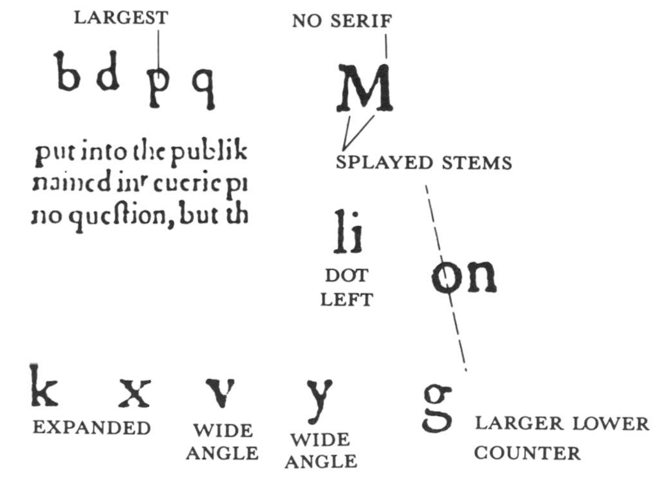

Lyon (b)

letters noted above. The 'bdpq' counters are each of a different relative size, with the 'p' now being the largest, 'b' and 'q' smaller and equal, and 'd' the smallest. The 'o' counter now has its axis tilted to the left, and the 'i' punch must have had a step-punch for the dot, as it floats usually somewhere to the left of centre. The 'k' is expanded to match the 'x'. A third design, 'Lyon (c)', is the same as (b) except that the 'i' dot is centred and sometimes high. This could be a variation obtained with the same kind of step-punch that produced the dot to the left, as there would have been room for movement in all directions. The 'w' used in (b) and (c) was the 'w–1' design in early years, and, from 1576, the 'w–3' form.

As one would expect, the popular Garamond pica was used in England at this time, having been introduced by John Day. Again, in the design the treatment of the diagonals is distinctive: the angles are more acute than in Lyon, giving a narrower set to the fount. The 'g' counters are the same size, as they are in all faces except Lyon. The 's' is slanted to the right, and this is a most useful distinguishing mark of the face. The 'w–2' form is associated with this face. There is little difference in the sizes of the 'bdpq' counters, all being fairly generous. The face has a slightly larger x-height than other picas, the difference being about a fifth of a millimetre, and, as a result, the 'i' dot appears to be higher than normal, and is often close to the ascender line. The 'o' counter is vertical or tilted very slightly to the left. The capitals are not quite the full height of the face, and the 'M' has the upper-right serif and vertical ascenders.

Haultin is similar in many ways to Garamond. Both faces are condensed because of the treatment of the diagonals. The Haultin face has a smaller x-height than Garamond, and the 's' is vertical. The 'bdpq' counters again are most useful in distinguishing the face: those of 'p' and 'd' are small, that of 'b' is larger, and that of 'q' is very much larger still, its relative size being the most easily recognizable feature of the face, although, of course, you may have to hunt through a few pages before you find one. As in the Garamond face, the 'g' in Haultin has equal-sized counters and the 'k' and 'x' are condensed. The normal 'w' is of the third design, and the 'o' axis is usually close to vertical, but can go either way. This last feature may be the result of poor casting. The capitals are similar in design to those in Gramond.

The most common of the lesser-known faces, Guyot, is similar to Garamond in the treatment of its diagonals, but has a more-expanded 'k', 'x' and 'v' (especially the 'v'). The 'i' dot is a bit high and the 'o' and 's' are vertical. The 'w', when it matches, is of the second design, but is slightly wider than that in Garamond, being based on Guyot's own wider 'v'. This is one face which is easily recognized by its capitals; for the 'M' has pronounced upper serifs which extend on both sides of the stem, and the 'G' is distinctive in that the stem almost reaches the height of the upper serif.

There were two founts of Tavernier pica in use during our period. This face has a 'g' with equal-sized counters, the 'i' dot centred and a vertical 'o'. The 'bdpq' counters are the same size and the 's' is vertical. The 'v' is wider than the 'x', which is unusual, as the two letters normally have similar angles to their diagonal strokes, and the 'y' is deep. The 'M' is similar to the Lyon form in that it lacks the upper-right serif, but it differs in that it is not splayed. Tavernier lacks both 'k' and 'w', and these had to be supplied separately.

The last type face found (and it is not found in works printed before 1602) is the pica illustrated in the Le Bé–Moretus collection of 1599. It is not exactly the same as earlier Garamonds, for there is a difference in the style of the 'y' and 'i', the dot of which is slightly to the right of centre. In addition, the 'bdpq' counters are slightly smaller than in earlier Garamonds.

To complete the record, there are two faces found in single examples. Reyner Wolfe had a Grapheus pica, and Hugh Singleton occasionally used Lambrecht's traditional pica in the early 1550s.

One must watch in all faces for the set of the face to be determined not only by the design of the letters but also by the casting process itself. Letters closer together or further apart look, on first glance, to be totally different, but in fact come from the same matrices. The mould's lateral opening, as we have seen, is determined by setting the sliding L-shaped register at the appropriate place for the letter to be cast. One may not get the opening exactly the same every time one recasts, so one fount may be cast on a slightly narrower or broader set than another. One way of checking the relative sizes of sets is to note the distance between two 'l's set together. The difference can be measured in tenths of millimetres, but this is quite enough to give different appearances to founts actually cast from the same matrices.

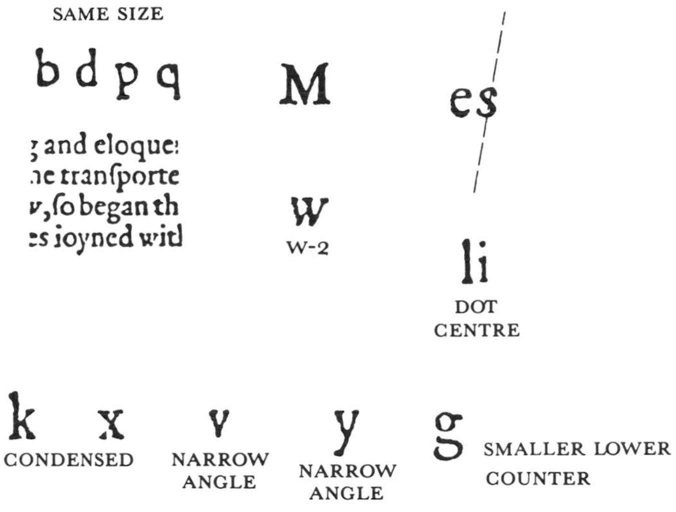

Garamond

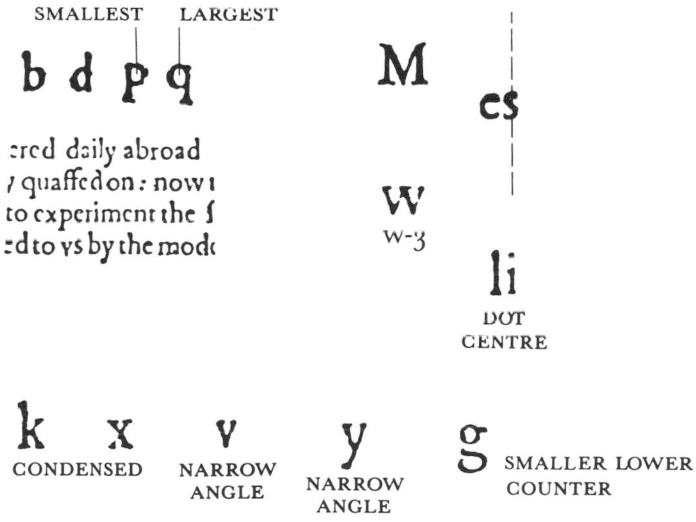

Haultin

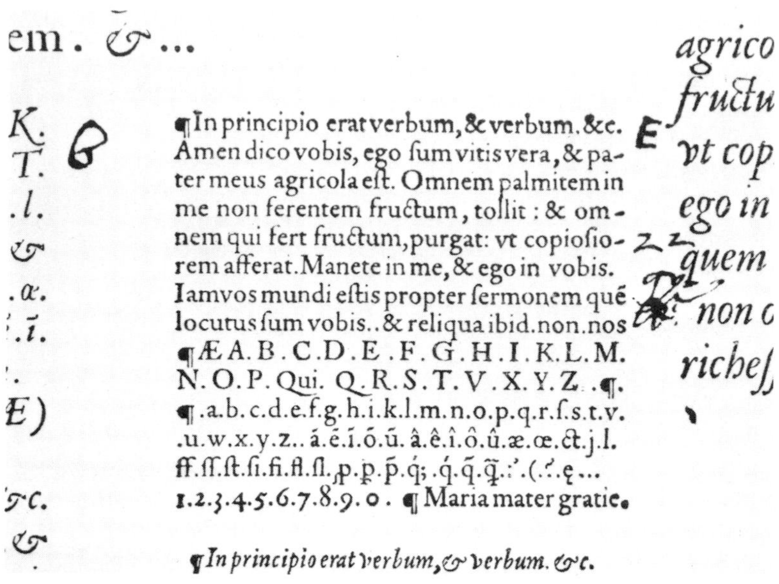

¶In principio erat verbum, & verbum. &c.
Amen dico vobis, ego ſum vitis vera, & pa-
ter meus agricola eſt. Omnem palmitem in
me non ferentem fructum, tollit : & omnem qui fert fructum, purgat: vt copioſio-
rem afferat. Manete in me, & ego in vobis.
Iam vos mundi eſtis propter ſermonem quē
locutus ſum vobis.. & reliqua ibid. non. nos
¶Æ A. B. C. D. E. F. G. H. I. K. L. M.
N. O. P. Qui. Q. R. S. T. V. X. Y. Z. ¶.
¶.a.b.c.d.e.f.g.h.i.k.l.m.n.o.p.q.r.ſ.s.t.v.
.u.w.x.y.z.. á.é.í.ó.ú. â.ê.î.ô.û.æ.œ.ct.j.l.
ff.ſſ.ſt.ſi.fi.fl.ſl.
1.2.3.4.5.6.7.8.9.0. ¶ Maria mater gratie.

¶In principio erat verbum, & verbum. &c.

Guyot pica in the anonymous Netherlands specimen sheet, *c.* 1565

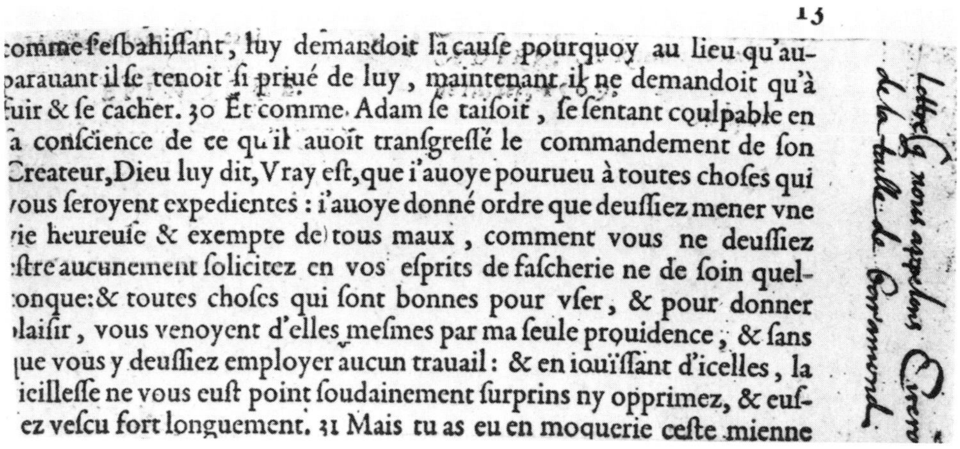

15

comme s'eſbahiſſant, luy demandoit la cauſe pourquoy au lieu qu'au-
parauant il ſe tenoit ſi priué de luy, maintenant il ne demandoit qu'à
fuir & ſe cacher. 30 Et comme Adam ſe taiſoit, ſe ſentant coulpable en
a conſcience de ce qu'il auoit tranſgreſſé le commandement de ſon
Createur, Dieu luy dit, Vray eſt, que i'auoye pourueu à toutes choſes qui
vous ſeroyent expedientes : i'auoye donné ordre que deuſſiez mener vne
vie heureuſe & exempte de tous maux, comment vous ne deuſſiez
eſtre aucunement ſolicitez en vos eſprits de faſcherie ne de ſoin quel-
conque: & toutes choſes qui ſont bonnes pour vſer, & pour donner
plaiſir, vous venoyent d'elles meſmes par ma ſeule prouidence, & ſans
que vous y deuſſiez employer aucun trauail: & en iouïſſant d'icelles, la
vieilleſſe ne vous euſt point ſoudainement ſurprins ny opprimez, & euſ-
ſiez veſcu fort longuement. 31 Mais tu as eu en moquerie ceſte mienne

The Le Bé–Moretus pica, 1599

4. THE ARRIVAL OF THE FOUNDERS

There were five main pica roman faces introduced into England between 1553 and 1574. All were well-known continental faces, so that punches or strikes had to be brought over to England by someone. What is remarkable is that within months of the arrival of a type founder, a new pica roman face appeared in English books, and in two cases the face was that associated with the name of the founder. We know a fair amount about the movements of these men, as they were registered aliens and in some cases quickly took out papers of denization, as there were tax advantages in doing so. Some of them came to England to escape religious persecution, and were associated with the French Church in London.

The first to arrive was Hubert Danvillier, who brought one or possibly two sets of the Lyon punches with him, for the face appeared in 1553 (see below). Then, in 1557, Poll Rotteford arrived, and Tavernier made its first appearance, and when in 1566 Charles Tressell came, Garamond appeared. Not at all surprisingly, the Guyot pica was seen shortly after François Guyot came in 1568. The Haultin face appeared in the works of Thomas Vautrollier within months of the acquisition of matrices by Jerome Haultin, who had been in the country for some time. It is an assumption of this study that the founts of these five faces used in England, in the initial years of this period at least, were the products of these five founders.

One might ask if the type could not have been imported direct from the Continent. I think this was a rare occurrence in the early days, and probably did not happen at all with common founts. The likelihood that the arrival of the five men and the immediate appearance of the five faces was not a coincidence is rather strong, it must be admitted. Later in this study we will see that at least two printers, John Kingston and Waldegrave, must have had their own matrices. There is further evidence of a circumstantial kind found in useful but little-known books, the *Rates of the Custome house* (STC 7687–95, various dates from 1545 to 1635), which give the duties to be charged on all imports and exports. There are very few copies of these left, as they were the kind of handbook which would be thumbed until it disintegrated. However, those that remain give us some indication of the goods which were traded. Unbound books are on the list of imports, as are various kinds of paper and, by 1582, ink. By 1609 the ink is designated as 'inck for Printers' and came in by the hundredweight. It was probably printer's ink right from the beginning, as ordinary writing ink was easily made from local materials. However, there is no mention whatever of type. Admittedly, most of the imports were trade goods, but even so, as both paper and ink were taxed, it is difficult to see how type would have been missed if it was imported in any quantity.

5. THE HISTORY OF THE FACES

Lyon (a)

The introduction of contemporary pica roman type faces into Elizabethan England began when Hubert Danvillier came to London from France in 1552 or early 1553. He had been apprenticed in 1545 to Robert Granjon and is listed in the *Returns of Aliens* on 28 January 1553. Immediately upon his arrival there appeared some interesting French type faces, including a pica roman.

It is not known where Danvillier acquired his materials, but it is probably no coincidence that his pica roman face is of a design found in the works of Jean de Tournes of Lyon in the 1540s. Granjon had close connections with the Lyon printer and one assumes his apprentice did too. In this study the face associated with Danvillier is referred to as 'Lyon' (as stated earlier, this being as close as I can come to identifying it). I think it probable that Danvillier possessed a set of punches for this face and that he obtained a set of very similar punches a few years later.

The first fount of Lyon pica from an English strike was used in 1553 in the work of Nicolas Hill. It was of the Lyon (a) design, a match for the de Tournes face. In Lyon it was cast on a generous, 88mm. body, but for Hill it was cast in a different mould, giving a much smaller, 75mm. body. The fount lacked both 'k' and 'w', so a 'k' from a smaller fount was supplied. Hill used this type only in 1553, and then only as a secondary fount for emphasis or for sidenotes in three books. Not much was needed, and it is probable that Danvillier did not provide Hill with matrices.

John Kingston was the next person to have a Lyon (a) fount, which he had by 1556. It was used cast on a large body in the setting of a single book, John Withals's *A Shorte dictionarie* (STC 25875). In 1558 it was used cast on a smaller body and in 1563 on a standard, 82mm. body. The 'k' used in each casting was the same: a smaller letter, with an expanded shape. It was the same 'k' as Hill's, which suggests that the source for both printers was Danvillier, who probably supplied Hill with sorts and Kingston more probably with a strike.

How can one tell when a strike has been supplied to a printer and not just a cast fount? One cannot, directly; the evidence must be circumstantial. In Kingston's case there is the fact that the type was recast several times, always from the same matrices. It happened that, except in one instance, new castings of the Lyon (a) face disappeared from the scene for almost thirty years. There was one more fount supplied, in 1561, and then the punches were set aside in favour of the (b) and (c) forms until 1589. Kingston, however, continued to use the same face until 1576. As it would have been necessary for him to replenish sorts from time to time, and as it is highly unlikely that Danvillier would have had a set of matrices set aside for Kingston's sole use, Kingston must have had his own matrices.

Kingston continued to use the fount, then, until 1576, but there were changes and additions. The original 'k' did not fit, and there was the problem of the 'w'. He made do with italic and black-letter 'w's for some years, but in 1568 he obtained some 'w–2', which he used together with a few italic sorts. This form of 'w' is the one normally associated with the Garamond face, and was almost never seen, except mixed with another form of 'w', in a Danvillier fount. Danvillier was already by this time supplying the 'w–1' form, but Kingston apparently did not go to him for it. It is quite probable that Kingston did not obtain a 'w–2' matrix, for only three years later 'w–3' sorts were added in with his 'w–2'. Had he had his own matrix for 'w–2' there would have been no call for him to create the mixture. As for the 'k', here he may have obtained a matrix from Danvillier, for the normal Lyon (b) expanded 'k' appeared in 1574.

The last person to obtain the (a) face at this time was Richard Jugge, who obtained his fount in 1561, cast on a standard pica body. There was in his fount the same small 'k' found in Hill's and Kingston's, and no 'w'. This type was used by Jugge only in this year, and when he again used a pica roman, he had obtained the (b) form, so it is unlikely that he had anything but a casting from Danvillier's (a) matrices.

The (a) face did not appear again until 1589. When it did reappear the founts always had a condensed 'k' and a 'w–3', although there were variant forms of this letter used. It may well be that the elderly Danvillier sold the punches of the (a) face, still without the 'k' and 'w', to another founder, sometime in the late 1580s. The punches, certainly, were discarded for some reason between 1561 and 1589, and one reason could be that the set lacked the vital letters which that of its sister face, (b), possessed. There was no reason for Danvillier suddenly to begin using the punches again in 1589 when he was still making strikes from the (b) punches, so a sale is quite possibly the way they came back into use. There is no good reason to suppose that Danvillier, had he retained the (a) punches, would not have used his excellent expanded 'k' punch with them. But, if the set was sold without the 'k' punch, then it would have been up to the new owner to obtain whatever 'k' he could. Orwin had been supplied with a distinctive curved 'k' in 1589, but from 1591 only the condensed form appears.

Lyon (b)

By 1557 Danvillier had a second set of punches, very similar to the first, but differing basically in the relative size of the 'bdpq' counters and in the position of the axis of the 'o'. The 'i' punch was stepped, and there was a very fine 'k' which fitted in well with the rest of the face. Did Danvillier cut these punches or did he purchase them? It is likely that he purchased them in France; for had he made them himself he surely would have included a 'w'. In fact, no 'w' was supplied with the fount until 1566, when the rather ill-fitting 'w–1' appeared.

The first purchaser of the (b) face was John Day, who acquired a fount cast on an 85mm. body and without a 'w' in 1557. Instead of using a double 'v' in place of 'w', Day from 1559 used an awkward four-pointed 'w' which makes his work unique. It was not until 1571 that he acquired a 'w–1' to go with the fount. As 'w–1' sorts were available by 1566, it is difficult to understand why he waited so long. Also, Day had some

Garamond with its standard 'w–2' by 1567, but he did not add a supply of this to his (b) fount either. There is no reason to suppose that Day possessed matrices for this face, although he probably did for others. It would have made sense for him to have acquired matrices in the late 1560s after the arrival of the Guyots. It is rather odd, one notes in passing, that he used his Lyon (b) pica for less than a year after he had obtained the missing 'w'.

The next person to obtain the (b) face was Rowland Hall, who, in 1563, used it on a large body and without the 'w'. Again, there is no reason to suppose he purchased anything other than a fount. This was the last year of his life, and thereafter his type disappeared from the scene.

Henry Denham obtained some (b) in 1565, cast on an 85mm. body and without the 'w'. He used this for two years and then replaced it with a normal, 82mm. fount with a 'w–1'. The only change through the years was the change in the 'w', for Denham added some 'w–2' to the fount in 1574 and some 'w–3' in 1580. Had he had a matrix, there would have been no need for this kind of mixture, for he would have had sorts cast from his single matrix.

There is something odd about the 'w–1'. It was introduced in 1566 and lasted for a decade, when it was driven out by the more harmonious 'w–3'. But in all its appearances the 'w–1' is unusual in that it is always very heavily inked, and stands out from the rest of the letters on the page. The problem appears to have been that the letter-form was the work of an inferior punch-cutter who did not have the wit or the skill to match the delicacy of design of the remainder of the face, but produced a rough-and-ready design with thick strokes and heavy serifs which stands out when combined with the other letters in the face. I may be being unfair to him, of course, for it is possible that he never saw the face for which he had been asked to provide the punch, although this is unlikely.

The gradual disappearance of the letter suggests that Danvillier had only a single matrix struck from the punch. This would have meant that no printer could have been supplied with a complete strike of matrices until after the mid-1570s, when an alternative letter-form became available. Time and again one finds mixtures like Denham's: one never finds a movement *toward* a 'w–1'; always away from it, either by replacing it altogether or, quite frequently, as Denham illustrates, by adding new and different sorts to the old supply. Charlewood and Jones both created such a mixture in 1585, and Watkins did so in 1579.

The last year in which 'w–1' was used unmixed with another 'w' was 1585, the year Charlewood and Jones created their mixtures. The letter-form was completely abandoned in 1591 (the last year in which it was used in a Jones book). And, indeed, from 1581 it was used only by Jones and by Charlewood, who dropped it in 1589. This means that any book in which the letter-form appears will have been printed after 1565 and will have 1591 as its terminal date, and if printed after 1581 will have come from one of these two presses.

Over the next few years Danvillier supplied more and more founts of Lyon (b), providing a dozen between 1566 and 1570. East's fount, cast in 1569 on an 88mm. body, lacked a 'w'; while Seres, in 1567, provided himself with a 'w–2'. All the others used a 'w–1', which Danvillier normally supplied at the time. No fount was provided in 1571, and from 1572 about a fount a year appeared. In 1576, Hugh Jackson obtained a fount which included a new 'w': the more harmonious 'w–3'. From this time on, no fount was provided with any other form of the letter: 'w–1' had been retired.

It is likely that with two exceptions (Vautrollier and, at a later date, Edward Allde) Danvillier supplied printers with founts and not strikes, for few of the later founts show evidence of having been recast from the same matrices. However, this must remain an open question.

Danvillier continued to provide a steady output of (b) founts until 1596, when, presumably, he retired or died. The last we hear of him is on 4 February 1594, when Thomas Grantham, an apprentice to Richard Watkins, was ordered to 'serue his yeres of [ap]prentiship with Hubert Dovilcy ffounder to learne the art of Casting of letters for printing and all the faculty which the said Hubert vseth.' It was further agreed that Danvillier would provide food and lodging for Grantham, so he must have stayed on the premises. Five years later Grantham was transferred from Watkins to Bishop, Newberry and Barker, and presented for his freedom by 'Master Watkins administrator' on 2 March 1601. No mention of Danvillier is made in either the transfer or the presentation entry in the Stationers' Register, and one may reasonably assume that he had died.

The supply of Lyon (b) founts stopped in 1596, and was not resumed until 1602, when a single fount was supplied (to Wight). However, the supply of Lyon (c), identical to (b) except for the position of the 'i' dot, began in 1601, the very year Grantham became free of the Stationers' Company, and continued regularly until 1608, by which time eleven printers had obtained the face.

The reason for the gap and the change is likely to have been that Danvillier ceased to provide founts after 1596 (he would by then have been well into his seventies). I assume that once Thomas Grantham was freed, he took over his old master's materials and began to provide founts from them. It is probable that he struck a set of matrices for his own use. The 'i' with the centred dot could have come from the same punch as the (b) variety, and may simply reflect Grantham's preference. There is no evidence that Grantham provided printers with anything other than castings.

Garamond

In 1567, after the arrival of Charles Tressell in 1566, the first Garamond pica appeared – in the work of John Day. Day's fount, a very fine casting, was used initially in the printing of one of his best-known books, *A testimonie of antiquitie* (STC 159) by Abbot Aelfric, where Day's new Anglo-Saxon types also appeared for the first time. Day continued to use the Garamond throughout his career.

The same face appeared in two other books printed in 1567 – both printed in the shop of Henry Bynneman – *The Manuell of Epictetus* (STC 10423) and Alexander Nowell's *A confutation* (STC 18739). In the first of these only a dozen lines of Garamond are found (on sig. C3v), while in the other it is used more extensively. One would be tempted to say that these books were printed by Day, except that the Garamond is used together with Bynneman's Lyon (b), which can be distinguished from Day's Lyon (b) by the letter 'w'. It is unlikely that the printing of the book was shared, for the change from Lyon to Garamond occurred within a forme: to be precise, between sigs. O1v and O2r, both on the inner forme. What is suspicious is that Bynneman did not use this handsome face again. The same problem occurs with a third printer who is supposed to have used Garamond in 1567: John Kingston. The face is found in only one of his books, Sir Thomas Wilson's *The rule of reason* (STC 25813), but the section in which it is found may well have been printed by one of the others. What makes me hesitate here in inferring that Kingston did not have a fount of Garamond is that the next year he had a supply of 'w–2' to go with his Lyon fount, and this is the form of that letter which from the beginning was provided in the Garamond fount. If he did possess Garamond, he could have discarded the fount for some reason, having first scooped up sorts of this single letter to add to his other fount, or, if he borrowed a fount, he could have kept some of the 'w–2' for his own use. All three books could do with being more fully investigated.

The next printer to obtain Garamond was Thomas Purfoot, sen., who obtained a fount in 1569, which within a year had become slightly mixed with Lyon (b) sorts, including some 'w–1'. This mixing was unusual in that Purfoot did not have a regular supply of Lyon (b) to mix in with the Garamond, for such mixing was much more likely to happen when two founts were being used within the same shop. This could, of course, be evidence that on occasion cases of type were moved around from shop to shop.

There was then a six-year halt in the supply of Garamond pica. Indeed, the early 1570s saw little activity from Danvillier either. The next Garamond was supplied in 1576 to Barker, and then it was supplied to others fairly steadily until the late 1580s. In most cases it can be assumed that founts only were supplied, but there are occasional instances in which strikes seem to have been sold.

Take the singular case of Robert Waldegrave. He had obtained a Garamond in 1584. In April 1588 he was raided by the Warden and other officers of the Stationers' Company for having printed, contrary to a Star Chamber decree, a seditious Puritan book by John Udall. Much of Waldegrave's printing equipment was carried off to Stationers' Hall. Included in the material were 'twoo paire of Cases wth Certen pica Romane & pica Italian letters . . .' These were ordered destroyed. However, it is known from Lord Burghley's report that Waldegrave saved some 'lettres' in a box which he concealed under his cloak. He took the box to a neighbour, and it was collected three months later by Waldegrave's wife. It has been assumed that this was the small type used to print two works in the Marprelate series, *Theses Martinianae* and *Just censure & reproof* (STC 17457 and 17458).

I think this version of the story is wrong. Surely Waldegrave would not have bothered to save a single case of type. To begin with, he would have needed to save two of them – they would have been in open cases, and one cannot imagine him taking time to look around for an appropriate cover – and voluminous as Elizabethan cloaks may have been, it would have been difficult to walk out with a full case hidden under it (and doubly so with two). Surely it is more likely that what Waldegrave was at pains to save were his matrices. The box that contained them would have been smaller, it would have had a fitted lid, and they would have been valuable, if not essential, to him. Waldegrave was a printer on the move, but the pica roman he used, whether in London before the raid, on the run with the Marprelate tracts (and the same pica appears in all of them somewhere), or in Edinburgh for the next decade and more, was always the same Garamond – the one he obtained first in 1584. It would have been nearly impossible for him to have supplied himself legitimately immediately after the raid, yet only six months elapsed between the seizure of the pica in April 1588 and the appearance of the same face in the first of the Marprelate tracts in October. I believe we have here a clear case of a printer owning his own matrices.

Garamond continued to be offered occasionally in the 1590s and beyond. Bourne obtained some in 1592 cast on an 86mm. body and containing some expanded 'k' and some 'w–3'. This was probably supplied by a different founder, one who lacked the matrices for these letters. The next to obtain Garamond also had problems: Legate obtained some in 1593 which was very short of 'w', and he made up the deficiency by using some 'w–3' obtained either from his supplier or by raiding his other pica founts. A very fine standard Garamond is found in the two books printed in 1597 under the imprint of Ballard, but I am quite sure that they were printed for him by Hatfield.

There was only one more fount of Garamond supplied in our period. This was a large order to some of the printers in the Eliot's Court group in 1602. This group had used Garamond extensively a few years before, and now it appeared again in books printed by Hatfield and the new partner, Bradwood. In these founts the 's' was vertical, and the capitals were Lyon (a), one of the few cases of a deliberate mismatching.

It would appear, then, that in the early days of Garamond a very good caster was available, and may indeed have been Charles Tressell himself. We do not know how long Tressell stayed in England, and I hesitate to trust Worman's judgement that he was the same person as 'Treasure' or 'Treswer' in the *Returns of Aliens* or even 'Tressa', who was listed in 1582 as 'a carver to the printers'. Certainly, though, Tressell was still in the country in 1571.

There was a gap in the supply of Garamond from 1570 until 1576, but, although when it reappeared there was a lower standard of casting, the popularity of the face remained high during the 1580s. Problems arose over the supply of certain letters, and a mixing of the face occurred in the 1590s, with the lower case finally being matched with Lyon (a) capitals. After this time, the face disappeared from the scene for decades.

Haultin

We know a considerable amount about the Haultin family of La Rochelle. Pierre Haultin was the guiding genius of the family, and lived in constant danger because of his Protestantism. His nephew, Jerome, worked in London with Danvillier and set up business on his own, most likely in 1574, when he bought matrices from his uncle. Jerome returned to La Rochelle in the late 1580s on the death of his uncle in order to take over the family business, and died there on 16 November 1600.

Very soon after Jerome Haultin purchased his uncle's matrices, the pica roman face called 'Haultin' appeared in the work of Thomas Vautrollier, like the Haultins a Huguenot who had fled religious persecution. The fount was set rather wide, and lacked a 'w'. The next fount was supplied in 1576, to John Kingston, and was complete with a 'w–3', which was the standard form of the letter by this time in founts with French originals behind them.

The records mention only matrices as being in Haultin's possession, but if, as is my belief, he also sold strikes, he probably had punches as well. The most interesting case is that of Henry Denham, who in 1581 obtained a fount of Haultin cast wide on the body. The fount had an unusual and distinctive ligature, consisting of two 'o's tied together. It is an awkward ligature, and, as it appears to have been provided for other Denham founts as well as the pica, it can be assumed that it was made to order. No other printer used it at that time. Peter Short took over Denham's business in 1589, and continued to use the Haultin, together with the double-'o' ligature. However, Short recast the type on a much narrower set, in fact, on probably the narrowest set seen in the period. To do this, it is likely that he had the matrices, including that for the double-'o' ligature, at hand to take to a caster; for by this time Haultin himself was no longer in London, although someone was carrying on his business.

One of the most interesting facts about Haultin faces is that they became more popular after Haultin himself had left the country. Six printers bought Haultin's pica between 1574 and 1582, after which there was a gap until 1588 (Garamond was the most popular face during these years). In 1588 one fount was provided, even though, we assume, Haultin himself was back in

France. Then in 1590 three founts appeared, two more appeared in 1591, and during the 1590s no fewer than fifteen printers began to use Haultin. There was a pause between 1601 and 1603, and then founts appeared again, at the rate of about one a year.

Obviously, Haultin had either sold his materials or set up a branch operation now that he was in control of the family business. One notes the uniformity of the founts through the years, which suggests that very few sets of matrices were in circulation. The quality of the casting was not uniform during the later years, and it may be significant that none of the founts provided after 1603 continued in use for more than a year or two. This suggests to me inferior casting, and quality control has always been a problem with a branch operation.

Guyot

There was a group of nine founts which, although they had several sets of punches behind them, were all recognizably Guyot founts. All but one had the most easily recognizable feature of a Guyot fount: the Guyot capitals, with the distinctive 'G' and 'M'. The Guyot face is seen in its purest form on the anonymous Netherlands specimen sheet of 1565 printed, it is believed, by François Guyot.

Henry Denham had the first fount of the Guyot family; its design did not resemble that of the later pica faces, or the specimen sheet, but was a faithful copy of another known Guyot face, his double pica. The 'y' is particularly distinctive in both the pica and double pica faces. Both faces can be seen side by side on sigs. A5v and A6r of Ovid's *Heroycall epistles* (STC 18940). Denham possessed his Guyot fount, but without a 'w', by early 1567; it was used in the printing of a book dated 6 May. This fount could have come from the Continent; for it was not repeated by any other English printer, which suggests that matrices were not available. Denham, like John Day, was known for his continental connections.

Henry Bynneman used a pica roman fount with a face the same as the one illustrated on the Netherlands specimen sheet (even though in his fount the ascenders and descenders appear to have been a very little bit shorter, the 'w' was not exactly the same and the 'i' dot was slightly lower). Bynnemen used this fount first in 1569, and continued to use it for a decade. It is quite likely that Guyot himself provided this fount, for it appeared just after his arrival in England.

The next fount of Guyot pica did not appear until 1577, when Thomas Marsh used one. There is no doubt about the capitals, but the lower case provides difficulties. The 'g' had a lower counter slightly larger than the upper, but not as much so as in the Lyon founts. The 'y' was very wide, suggesting Denham's letter. Again, it would appear that the same general design was behind the fount, but that some variant punches were used. Eight years later Abel Jeffes used a standard fount in a single book.

Again there was a considerable time lapse, twelve years, until James Roberts obtained the next fount in 1597. This was very close in design to the specimen, and measured about 76mm. for twenty lines. The 'k' was narrower than that in the fount used to print the specimen, as was the 'w'.

Eliot's Court was the next place for a Guyot to appear, in 1598. This fount, used by both Hatfield and Bollifant until 1602, and then in 1604 by both Dawson and Islip, had nearly the same face as the specimen. The distinguishing marks here are that the 'k' was expanded and too large for the face, and that the 'w' was the slightly condensed variant of 'w–3' which was to come into vogue a few years later. A fount with exactly the same characteristics appeared in 1600 in Waldegrave's Edinburgh shop, and this suggests a common Dutch source for all these late examples. The variety of the Guyot founts makes an interesting contrast with the Haultin face, where the very uniformity of the design of the founts suggests a steadier, local supply.

6. HOW PICA ROMAN WAS USED

Several well-known Elizabethan printers do not appear in this study because they did not use pica roman.[1] Other printers possessed only one fount of pica roman, which they used throughout their careers. What is of interest now is the remainder, comprising those printers who used more than one fount; for it might be instructive to see how they used the founts. There are only a few ways founts could be used: most obviously, a printer could discard one fount when he obtained another. Actually, a minority of printers adopted this method, the majority using the old as well as the new, although it was normal to phase out the old type. The questions arise: How did the printers use two founts? Did they ever use two distinct faces in one book? And if so, how? Did compositors stick to their own cases and distribute to them?

If one could find books from one shop in the printing of which two distinguishable founts were used by positively identifiable compositors, then that would be evidence that compositors sometimes worked from their own cases and distributed back to them. There is one book which is a perfect example of this. It is the second quarto of *Hamlet* printed in 1604 by James Roberts. Here we have displayed, as we will see, the relatively common practice of two faces being used within one book. In addition, we have a detailed compositor study of the same book, a study in which the stints of the two compositors are meticulously worked out by John Russell Brown.[2] Two founts of type were used in printing this book: Roberts's common Lyon (b) and his Lyon (a). The faces are not immediately distinguishable, but if one looks for the 'k', 'o' and 'bdpq' counters, one will see the difference. As it happens, the italics are markedly different too, but that is a bonus. What is fascinating here is that the use of the two founts corresponds almost exactly with the stints of the two compositors as worked out by Brown. According to his compositor study, compositor X set sheets B to D, F, I, the two outer pages of sheet L, sheet N and the last half-sheet, O. Compositor Y set the remainder. One finds that the Lyon (a) was used in the stints attributed to compositor X, and the Lyon (b) was used in the stints attributed to compositor Y. There is only one point of difference, and that is sheet L, which was printed throughout with the Lyon (b) fount. Brown is the first to admit that his evidence for attributing page L1r to compositor X is weak, and he may well be wrong about L4v as well, although it may be that here the compositors switched cases. Another interesting point is that the types did not at any time become mixed. Each time the Lyon (a) type was distributed back to the case, it always went back to the correct one.

There is one other book from Roberts's shop in the printing of which these two founts were used: William Perkins's *Of the calling of the ministerie* (STC 19733), printed in 1605. In this book the Lyon (b) was used for most of the work, but the Lyon (a) was used in the first half of sheets B and C. This book is an octavo, and sheet C is neatly divided between C4v and C5r, the centre of the sheet. The division in sheet B is not so neat: the Lyon (b) was used on B1r, the Lyon (a) was used to the middle of page B5r, and then the use of the Lyon (b) fount recommenced at a new paragraph. There is no evidence of mixing later in the book, so the seven and a half pages of Lyon (a) type must have been very carefully distributed back to its own cases. One can answer the question of whether compositors sometimes stuck to their own cases and distributed back to them in the affirmative. One could also use this evidence in tackling the question of whether compositors worked simultaneously on the same book.

There are many examples of two founts of type being used in printing the same book, but very few which are backed up by a compositor study to show that two compositors were at work. It was common practice, for example, in Thomas Orwin's shop to use two founts for the same book. Such a division of types suggests that two compositors were involved. If one insisted that a single compositor only was at work, then one must suppose that he had to use two different types for some reason, and was careful to distribute each back to the cases from which it had come.

As I mentioned, the use of two founts together was common practice in Orwin's shop. One straightforward example of his practice was the setting of Jean Taffin's *Of the markes of the children of God* (STC 23652), an octavo printed in 1590. Orwin's Garamond was used for sheets B to E. It was then more or less alternated with his distinctive Lyon (a), being used for sheets G, K, M, P and R; while the Lyon (a) was used for sheets F, H, I, L, N, O and Q. This was a fairly normal way of dividing a book, and gave nine sheets

1. They are: Berthelet, Brome, Caly, Colwell, Copland, King, Lacie, Lant, T. and W. Powell, Rogers, Singleton, Toy, Tysdale, Walley, Wayland and Whitchurch.

2. 'The Compositors of *Hamlet* Q2 and *The Merchant of Venice*', *Studies in Bibliography*, vol. VII, Charlottesville, 1955.

printed with one face, seven with the other. Surely it is reasonable to suppose that different compositors were at work here, each working from his own cases and distributing his type back to those same cases. The same kind of pattern can be seen in other Orwin books, such as Lyly's *Campaspe* (STC 17049: 1591), Perkins's *Treatise tending vnto a declaration* (STC 19753: 1591) and Willet's *Synopsis Papismi* (STC 25696: 1592).

In the setting of one of Orwin's books, Abraham Fraunce's *The Countess of Pembrokes Yuychurch* (STC 11340: 1591), the pattern was more complicated, but still made good sense: the division was normally in the middle of the outer forme, with one fount being used for the first four pages of the quarto sheet, the second fount for the last four, and then carrying on through to the middle of the next sheet – a stint of eight consecutive pages. This book used Orwin's mixed Lyon (a) and his Lyon (b). The (b) fount was used for A3r to B1r, the (a) fount for B1v to B2r, (b) for B2v to C3r, (a) for C3v to D2v, (b) for D3r to E2v, and (a) for E3r to F2v. The (b) fount was used for the remainder of sheet F, and the (a) for G1r to G2r. The (b) fount took over on G2v, and the normal pattern continued for the rest of the book, except that the (b) fount was used for K4r, where one would have expected the (a) fount. A similar pattern is found on sheets H to L of another Orwin book, Henry Smith's *The examination of vsurie* (STC 22661: 1591).

Of course, this juggling of types was almost bound to go wrong sooner or later, and Orwin did eventually mix his types, creating distinct mixtures. Still, he did use his founts side by side, and made a considerable effort to keep them separate by correct distribution.

Bibliographers are much happier if work stints and the appearances of founts and anomalies fall into patterns of sheets or inner and outer formes. These are our standard 'bibliographical units' and often strengthen our evidence. However, one thing that has become clear to me while working on types is that our neat units do not always apply. There are not very many examples of odd patterns, but they do occur frequently enough to give us pause.

One can begin with Henry Bynneman as an example. In his first year of printing, 1567, he printed Nowell's *A confutation* (STC 18739). We know that he had two founts of pica roman, a Lyon (b) and a Garamond. In *A confutation* the preface is printed in italic with Lyon (b) as the contrasting face. The text itself is black letter with roman as the contrasting face. For most of the book, up to sheet N, Garamond is used for contrast. Then, in sheet O, a switch occurs and Lyon (b) is found as the contrasting face, and is used as such to the end of the book. What is interesting here is that the change occurred in the middle of a forme, between O1v and O2r, so that one page of both the outer and inner formes had those portions that were to be in a contrasting face set in the Garamond, and the remainder had them set in the Lyon (b). This suggests that the book was set seriatim, beginning at the first page of the sheet and working forward, instead of being set one forme before the other.

John Kingston was another who used his types in this way, as can be seen in Vermigli's *Loci communes* (STC 24667: 1576). Here a Haultin and a Lyon (a) were used. The Haultin was used for the preface, then, for sheet A to 2F5v, the Lyon was used. The Haultin was used again for 2F6r to 2G3r, and then the Lyon for 2G3v to 2G5v. The Haultin was used for the remainder of the forme. From here on the two faces appear usually in complete sheets, although a considerable amount of mixing occurred in the founts through incorrect distribution.

John Legate printed at least one book in very irregular stints. It was Daneau's *A fruitfull commentarie* (STC 6227: 1594). All goes smoothly using his Haultin face through almost to the end of the third alphabet, then his Lyon (b) face appears, on 3X3v. It continues to 3X6r, and is used again on sheet 3Y for pages 3r to 5r, and 7r to 8v. On sheet 3Z it is found on pages 4v to 7r. Then in the fourth alphabet it is used from 4A3r to 5v, 8v to 4B3r, and so on, in completely irregular stints through the remainder of the book.[1] His Lyon (b) fount was not mixed with the Haultin on distribution, so some considerable care was taken to avoid such a mishap.

There are other examples of irregular stints, of course, and the reader may wish to look at *The raigne of King Edward the third* (STC 7502: 1599), printed by Stafford; Gyer's *The English phlebotomy* (STC 12561: 1592), printed by Danter; or the third edition of *The workes* of Richard Greenham (STC 12315: 1601), printed by Felix Kingston.

Another printer who repays attention is George Eld. He too used his founts together, and one sees interesting results. He printed one play, the Jonson–Chapman–Marston collaboration, *Eastward Hoe* (STC 4971: 1605), using both his founts: a Haultin and a Lyon (c). They were used in completely unbibliographical sequences, without too much apparent reason. The

1. *STC* gives this section of the book to Orwin, and certainly the mixing is in his style. If this is correct, then Orwin retained his Lyon (b) fount unused for two years before employing it in the printing of this book.

Haultin face appears on pages A2r, 3r, 4v, B1r, 1v, 2r, C1r to 2v, D4v, E1r, 1v, 2r, F2v, 3r, 3v, H2v to 4r, and I1r to 2r. As with Roberts's *Hamlet*, there exists a compositor analysis for this play, and again the results are most interesting in that the use of the types largely corresponds to the stints of the compositors. C. H. Petter in his analysis of 'this enigmatic compositorial pattern'[1] assigns to his compositor A most of the pages set in Eld's Lyon (c) fount. To compositor B he assigns the pages set in the Haultin fount and a few pages set in the Lyon (c): A4v (about which he is not positive), C3r, C4v and F2r. The remaining assignments fit the typographical pattern exactly.

I am afraid that analysis of type is going to call for a reappraisal of studies of Eld's compositors. Chapman's *Al Fooles* (STC 4963: 1605) was in fact set in three shops, not one, as all editors have assumed. Running-title evidence has already shown that the play was printed in three discrete sections, and the analysis of the type agrees with this division. Professor Akihiro Yamada came closest to the division warranted by the typographical evidence when he divided the play into six parts: sheets A–B, C–D, E–F, G–H, I, and K.[2] He thought further that sheet I was related to C–D, and K to either A–B or G–H. Analysis of the type shows that Eld's shop was responsible for A–B, G–H and K (all set in his Haultin type), so Yamada was very close to the solution. Sheets C–D and I, the second unit, were set by William White, using his Haultin mixture with the large 'k' and the distinctive double-'o' ligature. The compositor did not make much use of this rather awkward ligature, but it was used once, three lines from the bottom of C3r. Sheets E–F were printed by Simon Stafford, using his own mixture of types (which was close to White's in many respects, but lacked the large 'k', and had the expanded 'x' and high-dot 'i'), and were, as was usual with Stafford, fully signed.

Several plays in the 1604–1606 period were printed with Haultin faces. Standard Haultin was used during that period by Bradock, Eld, Field, Felix Kingston and Purfoot. It was also used by Barker, Barnes, Harrison and Legate, but these did not bother with ephemera. So, when one finds a standard Haultin in a play at this time, the hunt is narrowed to these five printers. However, Eld and Purfoot often did something else: they fully signed their quartos. Both Purfoot and Eld had cases of pure Haultin, but Purfoot also had one case in which there was a mixture of Haultin and Lyon capitals. To complicate matters further, Eld had a few Lyon 'M' sorts in his case in 1605, as can be seen in sheet I of *Eastward Hoe*, but these may have been borrowed for the occasion and most of them returned.

One finds fully-signed Haultin, consistent with Purfoot's mixture, in three other plays of the period: *The Fawne* (STC 17483: 1606), *The Malcontent* (STC 17479–81: 1604) and *The Honest Whore* (STC 6501: 1604). The three *Malcontent* quartos were shared with Simmes, who did most of the work, but in each of the three quartos a fully-signed section in Haultin is clearly distinguishable from the work of Simmes. In the first two quartos it is sheets B to E, and in the third, sheets H and I.

A second venture that Purfoot was involved in with Simmes was Dekker's *Honest Whore*. Greg noticed that it was printed in four sections, each in a different type. The first two sheets were printed by Simmes, and Purfoot was responsible for sheets G to K. John Windet's Lyon (c) face with the mixed 'M' is found on sheets C and D, and the odd mixture of Simon Stafford is found on sheets E and F. What complicates matters somewhat is that both Stafford and Purfoot fully signed their sheets, so that earlier critics were misled into thinking that a single shop was responsible for all four sheets.

Purfoot was involved in yet another shared venture, Marston's *The Fawne*. He printed only the first four, fully-signed sheets. Gerald A. Smith in his edition of the play[3] was on the right track when he divided the play between compositors at this juncture. We find that both of Windet's founts were employed in the setting of the remainder of the play. His Lyon face dominates, but the Garamond is found in odd places: beginning at the bottom half of E3v, it then composes all of F1r, the top of F2r, all of F2v, F3v to 4v, G1r, 2v and the bottom of G3v. And those are certainly odd enough units.

The last play to be considered here is Marston's *The Dutch courtezan* (STC 17475: 1605). It was probably printed throughout by Purfoot, with one compositor using the mixed capitals and fully signing sheets B to E, and another workman setting the remainder using the unmixed fount and signing only the first three leaves. There is always the possibility, however, that this was shared with another of the printers using Haultin, so a more careful study of the compositors would be in order.

1. See the New Mermaid edition, London, 1973, p. xli.
2. *Bibliographical Studies in the Plays of George Chapman*. Ph.D. thesis, University of Birmingham, 1976, p. 267.
3. Regents Renaissance Drama Series, London and Nebraska, 1964.

7. HOW TO USE THIS STUDY

One basic use of this study is to identify the printers of books. Here it is assumed that the reader knows the date of the book, and has been able to identify the type, or at least some of its characteristics. Let us assume that you have narrowed the type down to a particular design. The second set of tables (2–8) lumps together all founts of each of the designs, so your man should be there in the table for the design in the book. The first thing to do is eliminate all printers who did not have the face at the time the book in question was printed. This will eliminate many, probably most, of the printers. Then, concentrating on the remainder, look for anomalies both in the face of the text and among the founts of the printers. Perhaps the face of your text has only one form of 'k', for example. Therefore, any printer whose fount of this face while having the form of 'k' in your face had in addition another is eliminated. By this process of elimination one can usually narrow the field to a very few printers, and often to one. However, I cannot guarantee complete success every time, as the foregoing discussion of Haultin-set plays admits. Here too judgement, and one's knowledge of the printers of the period, can come into play. If one has a scurrilous pamphlet whose type is consistent with a face possessed by a disorderly printer and also with one possessed by one of the pillars of the Stationers' Company, one will argue, persuasively I would think, for the former. In the same way one can sometimes argue from the quality of press-work, or from the known habits of certain compositors.

Another way of using this study is to assist in the dating of books by known printers. If one finds that a book has no date, but does name the printer, it can be useful to check the printer's types to see when he used them. Sometimes this will give terminal dates. An example is Marlowe's *Massacre at Paris* (STC 17423) printed sometime by Edward Allde. The type is consistent with Allde's Lyon (a) but not with any other of his types. When one turns to the tables, or looks up Allde in the text, one will find that he used this particular face between 1591 and 1596, so one is able with some confidence to bracket the play within this time span.

This study may be used to check the conjectural assignment of printers of a fairly large number of books. But a word of caution: the identification of one printer at the beginning of a book is no guarantee that he printed the whole volume: one must check not only every gathering but also every page before one can be justifiably confident in the assignment.

To see how the process works, let us take a look at a well-known anthology, *England's Parnassus* (STC 378), edited by Robert Allot and printed in 1600. No printer is named on the title-page, but Nicholas Ling's familiar device is there, together with the initials of his co-publishers. At sheet B the work commences in a pica roman face. On this sheet the 'g' has a large lower counter, so that we know at once we are dealing with Lyon. But there are complications almost immediately; for on this sheet there are two sizes of counter to the 'p', the 'o' counter is decidedly to the left or just as decidedly to the right and the 'i' dot is centred or to the left of the stem. This should be enough to go on. We turn to the tables and ask ourselves who had, for example, two 'p' designs and two 'o' designs in a Lyon fount. There are several who had this mixture, but we want someone who not only had it, but also used it in the year 1600. Because of the dating factor we find that we have narrowed the search to two printers: Creede and Stafford. However, Stafford's 'g' does not fit the text, so by a process of elimination we come down on Thomas Creede with his peculiar mixture of Lyon (a) and (b) as our printer.

At least, he printed the first sheet. Let us now check through the book to see if he set the entire work. All goes smoothly until sheet T, where there is a complete change. The 'g' now has a small lower counter, the 'i' dot is centred, the 'o' axis vertical and the 'k' condensed: these features and the 'bdpq' counters suggest a Haultin face. The one oddity is that with the Haultin face there are some Lyon 'M's present. If we now turn to the table of Haultin types, and look for founts with such a mixture of 'M's, we find that there were in fact four of them, but that only one printer, Thomas Purfoot jun., had such a mixture in 1600. So now we have two printers, Creede and Purfoot.

Let us continue to check and see what happens. The Purfoot Haultin continues to the end of sheet Z, but at sheet 2A we have yet another face. This is in many respects similar to Creede's, but is nevertheless distinct. The Lyon 'g' form is again present, but the 'i' dot is left of centre only: a characteristic of Lyon (b). Also characteristic of Lyon (b) are the 'bdpq' counters; with the 'p' being the most prominent. When we look down the Lyon (b) table for a pure example possessed in 1600, we can eliminate all printers except John Legate and Valentine Simmes. Legate is unlikely, as he usually didn't print such books, but the notes on Simmes point out that some of the impressions of his 'p' are unusually heavy, and on the very first page of sheet 2A there is a heavily inked 'p'. So now we have three printers instead of one: Creede, Purfoot, and Simmes. Let us continue to look through the book. The Simmes Lyon (b) continues to the end of sheet 2F. At 2G1r we find another face, characterized by a Lyon 'g' and by 'p', 'o' and other letters each comprising a mixture of forms. This is familiar to us: we are back to Creede, who finished the book. So now one can say that *England's Parnassus* was divided among three printers. Thomas Creede was the main printer, being responsible for sheets B to S, 2G to 2K, and probably the preliminaries as well. Thomas Purfoot jun. printed five sheets, T to Z, and Valentine Simmes printed six, 2A to 2F.

The Printers

EDWARD ALLDE: Allde began printing in 1584 with a Lyon (c) fount [1] characterized by the inclusion of some dot-left 'i' and the use of 'w–1'. It was a battered fount, and was used in the printing of only one book, Baldwin's *Beware the cat* (STC 1245). Allde did not use pica roman again until 1587, when he used a Lyon (b) with a 'w–3' [2]. This fount became mixed when some condensed 'k' and 'x' were introduced in 1589. The contamination is more evident in some sheets of his books than in others, and this suggests that he had more than one pair of cases of the type, and that the sorts were more mixed in one pair than in the other or others. The fount was used regularly through 1590, and replaced during 1591. It appears in a single 1591 book, Phillips's *Ut hora* (STC 19876), in conjunction with a new type. This fount [3] was a Lyon (a). There was some mixing over the years – an expanded 'k' and a condensed 'x' were used occasionally in 1592 – and again the varying degree of contamination suggests that it was confined to a single case of type. For example, in Monardes's *Three bookes* (STC 18007: 1596) the contamination is apparent only in sheets R and S. This fount did not appear later than 1596, and its disappearance from the scene could be linked either to the Stationers' Court decision of 10 April 1597 to deface his type for his having printed what he should not, or to his having moved his shop.

A fourth fount, a Haultin design [4], but one not free from some mixture, especially of 'g's, 'k's and 'M's, appeared in 1597. This fount was used until 1604, when a fifth fount was introduced. In that year, according to McKerrow's *Dictionary of Printers*, Allde again moved to new premises, and he may have discarded his type on that occasion. The fifth fount [5], marking a return to the Lyon style, was basically a Lyon (c) because the 'i' dot was centred and high. There was a mixture of 'p's, and some of the 'k' was condensed. Occasionally one spots the use of a narrow 'w–3'. This fount was used through 1610.

At first, Allde preferred to use pica roman only in prefatory matter, using either a pica or larger black letter for the text. In 1589 he produced his first book set entirely in roman (with italic as the secondary face), and from then on stuck quite consistently to pica roman as his normal face and size. Black letter appeared in, on average, about a book a year from 1591 on. From 1605 a larger roman, measuring 94mm. for twenty lines, and termed 'english', was used with increasing frequency as the primary fount.

JOHN ALLDE: John Allde did not make much use of pica roman, but did possess some Lyon (b) cast on a 78mm. body. This he used as a secondary fount from 1569 until probably 1580, although he was just as likely to use italic as the contrast to his normal black letter. The fount contained some 'w–1', but it was in short supply.

JOHN AWDELEY: Awdeley began using a Lyon (b) fount cast on a 79mm. body in 1570, and continued using it until 1575. He was forced by a shortage of 'w–1' to add an older style, four-pointed 'w' to the fount in 1575, and this is found on sig. C5r of the *Catechism* (STC 6679.5). It would be tempting to assign the printing of this book to John Day, if Day's type had been cast on a 79mm. body and not, as it was, on a standard, 82mm. body. Awdeley's roman was used only for prefatory matter and quotations: he used black letter for the main text almost exclusively, moving between pica and a larger size.

HENRY BALLARD: Ballard almost certainly did not print the two 1597 books attributed to his press, for these show clear signs of being Hatfield's work. Ballard disappeared from the scene for a decade, and then he reappeared in 1607. The following year he used a Lyon (c) [1] with the 'i' dot slightly higher than usual. This fount had belonged to Valentine Simmes. Ballard also used a second fount which he also obtained from

Simmes. This was a Lyon (b) [2] design, in rather battered condition, with mixtures of 'i' and 'p' and occasionally of other letters. It was used to print *The merry devill of Edmonton* (STC 7493: 1608). No Ballard books are known to have been printed after 1608. Most of his output was in pica roman, but he did use black letter or larger roman in a few books.

CHRISTOPHER BARKER: Barker did not make much use of pica roman type; he used it only for prefatory material and as a contrasting fount, preferring to set the body of his books in black letter. He obtained a fount of pica roman in 1576, a Garamond design [1], but by 1578 had created a distinct, second fount [2] by mixing it with a Haultin fount. The two faces in this mixture are difficult to distinguish; but as the x-height of the Garamond letters is slightly greater than that of the Haultin, and as the 'p's and 's's are different, it is possible. The 'w' was at first a 'w–2', but in 1580, with the addition of some 'w–3', it became mixed. Haultin forms dominated the fount; Barker probably began with a small amount of Garamond which he then mixed with a much larger amount of Haultin (which did not at any time appear in its pure form). The fount was used until 1587, and probably passed to Robert Robinson; certainly not to any of Barker's own deputies.

ROBERT BARKER: Robert Barker's early work was done in conjunction with Bishop and Newberry; he then had no distinctive types. However, from 1600 onwards, after he separated from them, he possessed a Haultin face. It may have been recast in 1608, for the type in Abbot's *Antichristo demonstratio* (STC 44) appears to be unusually crisp. (*STC* suggests it may have been printed in Frankfurt.) As much of Barker's work was on bibles and proclamations, black letter was his usual face. When roman was used, he preferred a large roman, a gros romaine, to pica.

JOSEPH BARNES: Barnes began in 1585 with a Haultin face [1]. This was replaced in 1591 with a Lyon (a) [2], which he used throughout the period. He probably transferred some of his old Haultin sorts to at least one pair of cases of the new fount. Over the years the fount lost its crispness, probably because, being in Oxford, he was at an inconvenient distance from the source of supply. Another feature of Barnes's work is that the ink is often poor in quality, tending to give a grey cast to his work. Barnes used his pica as one of his basic faces. However, he also used an english (measuring 88mm. for twenty lines) throughout the period, and with greater frequency from about 1603, so that by 1610 all the books being printed that can be assigned to him were being printed in sizes larger than pica.

GEORGE BISHOP: Bishop, one of the deputies of Christopher Barker, did not use a pica roman before 1590. Whenever a pica roman is found in his earlier books, it turns out that the book was printed for him by someone else, usually Middleton or one of the Eliot's Court group. Bishop's own pica was a Haultin very like Christopher Barker's. There was, in the early years, a mixture of 'p' and a mixture of 'x'; but as the years progressed the large 'p' and square 'x' became less common, probably because of replacement over the years from Haultin matrices. Most of Bishop's work was in roman, with a smaller size preferred in the early years, but later ranging over many sizes.

RALPH BLOWER: The type used by Blower is difficult to classify, for it was little used and had odd mixtures. A page or two from one of his books will exhibit a run of condensed 'k', for example, while another page will exhibit the expanded form. However, from 1603 to 1607 (I have not seen the two books printed in 1608 and 1609) his type was basically Lyon (c) with 'g', 'k', 'o', 'p', 'y' and 'M' each comprising a mixture of forms. These mixtures suggest contamination with Haultin sorts; for these would be the most likely source of condensed letters and a small 'p'.

EDMUND BOLLIFANT: See ELIOT'S COURT PRESS

ROBERT BOURNE: Bourne did little printing, but more of his books are coming to light. He was not allowed to be a master printer as he had, in 1586, contravened the monopoly on grammars, which belonged to Francis Flower. However, there are some books of the early 1590s, printed by 'RB', previously thought to be Ralph Blower, that are now assigned by *STC* to Bourne. Where a pica roman fount was used it was a Garamond cast on a large, 86mm. body, with some expanded 'k', and some 'w–3' mixed with the normal 'w–2'.

RICHARD BRADOCK: Bradock did not begin printing until 1597, in which year he used a Haultin face. He continued to use it until 1609. The 'o' was basically vertical but wavered a bit, possibly due to less-than-perfect casting. From 1605 there was some expanded 'k' in at least one case of the type. Sir John Lambe claimed that Bradock married the widow of Robert Robinson; and the fact that the type is the same as one of Robinson's seems to corroborate this. This type was also the same as that used later by George and Lionel Snowden, both of whom had been apprenticed to Robinson and presented for their freedom, in 1603, by Bradock. Bradock printed most of his books in pica roman, but used both larger and smaller faces occasionally. He used very little black letter.

MELCHISIDEC BRADWOOD: See ELIOT'S COURT PRESS

HENRY BYNNEMAN: Bynneman began in 1567 with two founts of pica roman. The first was a Lyon (b) [1a]. He used this fount most between 1568 and 1573, but kept it until 1583. He appears to have recast it on an 85mm. body and with a 'w–3' in 1578 [1b]. The upper case which he used with it also underwent a change, for in 1580 he began using Garamond capitals [1c]. The second fount which he began with in 1567 was a Garamond [2], but this he used in only two books. The fact that matrices and moulds are mentioned in the inventory of his goods made after his death,[1] and the activity indicated by the states of Lyon (b) in particular, both suggest that he possessed the matrices for at least this face.

Bynneman obtained a Guyot pica [3], probably in 1569 (when it appeared in the running-title of John God's *Discourse of the great crueltie of a widowe towardes a yong gentleman* (STC 11927)), and another fount, a Tavernier [4], in 1570 (although this may have been obtained earlier if the queried date of 1568 for Alessio's *Secrets* (STC 302) is correct). The Guyot, with its distinctively angled form of 'w–2', was used until 1578, the Tavernier until 1574. The Tavernier lacked a 'w', and there was some expanded 'k' in the fount. Bynneman also owned a small Guyot face, cast on a pica body, used in 1567 in the setting of *The treasurie of Amadis* (STC 545). This face is not illustrated or catalogued. Bynneman used his pica roman as a secondary fount, usually with black letter, although in the early 1580s he often used romans smaller than pica.

JOHN CAWOOD: Cawood practically never used a pica roman, using black letter almost exclusively, but he did possess some, a Lyon (b), which he used occasionally in marginal notes between 1569 and 1571.

JOHN CHARLEWOOD: Charlewood used basically the same Lyon (b) from 1570 until 1592. The first form [1a] had a 'w–1', which by 1585 had mixed in with it some 'w–2' and 'w–3'. By 1589 he had had it recast, using only 'w–3' [1b]. The fount passed to James Roberts when he married Charlewood's widow and succeeded to the business.

THOMAS CREEDE: Creede's pica romans have been dealt with at greater length than they will be here (but not using the present terminology, which had not been developed at that time) in *Studies in Bibliography* XXIII (1970). Creede's first four types were related in that they were all of Lyon design. His first fount, used in 1593 and 1594, was a Lyon (b) [1] with some mixture of 'i's. His second fount, used in 1594, was a Lyon (a) [2] with the usual condensed 'k' but some slightly large 'w'. This fount appears in its pure form in only a few pages of *The first part of the Tragicall raigne of Selimus* (STC 12310a). In that book the first fount was also used, and about half-way through the work the founts were mixed through faulty distribution, bringing a third fount [3], a mixture of the first two, into being. This was used certainly until 1602, and probably until 1603, when it was used in the setting of two books, Barckley's *Discourse* (STC 1382) and Dent's *The ruine of Rome* (STC 6640). Some small-bowl 'g' was mixed in in 1598.

The fourth fount was a Lyon (c) [4] with the 'i' dot a trifle high, but not quite at the ascender line. This was replaced in 1609 by a fifth fount [5], similar to standard Garamond in design, with a small-bowl 'g' and a 'w–2'. There was a mixture of condensed 'k' with a few sorts of the expanded form, a small amount of slanted 's' (a Garamond characteristic) and a wide-angled 'y' in which the diagonals met above the base line. This face is the variant of Garamond found in the Le Bé–Moretus specimen of 1599.

Pica roman was Creede's usual type, although he made considerable use also of the larger english size (with a 'k' whose upper diagonal did not reach the mean line, a common anomaly at this time), especially in what could be called 'literary' works. In 1595, for example, Creede used the larger type to print the poets Sidney and Spenser. (Shakespeare, however, normally had to be content with pica.)

JOHN DANTER: Danter was a disorderly printer in more ways than one. His types were so badly mixed that they challenge description. He began in 1591 with a Lyon (a) [1a] with some mixing of 'g' and some mixing of 'k', and with both 'w–2' and 'w–3'. The 'p' was smaller than usual, and the principal 'w–3' was shallow, not touching the base line. This type was used until 1597, when, presumably, it was destroyed by order of the Stationers' Court in April. A variant [1b]

1. Mark Eccles, 'Bynneman's Books', *The Library*, Fifth Series, vol. XII, no. 2, 1957.

had been used in the setting of a single book in 1592: Gyer's *The English phlebotomy* (STC 12561). This fount is characterized by its 'g', 'p' and 'x' each being mixed, and had the same mixture of 'w's as [1a], with perhaps more 'w–2' present. It differed from the first fount in having a narrow 'y' and in the preponderance of small-bowl 'g'. It was used in conjunction with the first fount in units which rule out shared printing. Both founts seem to have been formed by varying degrees of contamination, mostly from Haultin sorts, but also from others he obtained here and there.

A second fount [2] was used in sheet F of *The coblers prophesie* (STC 25781:1594). (Shared printing cannot be entirely ruled out here.) It was a Haultin face, with 'o' basically vertical but some sorts to the right, and a 'w–3' which appears to have had some sorts of Danter's shallow form of the letter mixed in with it. While pica roman was Danter's standard face, he occasionally used a larger, english roman, similar to Creede's, and used for similar purposes.

THOMAS DAWSON: Dawson began in 1577 with a Garamond [1]. He continued to use this fount alone until 1587, when he obtained a Lyon (b) [2]. This was used in its pure form in the setting of only two books printed that year: Everard Digby's *De arte natandi* (STC 6839) and Reniger's *Treatise* (STC 20888). He began mixing the two founts slowly during the next two years to create a third [3]. The Lyon fount was again used in its pure form in a book printed in 1588, Philip Jones's *Certaine sermons* (STC 14728), so Dawson must have kept at least one pair of cases unmixed. From this point on, however, they were inextricably mixed. The mixture continued in use until 1598.

Dawson printed little at the turn of the century, but in 1604 a Guyot fount [4] appeared that was identical to Bollifant and Hatfield's Guyot with the large 'k' and 'w'. It is possible that the fount came from one of these printers, who were by then no longer using it.

Throughout the period Dawson used another type which was technically a pica. It was a much smaller letter cast on a pica body. It was not a leaded type, as it did not have a 'w', and a 'w–2' of regular pica size was used with it. This fount is not included in the catalogue. Dawson used a considerable range of types, often black letter but sometimes italic. Until 1590 he preferred to use his pica roman as a secondary fount.

JOHN DAY: Day was the second printer to use a Lyon fount, and the first to use Lyon (b) [1]. It did not appear in an acknowledged Day book until 1558, but it was used a year earlier in the setting of *The prymer* (STC 16080), which, according to the imprint, was printed by 'the assygnes of' John Wayland, in this case almost certainly Day. The fount continued in use until 1571. It was cast on a large, 85mm. body, and at first did not have a 'w'. In 1559 Day obtained an awkward, four-pointed 'w' which he used with both his pica and his larger, english fount. In one book, Bishop Aylmer's *An harborowe for faithfull and trewe subjects* (STC 1005: 1559), one can see how he shifted the letter from one case to the other. Sheet A is in pica roman, and uses the 'w'. Sheet B is in english roman and is without the letter, which reappears in sheet C. What has happened is that the 'w' sorts had at first been placed in the pica case; then, once the type for sheet A had been distributed (during which time sheet B was being set), the 'w' sorts were transferred to the english case, where they remained for the printing of the remainder of the book. It was not until 1571 that Day obtained a 'w–1' to use exclusively with his pica.

A second fount of pica roman was introduced in 1567. This was a handsome Garamond [2], and was used with Day's celebrated Anglo-Saxon types. The fount was very well cast, and Day was not the only printer to obtain the face in 1567; for both Bynneman and John Kingston acquired a fount in that year. Day continued to use his Garamond for the remainder of his career, although by 1577 there was some mixing of 'w–3' with 'w–2' and, by 1581, there were some Lyon 'g' and 'k' sorts mixed in as well.

HENRY DENHAM: Denham in 1565 obtained some Lyon (b) [1a] on an 85mm. body, but without a 'w'. In 1568 appeared a Lyon (b) [1b] on an 82mm. body with a 'w–1', and in 1574 a 'w–2' became mixed in with it. From 1579 a case of Lyon seems to have had added to it some condensed 'y' and high-dot 'i', and in 1580 some 'w–3' as well.

Denham had a second fount [2], which he used for six years, from 1567 until 1572. He used it alongside his Lyon fount, and in at least one instance, Salesbury's *A playne and a familiar introduction* (STC 21615: 1567), together with it in setting the same book. This is an unusual face; it looks like a copy of Guyot's double pica, which indeed Denham possessed a fount of at the time (both faces are found in Ovid's *Heroycall epistles* (STC 18940: 1567)). The most distinctive letter is the 'y', which is awkwardly wide. This fount [2] contained a normal 'w–2', characteristic of Dutch founts, and not a copy of the wider letter in Guyot's double pica.

A third fount, a Haultin cast fairly wide on the body [3], was introduced in 1581. The identifying mark here is the presence of unusual ligatures. There was a 'ch' ligature and an awkward double-'o' ligature. The double-'o' ligature was in other Denham founts, and was probably the result of an innovation peculiar to him. The matrices for this fount must have passed to Peter Short when he took over Denham's business in 1589, for Short recast it on a narrower set. Denham used a large range of sizes and faces, and usually restricted his pica roman to a secondary role.

THOMAS EAST: East introduced a Lyon (b) pica [1a] in 1569, characterized by the absence of 'w' and by being cast on an 88mm. english body. This was replaced in 1571 with another casting [1b] on a normal, 82mm. body, probably from the same punches, and with some 'w–1', although he often ran short. In 1580 appeared another form [1c] with the 'i' dot almost centred, and a 'w–3'. From now on the only changes were in the position of the 'i' dot, suggesting the possibility that East owned punches. This view is strengthened by the fact that different matrices would have had to be struck to provide castings on the different body sizes. An 'i' with a centred dot appeared in 1594, with some cases of type having more of it than others; by 1603 the 'i' was all centre-dot. East continued to print until 1609. He used his pica roman usually as a secondary fount and usually with black letter. He was a printer of music, and normally used pica roman for the words.

GEORGE ELD: Eld used two founts of pica roman at the same time, and managed to keep them more or less separate. The first one, a rather worn Haultin [1], appeared in 1604. By 1605 it had at most three Lyon 'M' sorts in it. It was used throughout the period. The second fount was a Lyon (c) [2] with the 'i' dot high. This was used from 1605 until 1608, when it appeared in only one book. Throughout the period Eld frequently used both founts in printing the same book, which suggests a method of sharing by his compositors.

It is probable that both faces came to Eld through marriage, for he was his wife's third husband. Her first husband had been Gabriel Simson, and her second had been Richard Read (q.v. for details of the types).

Pica was Eld's usual size; but he made considerable use of english, having a fount with the small-armed 'k', which he used with increasing frequency as the years went on. He seldom used black letter.

ELIOT'S COURT PRESS: The four printers who combined in 1584 to form this press, Bollifant, Hatfield, John Jackson and Newton, all began with a Garamond type [EC1] distinguished by a slightly small 'v' and 'x'. Jackson used it from 1586 until he dropped out of the partnership in 1595. Bollifant used it from 1584 until 1598. In 1600 (he did not use a pica in 1599) he began using a Guyot [EC2] with a large 'k' and condensed 'w–3' that Hatfield had begun using in 1598 (so it was available from that earlier date). Hatfield used the Garamond from 1584 until 1588, but did not employ a pica roman from 1589 until 1597, during which period, indeed, few books appeared over his imprint. In 1602 both Bollifant and Hatfield introduced another face [EC3]. This was possibly continental, and had a distinctive lower case which was very much like the Le Bé Garamond, except that the 'x' was expanded and the 'y' condensed. The 'i' dots were basically slightly to the right. The capitals were different from those of the Le Bé, being of the Lyon (a) design. Bollifant used it in the setting of only one book, his last (which could indeed have been printed for him by Hatfield). Hatfield continued to use the fount until 1607.

Ninian Newton is associated with the Garamond face, found in two books printed early in the partnership; however, these were probably printed for him by Hatfield. When Bradwood joined the group in 1602 he used the same face [EC3] as Hatfield. Then, in 1608, he replaced it with a Lyon (c) [EC4] characterized by a high-dot 'i' and Guyot capitals with the second, less massive, Guyot form of 'M'.

According to Plomer, this group obtained its printing materials from Bynneman's shop. Whatever else they may have obtained in this way, they did not take over his pica roman, unless years later stray matrices or sorts from his Guyot face were pressed into use, for that is the only face they had in common with him.

RICHARD FIELD: Field began well by marrying the widow of his master, Thomas Vautrollier, to whom his first pica, a Lyon (b) [1], had belonged. This fount was used from 1589 until 1599, when it was replaced by a Haultin [2] which had come into the shop the previous year. Field continued to use this Haultin face until 1610, often in French books. Field did a fair amount of shared printing, and other faces will often be found in books attributed to him. Close scrutiny will determine the existence and stints of such sharing.

From the beginning Field had a large number of faces and sizes available to him, and he used them all; often using larger faces for literary works, as seems to have been the general practice in the 1590s. Both *Venus and Adonis* and *The Rape of Lucrece* (STC 22354–7,

22345), for example, are in great primer. As the period progressed, Field used his larger sizes more frequently.

WILLIAM GRIFFITH: Griffith used virtually no roman type at all, preferring black letter. It was not until 1570 that he acquired some Lyon (b), to be used solely as a secondary fount, and which he sold the next year to Henry Middleton.

THOMAS HACKET: Duff reports that Hacket 'seems to have been a prolific printer', but Morrison records only seven books printed by him. Pica roman was used only in 1574. It consisted of a small amount of Lyon (b), used for preliminaries, and even that was short of 'w'.

ROWLAND HALL: Hall was in the last year of his life when he acquired in 1563 a Lyon (b) fount. Used only for preliminaries, it lacked a 'w' and was cast on a very large, 92mm. body.

WILLIAM HALL: In 1609 Hall used a battered Le Bé Garamond [1]. The 'i' dots were mostly centred, but some were to the right. The 'k', while condensed, was in several shapes, probably due to poor casting. The 'o' counter, while basically vertical, could be slanted either way, which was also likely to have been due to poor casting. There was more 'w–2' than 'w–3' in the fount, but both were there. This type was used also by Hall's associate, Thomas Haviland, whose use of it was neater and more competent than Hall's.

At the same time Hall was using a second fount, which was basically Haultin [2]. There was a mixture of 'k', with most sorts being expanded and rather large on the body. There was a mixture of 'p', a mixture of 'v', and some 'G' in the Guyot form. Pica roman was his normal text-face, although he did use a great primer in 1610.

JOHN HARRISON III: Harrison had what was basically a Haultin fount, which he used from 1600 to 1606. It was the same as Judson's, and, as Harrison succeeded Judson as a master printer in 1600, it is reasonable to assume that Judson was the source of this type. Pica roman was his most frequently used text-face.

LUCAS HARRISON: Harrison used a pica roman, a Lyon (b) with the 'i' dot only slightly to the left, only in 1578. It was used as a secondary fount with black letter.

ARNOLD HATFIELD: See ELIOT'S COURT PRESS

THOMAS HAVILAND: Associated with William Hall (q.v.).

NICHOLAS HILL: Hill was the first printer to use a Lyon fount in England, introducing it in 1553. As one would expect in a continental fount, there was no 'k' or 'w'. Hill made do with an expanded 'k' from a fount of a smaller type-size. Hill's pica was the Lyon (a) face, cast on a small, 75mm. body. The type was used only in 1553, and then only as a secondary fount. Because of its body size the descenders were kerned, and often became bent or broken as a result.

WILLIAM HOW: How had been printing for several years before he finally acquired a pica roman in 1569 (the year, coincidentally, in which he married). He used the fount, a Lyon (b) [1a], only in Latin texts until 1571, so one cannot tell if he had 'k', 'y', or 'w' sorts before that date. Certainly by 1571 he had a 'w–1'. But sometime between 1579 and 1582 he replaced the 'w–1' with a 'w–3' [1b]. As the fount was not used during these years, it is not possible to be more exact in dating the change. The 'i' dot was only slightly to the left throughout. The fount was used until 1588, always as the secondary face with his black letter.

ADAM ISLIP: From 1592 until 1599 Islip used a Lyon (a) fount. It existed in two states. The first [1a] was standard, while the second [1b] was cast on an 86mm. body and contained a supply (which sometimes ran short) of the condensed 'w–3'. Both faces can be seen in John Udall's *Certaine sermons* (STC 24491), most conveniently on sheet F, of which the inner forme was printed with the larger-bodied type, and the outer forme with the regular. To my knowledge Islip did not use pica in setting more than two books between 1599 and 1602, preferring his great primer type. However, in 1602 another pica was used. It was a Lyon (c) [2] with the 'i' dot just a trifle high, and with a very generous 'k'. This was used through 1610. Also in 1602 he used a Guyot [3] with the same admixture of large 'k' and condensed 'w–3' as that found in the Eliot's Court Guyot face. Islip used it until 1604. It is possible that this was in fact the Eliot's Court fount, and that it passed from Islip to Dawson in 1604. Otherwise, it would be odd that the dates of use should coincide so exactly.

HUGH JACKSON: Jackson used a Lyon (b) from 1576, and was the first printer to use a 'w–3'. His Lyon (b) continued in use until 1594, always secondary to black letter.

JOHN JACKSON: See ELIOT'S COURT PRESS

WILLIAM JAGGARD: The celebrated Jaggard used very little pica in the early part of his period. His first fount of pica roman, a Haultin [1], appeared in 1604 and was used through 1610. A second fount [2] was used in the setting of a single book, Attersoll's *The badges of christianity* (STC 889), printed in 1606. This appears to have been basically a Haultin, with 'g', 'p', 'v' and 'x' each comprising a mixture of forms (which suggests a Lyon (a) mix), and, along with them, a black-letter ampersand and 'y^{e}' contraction. Most of Jaggard's books were set in roman type, with a preference for the larger, english body.

ABEL JEFFES: If Jeffes did in fact print the first book ascribed to him, *Articuli per archiepiscopum* (STC 4584) (and even the date, 1585, is conjectural), he began with a presentable Guyot [1] which he never used again. His second fount, dating from 1587 and used until 1590 (although not in 1588), was a mixture which defies description [2]. It appears to have been basically Haultin, with Lyon and possibly Garamond sorts mixed in. The 'i' was always centre-dot, the 'g' usually the small-bowl variety and the 'k' usually condensed; some 's' sorts were slanted, and the 'w' was equally divided between the second and third forms. Some black-letter sorts were used, and the use of the black-letter 'y^{e}' contraction was common. Happily, this fount appears not to have survived his move from Philip Lane to St Paul's Churchyard. In 1591 a Lyon (a) [3] appeared, and was used until 1598.

Jeffes usually used his pica as a supplement to his black letter; it was not until 1593 with the printing of Peele's *King Edward I* (STC 19535) that a roman face was used throughout a book, and to my knowledge that was the only book he printed throughout in roman.

RICHARD JONES: Jones did not use much pica roman, and, although he may have had his fount, and have used it in the margin in 1571, it cannot be firmly established that he actually possessed it before 1573. His pica was a standard Lyon (b) with a 'w-1' [1]. By 1585 he had mixed in some 'w-3', and in 1587 there were also some 'w-2' sorts, together with a very wide 'y'. By 1590 the 'w-1' and the wide 'y' had disappeared. After 1591 the fount was put aside for three years, to be used again in the setting of one book in 1595, Robert Parry's *Moderatus* (STC 19337). It is difficult to be more precise in dating these changes, as the type was seldom used, and then only as a secondary fount.

Jones used a second fount from 1595 until 1597. This was a Haultin [2] which contained the unusual double-'o' ligature, and used mostly Lyon capitals, which may have come from his old Lyon pica. Both founts passed to William White when he bought Jones's business in 1598. Jones preferred to use black letter as his principal fount, although he developed a taste for english roman, using it more and more frequently in the mid-1590s.

THOMAS JUDSON: Judson did little printing, but he did have a Haultin fount, which he used in 1598 and 1599. It passed to John Harrison III.

RICHARD JUGGE: It was very seldom that Jugge had any use for pica roman. It occurs only sporadically in his work, never replacing black letter as his principal face. He had a Lyon (a) [1] in 1561, without 'k' (he substituted a smaller 'k' for the missing letter) or 'w'. This fount was not used in any other year. A second fount, a complete Lyon (b) [2] with 'w-1' (its earliest occurrence), was used in 1566 and remained in use until 1579. (There is a possibility that this fount may have been possessed by Jugge at an earlier date, if the date of the 1563 *Statutes* (STC 9467) is to be credited. However, as the other edition of the 1563 *Statutes* (STC 9466) is wrongly dated – it uses a Lyon (b) with a 'w-3' that was not available until several years after the date given – it need not be credited. *STC* suggests the possibility that these both belong to the 1570s.)

WILLIAM KEARNEY: Kearney did not print many books in London in the early 1590s, but he nevertheless possessed two founts of pica roman, both used as his principal founts in 1591 and 1592. The first was a Haultin [1] with some slight mixing of Lyon letters, as if a small amount of type had been mistakenly distributed. The second fount was a Lyon (b) [2]. He may have used the same capitals, basically Haultin with again a mix of Lyon, with both lower cases. *STC* tentatively suggests that the two books in the setting of which the second fount was used, both sermons by Henry Smith (STC 22663, 22684), were printed by Allde. However, Allde did not at any time use Lyon (b).

FELIX KINGSTON: Kingston was one of the most active printers of the period, but despite this activity he used only two founts of pica roman between 1597 and 1610. The first, a Haultin [1], was used throughout the period. The second, a fount [2] resembling the Le Bé Garamond, was introduced in 1599. It was used extensively until 1602, but very little after that. In 1607 it became mixed with some of his Haultin and then dropped from use. It used a slightly large, expanded 'k', an expanded 'x', a small-bowl 'g', a high-dot 'i' and the condensed form of 'w-3'. The 'k' and 'w' both suggest that it was a Dutch import.

Kingston used pica roman as his principal fount,

but often employed english or great primer as principal founts as well, particularly in 1600. He also made use of long primer, and all four were used in printing one of his 1609 books, Calvin's *A commentary upon the prophecie of Isaiah* (STC 4396).

JOHN KINGSTON: John Kingston did not acquire a pica roman until 1556, when he used a Lyon (a) design cast on a 92mm. body [1a]. In 1558 he possessed it on a much smaller, 74mm. body [1b]. There is a slight possibility that he may have had this as early as 1554, if the *STC* attribution and dating of Montulmo's *Treatise of astronomie* (STC 18054) are correct. Unfortunately, there are only four fragmentary lines to go on in this book. In 1562 Kingston had the fount recast on a standard, 82mm. body [1c]. The fount lacked both 'k' and 'w' – a small 'k' was used until 1574, when he obtained the expanded form of the letter. He added some 'w–2' (sometimes supplemented with an italic) in 1568, and from 1571 a 'w–3' was mixed in with it. The fount was used until 1576.

A second fount, a Haultin [2], was used from 1576 until 1583. This fount had a rather deep 'y' and a few Lyon sorts as well. The mixing in of some Lyon sorts is not surprising: both founts were on occasion used together and could easily have been mixed on distribution.

A handsome Garamond [3] was used in printing only one of Kingston's books, in the introduction to Sir Thomas Wilson's *The rule of reason* (STC 25814). This fount presents a bit of a problem. The face is the Garamond that Day and Bynneman introduced into England in that year, and one wonders if Day, perhaps, printed this section for Kingston. What gives one pause in actually stating that Kingston did not print it (given that it is found used in only one book with his imprint) is the presence shortly after of a number of 'w–2' sorts in Kingston's Lyon (a) case, which could very easily have come from the Garamond. Perhaps he borrowed some Garamond from Day or Bynneman for this job, and borrowed a handful of 'w–2' sorts more permanently.

Kingston always used black letter as his principal face, using either roman or italic as secondary faces. In one book, Du Ploiche's *A treatise in Englishe and Frenche* (STC 7364: 1578), in which the two languages are in parallel columns, roman is used for the French, black letter for the English.

JOHN LEGATE: Legate first used a pica roman, a Haultin [1], in 1590. The 'o' was poorly cast, and leaned in either direction. The fount was used extensively until 1599 and then put away until 1604, when it was used again. It continued in use through 1610. His second, seldom-used fount was a Garamond [2] that was very short of 'w–3'. It was used in the printing of only three books, one in 1593 and two in 1599.

Legate's third fount [3], used first in 1594 and then more extensively from 1600 until 1604 (effectively replacing the first fount for this period), was a Lyon (b). In 1603 it was showing signs of wear, and the following year was replaced by the older fount. Other founts are found in books attributed to Legate, but close examination shows that they were printed by others. Pica roman was Legate's normal principal fount, although in 1598 he printed several books in english roman. I have not seen any black letter in his work.

CANTRELL LEGGE: Legge was apprenticed to Legate, and shared the Cambridge printing with him. It is not surprising, therefore, to find that in 1607 Legge used the same Haultin face as Legate. As Legate used the face for such a long time, and was at such an inconvenient distance from the source of supply, it is probable that he had matrices and that he allowed Legge to use them. Legge's 'o' was better cast. Legge's type preferences were the same as his master's, with an english roman used in about half of his books.

HUMPHREY LOWNES: Lownes, although free of the Stationers' Company in 1587, did not begin his extensive printing business until 1604, when he married Peter Short's widow and took over that business. His first pica roman was Short's Haultin [1] recast on a wider set and with a wandering 'o'. The double-'o' ligature which Short had inherited from Denham was discarded. This fount was used until 1608, by which time it had acquired a few sorts from Lownes's other fount, a Lyon (c) [2] with a high-dot 'i'. This second fount had been used since 1606, and continued in use through 1610. In 1608 there had been some mixing in at least one case of type, notably of some condensed 'k' and small-counter 'p' from the Haultin fount. Fewer than a third of Lownes's books used pica as the principal fount: he preferred larger roman faces, up to great primer. Only occasionally did he use black letter.

THOMAS MARSH: Several years after he began printing, Marsh replaced his old-style pica with some Lyon (b) [1]. He did this probably in 1567, when a Lyon (b) fount was used in setting one page (sig. D2v) of a prognostication (STC 435.43). Here it was either on a large body or, more likely, leaded. The face is found in single lines elsewhere in the book. He had some 'w–1' for the fount from this time, although it was used without the letter in some of the 1568 books. He continued to use the fount, though sparingly, until 1579.

Marsh's second face, used occasionally with his standard black letter from 1577 until 1587, appears to be a Guyot [2] with a rather large lower counter to the 'g', a high-dot 'i', a 'w–3' which is a bit lower on the face than the other letters (so that it often cuts the base line and does not touch the mean line) and a very wide 'y'.

HENRY MIDDLETON: Middleton's collection of pica romans to some extent paralleled that of his partner, Thomas East. He began with a Lyon (b) [1a] with some 'w–1' in 1570. It was the same face as that possessed by Griffiths, so when he bought Griffiths out the following year he probably simply combined the two founts. In 1576 the 'w–1' was replaced with a 'w–3', probably as the result of a complete recasting [1b]. The fount was used, though sparingly, until 1582, when the lower case was used with the capitals of his second fount. The second fount, a Haultin [2], had appeared in 1579, and was used until 1586. In 1579 some Lyon (b) and the Haultin were mixed, probably to set sheet 3V of Calvin's *Sermons on the epistles* (STC 4441), and this distinct, third fount [3] was used until 1581. Middleton used a variety of faces and sizes without seeming to have any one preference. Books printed by Middleton entirely in roman had appeared by 1579.

NINIAN NEWTON: See ELIOT'S COURT PRESS

NICHOLAS OKES: Okes used his Haultin fount [1] in setting only two of his books, one printed in 1606 and the other in 1607. At the same time he used a Lyon (c) [2] with the 'i' dot a trifle high, and a very large 'p'. This fount, used until 1610, was made more singular by being used with Guyot capitals. The type from this fount used to print sheet L of Sarpi's *Apology* (STC 21757: 1607) had some condensed 'k' and some 'w–2' mixed in, but this is the only book of his in which this mixing has been seen. Most of Okes's books were printed in pica roman, although he printed a number in english roman. Only a few were printed in black letter.

THOMAS ORWIN: Orwin began in 1587 with a Garamond [1], which he used extensively until 1589, but then only occasionally in 1590 and 1591. Presumably he obtained it from George Robinson's stock when he married Robinson's widow. In 1589 he acquired a Lyon (a) [2a] with a distinctive 'k'. This 'k' had curved diagonals, and he was the only printer of the period to possess it. The variety of 'w–3' in his fount was a shallow letter. In 1590 he mixed in with it some 'w–2' from his first fount, together with a few 's' and 'y' sorts, and perhaps a few sorts of other letters (but not 'k'), making a distinct variant [2b] of his second fount.

In 1591 Orwin obtained a third fount, a Lyon (b) [3a]. In the same year he contrived to mix with it some of his Lyon (a) variant [2b], making yet another distinct fount [3b], a variant of the Lyon (a). In 1592 he obtained a Haultin fount [4], which replaced all but his unmixed Lyon (a) and (b) (those designated [2a] and [3a]), and in 1593 this was the only pica he used. His widow, Joan, continued using the Haultin until 1597.

Orwin more than most other printers used two pica founts in the same book, keeping them reasonably apart, but with some mixing. In the 1580s, he used pica roman primarily as a secondary fount with black letter, and continued to use a considerable amount of black letter through to 1593. A few books, mostly printed in 1590, were printed with an english roman fount.

THOMAS PURFOOT: As both father and son were in business together and as their work cannot be distinguished typographically, they will be treated as a single shop. Purfoot sen. obtained a Garamond [1] in 1569, and used it until 1582. Fairly early on, probably in 1570, some Lyon forms and some 'w–1' were added, and one finds thereafter a light sprinkling of these letters throughout.

During 1582 a second fount, a Haultin [2] with a deep 'y', was substituted for the Garamond, and was used through 1610, by which year the occasional Lyon 'g' was appearing. Purfoot sen. died in 1591, and there was then a gap in the shop's output, with no books being issued in either 1592 or 1593. From 1594 there was a mixture of 'M's in at least one case of the Haultin, but Purfoot kept at least one case unmixed. The length of time the same face was used suggests that Purfoot had his own matrices. One has to be on one's guard with Purfoot jun., for he did a large amount of shared printing, including that of some of our more important dramatic texts.

Purfoot sen. preferred to use black letter as his principal face, using pica roman for preliminaries. His son continued this practice for several years, printing only two books entirely in pica roman before 1604; from that year on, although he used larger romans as well, and continued to use black letter as a principal face, he used pica roman more frequently.

ROBERT RAWORTH: Raworth did little printing during our period, but he did have a Lyon (c) with a high-dot 'i' and a mixture of 'k's, which he used in 1608.

RICHARD READ: *STC* is rather hesitant about assigning books to this press. However, although one should approach the assignment of types to Read with caution, the two types used do seem to create a reasonably clear pattern of use. Read married the widow of Gabriel Simson, and Simson's face is found in Read books. Next, Read's widow married George Eld, and in Eld books one finds the Simson–Read face together with a Haultin which had been used in books attributed to Read. So it seems probable that Read had two founts – the Simson fount brought by his wife, and the Haultin which he acquired himself – and that both founts were subsequently taken by his widow to Eld. The Haultin face [1] is the earlier fount, being used in the single 1600 book attributed to Read, the second part of Cornwallis's *Essayes* (STC 5775). We assume it was Read who in 1601 used Simson's Lyon (b) [2]; an undistinguished fount in which 'i', 'k', 'p' and 'M' each comprised a mixture of forms. When Eld obtained the materials he discarded those letter forms which did not belong, and produced an 'i' with the dot a trifle higher. Several of the books assigned to Read are printed in english roman.

JAMES ROBERTS: During his distinguished career Roberts used four pica roman founts. The first one, obtained in 1593, had belonged to Charlewood, whose widow Roberts married. He remained faithful to the fount, a Lyon (b) [1], throughout his career. It was a standard fount, although many of the 'i' dots were centred. He used a small Guyot [2] in 1597 in one book, a reprint of Lyly's *Euphues* (STC 17075), and again in 1602 and again in a single book, a reprint of Drayton's *Englands heroicall epistles* (STC 7197). In 1599 he used a Haultin [3] in a single book, Marston's *The scourge of villanie* (STC 17486). His last fount, a Lyon (a) [4] with a narrow 'w–3', was used together with his Lyon (b) in printing the second quarto of *Hamlet* (STC 22276: 1604) and again the two were used together in printing William Perkins's *Of the calling of the ministerie* (STC 19733: 1605). Roberts was able to keep his types in their separate cases, although there was some mixing of 'M' in his Lyon (b) by 1605.

Roberts did not settle on any one type-size for his books, and ranged more widely than most of his contemporaries. He used black letter throughout his career, together with pica and english roman, and printed a fairly large number of books with his small pica, which had a slightly outsized 'w'.

GEORGE ROBINSON: Despite the fact that he married John Kingston's widow, Robinson did not use any of Kingston's pica roman. Instead, he obtained a standard Garamond and used this fount from 1585 until 1587, when it passed to Orwin, who had married his widow. Robinson used pica roman as a supplement to his black letter.

ROBERT ROBINSON: Robert Robinson began in 1585 with a Garamond [1]. He used it very little, and in 1587 began to use a second fount [2], a mixture of Garamond and Haultin sorts, which he probably purchased from Christopher Barker, who ceased using such a mixture in the same year. Robinson used it only until 1588, and then replaced it with the Haultin which had belonged to Middleton [3], obtained when he bought Middleton's equipment from his widow. This fount passed in turn to Bradock when he married Robinson's widow in 1597.

Black letter was Robinson's standard type in the late 1580s, with pica roman used as a secondary fount. However, by 1592 pica roman had become his standard size and face, although he continued using some black letter, and also some romans larger and smaller than pica.

THOMAS SCARLET: Scarlet printed from 1590 until 1597, using only one style of pica roman: a Haultin made identifiable by the distinctive presence of several Lyon 'g' sorts. He seldom used it, preferring great primer and english romans.

WILLIAM SERES: Seres seldom used pica roman, preferring black letter. However, by 1567 he had in his shop a Lyon (b) [1a] with a 'w–2'. In 1575 the face was recast as a Lyon (c) [1b] with a high-dot 'i' and had added to it the distinctive Guyot capitals.

PETER SHORT: Short took over Denham's business in 1589, and in 1590 books bearing his imprint appeared. He used Denham's Haultin face, recast on a much narrower set, and included the double-'o' ligature. He used the ligature sparingly, as can be seen in the first quarto of *1 Henry IV* (STC 22280: 1598). He continued to use the fount until 1603. Short used pica roman as his principal fount in about half his books. He also made frequent use of both larger and smaller sizes of roman, making full use of the wide range of founts he had obtained from Denham.

VALENTINE SIMMES: Simmes began in 1594 with a

Lyon (b) [1a]. Its 'i' dot was very much to the left, and many of its 'p' sorts were very heavy in their impression. Some centre-dot 'i' appeared in 1604. He continued to use this until 1606, when he had at least the lower case recast on a slightly wider set, and the 'i' dot centred and placed a bit high, creating by the alteration to the 'i' a Lyon (c) [1b]. It was used until 1607. Both founts were used in printing John Hind's *Eliosto Libidinoso* (STC 13509: 1606), the older type being used for sig. D3r to E4v. Both founts passed to Ballard.

Simmes increased his use of pica roman during his career. He had begun by using it as a secondary fount with black letter, but by 1597 it had become his most important fount. He continued to make use of black letter, and used romans both larger and smaller than pica as well.

GABRIEL SIMSON: There are very few books printed between 1595 and 1600 that are assigned to Simson. He used a Lyon (b) with considerable mixing. One case at least seems to have contained more centre-dot 'i' and condensed 'k' than the others, but they too had these letters well mixed in by 1600. There was no marked preference of sizes or faces in Simson's work: he used black letter and english roman as often as pica roman.

THOMAS SNODHAM: There are not many books from this press printed before 1610, but two pica founts were nevertheless used before then. The first, used in 1603 and then again in 1609 and 1610, was a Lyon (c) [1] with the 'i' dot a trifle high, and could easily have come from East's punches. Snodham's second fount, used in 1609 and 1610, was a Le Bé Garamond [2] with an anomalously high shoulder to the 'h'. The 'k' was between expanded and condensed, the 's' was slightly slanted and 'w–2' was used. Snodham did not make much use of his pica roman, using black letter just as frequently and, of course, concentrating on music.

GEORGE & LIONEL SNOWDEN: This shop operated for only a short time, printing only five books. The pica roman used was a Haultin. The first part of Tilenus's *Positions lately held* (STC 24071: 1606) was probably printed for them by Bradock, who used a Haultin with a mixture of 'k', while the second part was shared with a printer employing a Lyon (c) with a high-dot 'i', which narrows it down to Allde, Eld, or Lownes. The Snowdens printed only during 1605 and 1606, using their pica roman as the principal fount in the printing of all five books.

SIMON STAFFORD: From 1598 through to 1610 Stafford used a pica roman fount which was very much a jumble. The 'g' was mostly condensed, but there were some sorts of the Lyon form. The 'i' was equally divided between centre-dot and high-dot. The 'k' was mostly of the condensed form at the beginning of the period, but the amount of the expanded form increased as time went on. In addition to a mixture of 'p' there were at least two varieties of 'w–3', including the condensed variant. Behind the mixture probably lay some Haultin sorts and some Lyon (a) (which were used more or less unmixed in printing parts of the 1599 edition of *The raigne of King Edward the third* (STC 7502)), into which was mixed some Lyon (c) as time went on. This would explain the expanded 'k' and the constancy of the 'i' dot.

When he began printing, Stafford used pica roman as his principal fount, but as time passed he came to use more black letter, which is a reversal of the usual pattern. He also came to use more english roman.

WILLIAM STANSBY: Many of the books formerly attributed to Stansby have been reassigned to John Windet, his partner and former master. However, there remain a few Stansby books, printed in 1609 and 1610, that employ a Haultin face, which Windet did not have. Stansby seldom used pica roman as a principal fount, preferring english or great primer roman, or black letter.

HENRY SUTTON: Sutton used very little pica roman, and then only as a secondary fount. The pica roman that he used, from 1557 until 1559, was a Tavernier without 'k' or 'w'. The face is illustrated in Isaac (volume 2, fig. 151), where it is incorrectly called a Garamond. It is the earliest use of Tavernier in England I have seen. The capitals of the face are a trifle small, and the 'M' is very close to the Lyon style, the only difference being that the stems of the Tavernier capitals are closer to the vertical.

RICHARD TOTTEL: Tottel seldom used roman types, for most of his trade was in law books, traditionally printed in black letter. It was not until 1587 that a pica roman appeared, a Garamond with the 'i' dot mostly high. He used it until 1593, his last year, but never as a principal fount.

THOMAS VAUTROLLIER: Vautrollier did not use a pica roman before 1574. In that year he obtained a Haultin without a 'w' [1a]. This was the first Haultin pica roman to be used in England, and, as both Haultin (who had just acquired his uncle's matrices) and Vautrollier were Huguenots, it is not surprising that

Vautrollier patronized him as soon as he did. The fount was set rather wider than later Haultins. A 'w–3' was added in 1577, and the type [1b] was used until 1588, although it was largely superseded in 1587 by a second fount, a Lyon (b) [2] with the 'i' dot just slightly off-centre, which later passed to Richard Field. There was no one fount which Vautrollier used more regularly than the others; he ranged through various sizes and faces, using more italic than was usual.

ROBERT WALDEGRAVE: Waldegrave did not use a pica roman until 1584, when he began with a standard Garamond [1]. He used this through to 1598 or possibly 1600, and almost certainly had matrices for it. (See discussion in Introduction, pp. 12-13.) In 1600 (or possibly 1598 – I have not seen all his books for those years) he obtained what appears to have been a poorly made Dutch fount, basically Guyot [2] with a large 'k' and 'w', which he used until his death in 1603. I assume, because of the difficulty he apparently had in obtaining proper-fitting 'k' and 'w', that he bought this on the Continent.

In the 1580s Waldegrave preferred to use black letter as his principal face; but he gradually moved to roman, although not exclusively to pica – indeed he frequently used romans both larger and smaller than pica.

ROGER WARD: From 1580 until 1585 Ward used a Lyon (b) [1] in which some of the expanded-'k' sorts were slightly smaller than the rest. After 1585, when Ward was imprisoned and his printing materials seized, there was a gap until 1589, when, not unexpectedly under the circumstances, his reappearance brought with it a badly-mixed type [2]. Behind it lay some Lyon (a) and some Haultin. The 'g', 'p' and 'v' each comprised mixed forms, he was short of 'w', and the 'k' and 'x' sorts were all of the condensed form, unlike those in Danter's mixture, for example. The capitals were Haultin. Ward used the fount until 1592.

Ward preferred black letter as his principal face, using pica roman as a secondary fount until 1589, when he began occasionally to use it as the principal fount.

RICHARD WATKINS: The first of Watkins's books was printed in 1561, after which there was a gap until 1570. This first book used pica roman basically for sidenotes. The fount was the same as Nicholas Hill's: a Lyon (a) on a 75mm. body with a small 'k' and no 'w' [1], and one wonders if it was the same type. As in Hill's fount, many of the tails of the 'y' were bent because of the kerning made necessary by such a small body.

When he printed again in 1570, Watkins used a Lyon (b) [2] with a 'w–1'. In 1579 some 'w–3' was mixed in with it. The fount disappeared during the 1580s, but was used again for some of the books printed in 1591, 1594 and 1598. When these books were printed the 'w–1' had been completely replaced by the 'w–3'. From 1579 until 1583 Watkins used a Garamond [3] with the 'i' dot a trifle high. He printed very little in the next seven years, and most of that was in collaboration with Roberts. It was not until 1591 that Watkins used pica roman as a principal fount, preferring to use black letter.

WILLIAM WHITE: White bought Richard Jones's business in 1598, and quite simply mixed together Jones's Lyon (b) and Haultin with the distinctive double-'o' ligature [1]. There was very little 'w–2' left by then. He used this fount until 1606. In 1607 he replaced it with a Lyon (c) [2] with a high-dot 'i', which he used through 1610. White used pica roman as his principal fount in about half his books, using a fair amount of black letter and some larger romans as well.

THOMAS WIGHT: Wight used two founts, beginning in 1598 with a Haultin face [1], to which was added in 1601 some 'w–3' that was slightly larger than normal and a few other sorts, probably Dutch. In 1602 and 1603 he used a Lyon (b) [2]. As a printer of law books, Wight worked principally with black letter: I have not seen any of his books in which pica roman was used as the principal face.

WILLIAM WILLIAMSON: A little-known printer in the early 1570s, Williamson occasionally used a small amount of Lyon (b), with black letter, from 1572 to 1574.

JOHN WINDET: In 1584, his first year of business, when he was working with Thomas Judson, Windet used a Lyon (b) [1] cast on an 85mm. body. The next year he used a Garamond [2a] with some expanded 'k', also cast on an 85mm. body. He continued to use this until 1591, after which time it was superseded for several years by a Lyon (a) [3], used until 1599. In 1600 he began using his Garamond again, now cast on an 82mm. body [2b], but without the expanded 'k'. In 1606 he also used a Lyon (c) [4] which had a few condensed-'k' sorts and some 'w–2'. In 1607 a fifth fount [5] was created by mixing together the recast Garamond and the Lyon (c), and this was used until 1609. Pica roman was one of Windet's preferred principal founts, although he came to use more english roman as the years progressed.

JOHN WOLFE: Wolfe began in 1581 with a Garamond [1a] cast on a 79mm. body and with some slight mixing of 'k'. In 1591, in the printing of Leonard Wright's *The pilgrimage to paradise* (STC 26032), a Garamond with the same characteristics but cast on an 85mm. body [1b] and with some 'w–3' was used. However, this could be the work of Robert Bourne, so the attribution of this fount to Wolfe must remain conjectural. Another fount used in 1591 was a Lyon (a) [2]; however, this could well have belonged to Windet. The relationship between these two printers was probably much closer than has been thought, and probably began much earlier than 1603, when Windet succeeded Wolfe as printer to the City of London. Wolfe did not use much pica roman, preferring black letter, and sometimes using italic or, more often than italic, a larger roman.

REYNER WOLFE: Reyner Wolfe's pica roman has been identified by Vervleit as a Grapheus. Wolfe had it in 1556, cast on an 85mm. body with an awkward 'w' [1a], but in 1564 it appeared on a 76mm. body and with a 'w–2' [1b], the first appearance of this letter form in England. Wolfe used the fount until 1573. He did not use pica roman as a principal fount until 1570, but it was used occasionally from then on.

HENRY WYKES: Wykes did not use a pica roman until 1569, when he acquired a Lyon (b), which he used until 1571. Wykes did not use his pica roman much, and often preferred instead to use italic as a secondary face with his black letter.

CHARLES YETSWEIRT: The few books from this shop usually use some pica roman, but seldom as the principal fount. The fount possessed was a Lyon (b) with some centre-dot 'i' and a mixture of 'p'. It was used from 1594 until 1596.

Bibliography

Arber, E. — *A transcript of the registers of the Company of Stationers of London 1554–1640*, 5 vols. London and Birmingham, 1875–94

Brown, J. R. — 'The Compositors of *Hamlet* Q2 and *The Merchant of Venice*', *Studies in Bibliography*, vol. VII, Charlottesville, 1955

Carter, H. G. — *A View of Early Typography*. Oxford, 1969

Desgraves, L. — *Les Haultin 1571–1623*. Geneva, 1960

Dreyfus, J. G. (ed.) — *Type Specimen Facsimiles*. London, 1963

Duff, E. G. — *A Century of the English Book Trade* [1457–1557]. London, 1905

Eccles, M. — 'Bynneman's Books', *The Library*, Fifth Series, vol. XII, no. 2, 1957

Ferguson, W. C. — 'Thomas Creede's Pica Roman', *Studies in Bibliography*, vol. XXIII, Charlottesville, 1970

Gaskell, P. W. — 'A Nomenclature for the Letter-Forms of Roman Type', *The Library*, Fifth Series, vol. XXIX, no. 1, 1974

Greg, W. W., and E. Boswell — *Records of the Court of the Stationers' Company 1576–1602*. London, 1930

Isaac, F. S. — *English and Scottish Printing Types 1535–58, 1552–58*. Oxford, 1932

McKerrow, R. B. — *A dictionary of printers and booksellers in England, Scotland and Ireland, and of foreign printers of English books 1557–1640*. London, 1910

Morrison, P. G. — *Index to printers, publishers and booksellers* [in *STC*]. Charlottesville, 1950

Petter, C. G. (ed.) — Ben Jonson, George Chapman, John Marston, *Eastward Ho!*, The New Mermaids. London, 1973

Pollard, A. W., and G. R. Redgrave — *A short-title catalogue of books printed in England, Scotland, & Ireland and of English books printed abroad, 1475–1640*. Second Edition, revised by W. A. Jackson, F. S. Ferguson, and K. F. Pantzer, London, 1976, 1986

Smith, G. A. (ed.) — John Marston, *The Fawne*, Regents Renaissance Drama Series. London and Nebraska, 1964

Vervliet, H. D. L. — *Sixteenth-century printing types of the Low Countries*. Amsterdam, 1968

Worman, E. J. — *Alien members of the book-trade during the Tudor period*. London, 1906

Yamada, A. — *Bibliographical Studies in the Plays of George Chapman*. Ph.D. thesis, University of Birmingham, 1976

Tables

Explanation of symbols used in the following tables

g1	small bowl	s2	slanted to right	G	Garamond
g2	large bowl	v1	condensed	Gra	Grapheus
i1	dot left	v2	expanded	Gu	Guyot
i2	dot centre	w1	heavy (see p. 4)	H	Haultin
i3	dot right	w2	arms meet (see p. 4)	H(oo)	Haultin, double-'o' ligature
i4	dot high	w3	normal (see p. 4)	L(a)	Lyon (a)
k1	condensed	x1	condensed	L(b)	Lyon (b)
k2	expanded	x2	expanded	L(c)	Lyon (c)
o1	slanted to left	y1	condensed	T	Tavernier
o2	upright	y2	expanded	mm	Measurement of 20 lines, if not between 81 and 83mm.
o3	slanted to right	M1	no upper-right serif, splayed		
p1	small counter	M2	normal serifs, upright	n	See notes in text
p2	large counter	M3	heavy serifs	EC	Eliot's Court Press
q	large counter	B	Le Bé Garamond	[ ]	Capitals only
s1	upright				

Table 1. *Printers*

		1 g	2 g	1 i	2 i	3 i	4 i	1 k	2 k	1 o	2 o	3 o	1 p	2 p	q	1 s	2 s	1 v	2 v	1 w	2 w	3 w	1 x	2 x	1 y	2 y	1 M	2 M	3 M	mm	FACE	DATES
Edward Allde	1		•	n	•				•	•				•		•			•	•				•		•	•				L(c)	1584
	2		•	•				n	•	•				•		•			•			•	n	•		•	•				L(b)	1587–91
	3		•		•			•	n			•	•			•			•			•	n	•		•	•				L(a)	1591–96
	4	•	n		•			•	n		•		•		•	•		•				•	•		•		n	•			H	1597–1604
	5		•				•	n	•	•			•	•		•			•			n		•		•	•				L(c)	1604–10
John Allde			•	•					•	•				•		•			•	n				•		•	•			78	L(b)	1569–80
John Awdeley			•	•					•	•				•		•			•	n				•		•	•			79	L(b)	1570–76
Henry Ballard	1		•		n				•	•				•		•			•			•		•		•	•				L(c)	1608
	2		•	•	n				•	•			n	•		•			•			•		•		•	•				L(b)	1608
Christopher Barker	1	•					•	•			•			•			•	•			•		•		•			•			G	1576–77
	2	•			•		•	•			•		•	•	•	•	•	•			•	n	•		•			•			H+G	1578–87
Robert Barker		•			•			•		•			•		•	•		•				•	•		•			•			H	1600–10
Joseph Barnes	1	•			•			•			•		•		•	•		•				•	•		•			•			H	1585–91
	2		•		•			•				•	•			•			•			•	•	•		•	•				L(a)	1591–1610
George Bishop		•			•			•			•		•	n	•	•		•				•	•	n	•			•			H	1590–99
Ralph Blower		n	•		•			n	•	•	n		n	•		•			•			•	n	•	n	•	•	n			L(c)+H	1603–07(?)
Edmund Bollifant	EC1	•			•			•		•				•			•	n			•		n		•			•			G	1584–98
	EC2	•					•		n		•			•		•			•			n		•	•				•		Gu	1600–02
	EC3	•				•		•		•				•		•		•			•			n	n		•				B(?)+[L(a)]	1602
Robert Bourne		•			•			•	n		•			•			•	•			•	n	•		•			•		86	G	1592–93
Richard Bradock		•			•			•	n		n		•		•	•		•				•	•		•			•			H	1597–1609
Melchisidec Bradwood	EC3	•				•		•		•				•		•		•			•			n	n		•				B(?)+[L(a)]	1602–08
	EC4		•				•		•	•				•		•			•			•		•		•			n		L(c)+[Gu]	1608–
Henry Bynneman	1a		•	•					•	•				•		•			•	•				•		•	•				L(b)	1567–78
	1b		•	•					•	•				•		•			•			•		•		•	•			85	L(b)	1578–80
	1c		•	•					•	•				•		•			•			•		•		•		•		85	L(b)+[G]	1580–83
	2	•			•			•			•			•			•	•			•		•		•			•			G	1567
	3	•			•			•		•				•		•			•		n			•	•				•		Gu	1569–78
	4	•			•			•	n		•			•		•			•	–	–	–	•		•			•			T	1570–74
John Cawood			•	•					•	•				•		•			•	•				•		•	•				L(b)	1569–71

		1 g	2 g	1 i	2 i	3 i	4 i	1 k	2 k	1 o	2 o	3 o	1 p	2 p	q	1 s	2 s	1 v	2 v	1 w	2 w	3 w	1 x	2 x	1 y	2 y	1 M	2 M	3 M	mm	FACE	DATES
John Charlewood	1a		•	•					•	•				•		•			•	•	n	n		•		•	•				L(b)	1570–89
	1b		•	•					•	•				•		•			•			•		•		•	•				L(b)	1589–92
Thomas Creede	1		•	•	n				•	•				•		•			•			•		•		•	•				L(b)	1593–94
	2		•		•			•			•	•	•			•			•			n		•		•	•				L(a)	1594
	3	n	•	•	•			•	•	•	•	•	•	•		•			•			•		•		•	•				L(a) + L(b)	1594–1603
	4		•		n				•	•				•		•			•			•		•		•	•				L(c)	1603–09
	5	•			•			•	n	•	•			•		•	n		•		•		•			n		•			B	1609–
John Danter	1a	n	•		•			•	n			•	n			•			•		•	n		•		•	•				L(a)	1591–97
	1b	n	•		•			•			•	•	•	n		•			•		n	•	n	•	n		•				L(a) + H(?)	1592
	2	•			•			•			•	n	•		•	•		•				n	•		•			•			H	1594
Thomas Dawson	1	•			•			•		•	•			•			•	•			•		•		•			•			G	1577–87
	2		•	•					•	•				•		•			•			•		•		•	•				L(b)	1587–88
	3	•	•	•	•			•	•	•	•			•		•	•	•	•		•	•	•	•	•	•	•	•			G + L(b)	1587–98
	4	•					•		n		•			•		•			•			n		•	•				•		Gu	1604–
John Day	1		•	•					•	•				•		•			•	n				•		•	•			85	L(b)	1558–71
	2	•	n		•			•	n	•				•			•	•			•	n	•		•			•			G	1567–81
Henry Denham	1a		•	•					•	•				•		•			•	–	–	–		•		•	•			85	L(b)	1565–68
	1b		•	•			n		•	•				•		•			•	•	n	n		•	n	•	•				L(b)	1568–80
	2	•			•			•		•				•		•			•		•			•		n		•			Gu(?)	1567–72
	3	•			•			•			•		•		•	•		•				•	•		•			•			H(oo)	1581–89
Thomas East	1a		•	•					•	•				•		•			•	–	–	–		•		•	•			88	L(b)	1569–70
	1b		•	•					•	•				•		•			•	•				•		•	•				L(b)	1571–79
	1c		•	n	n				•	•				•		•			•			•		•		•	•				L(c)	1580–1609
George Eld	1	•			•			•			•		•		•	•		•				•	•		•		n	•			H	1604–10
	2		•				•		•	•				•		•			•			•		•		•	•				L(c)	1605–08
For Eliot's Court *see* individuals																																
Richard Field	1		•	•					•	•				•		•			•			•		•		•	•				L(b)	1589–99
	2	•			•			•			•		•		•	•		•				•	•		•			•			H	1598–1610
William Griffith			•	•					•	•				•		•			•	•				•		•	•				L(b)	1570–71
Thomas Hacket			•	•					•	•				•		•			•	n				•		•	•				L(b)	1574
Rowland Hall			•	•					•	•				•		•			•	–	–	–		•		•	•			92	L(b)	1563

		1 g	2 g	1 i	2 i	3 i	4 i	1 k	2 k	1 o	2 o	3 o	1 p	2 p	q	1 s	2 s	1 v	2 v	1 w	2 w	3 w	1 x	2 x	1 y	2 y	1 M	2 M	3 M	mm	FACE	DATES
William Hall	1	•			•	n		n			n			•		•			•		•	n	•			•		•			B	1609–10
	2	•			•			•	n		•		•	n	•	•		•	n			•	•		•			•			H	1609–10
John Harrison III		•			•			•			•		•		•	•		•				•	•		•			•			H	1600–06
Lucas Harrison			•	n					•	•				•		•			•			•		•		•	•				L(b)	1578
Arnold Hatfield	EC1	•			•			•		•				•			•	n			•		n		•			•			G	1584–88
	EC2	•					•		n		•			•		•			•			n		•	•				•		Gu	1598–1602
	EC3	•				•		•		•				•		•		•			•			n	n		•				B(?)+[L(a)]	1602–07
Nicholas Hill			•		•				n			•	•			•			•	–	–	–		•		•	•			75	L(a)	1553
William How	1a		•	n					n	•				•		•			•	n				•		n	•				L(b)	1569–78
	1b		•	n					•	•				•		•			•			•		•		•	•				L(b)	1582–88
Adam Islip	1a		•		•			•				•	•			•			•			•		•		•	•				L(a)	1592–99
	1b		•		•			•				•	•			•			•			n		•		•	•			86	L(a)	1592–99
	2		•		n				n	•				•		•			•			•		•		•	•				L(c)	1602–10
	3	•					•		n		•			•		•			•			n		•	•				•		Gu	1602–04
Hugh Jackson			•	•					•	•				•		•			•			n		•		•	•				L(b)	1576–94
John Jackson	EC1	•			•			•		•				•			•	n			•		n		•			•			G	1586–95
William Jaggard	1	•			•			•			•		•		•	•		•				•	•		•			•			H	1604–10
	2	•	n		•			•			•	•	•	n	•	•		•	n			•	•	n	•			•			H+L(a)	1606
Abel Jeffes	1	•					•	–	–		•			•		•			•	–	–	–		•	–	–			•		Gu	1585
	2	•	n		•			•	n	•	•	•	•	•	•	•	n	•			•	•	•		•			•			H+L+G	1587–90
	3		•		•			•				•	•			•			•			•		•		•	•				L(a)	1591–98
Richard Jones	1		•	•					•	•				•		•			•	n	n	n		•		n	•				L(b)	1573–95
	2	•			•			•			•		•		•	•		•				•		•	•		n				H(oo)+[L(b)]	1595–97
Thomas Judson		•			•			•			•		•		•	•		•				•	•		•			•			H	1598–99
Richard Jugge	1		•		•			n				•	•			•			•	–	–	–		•		•	•				L(a)	1561
	2		•	•					•	•				•		•			•	n				•		•	•				L(b)	1566(?)–79
William Kearney	1	•			•			•			•		•		•	•		•				•	•		•		n	•			H	1591–92
	2		•	•					•	•				•		•			•			•		•		•	n	•			L(b)	1591–92
Felix Kingston	1	•			•			•			•		•		•	•		•				•	•		•			•			H	1597–1610
	2	•					•		n		•		•			•			•			n		•	•			•			B(?)	1599–1607

		1 g	2 g	1 i	2 i	3 i	4 i	1 k	2 k	1 o	2 o	3 o	1 p	2 p	q	1 s	2 s	1 v	2 v	1 w	2 w	3 w	1 x	2 x	1 y	2 y	1 M	2 M	3 M	mm	FACE	DATES
John Kingston	1a		•		•			–	–			•	•			•			•	–	–	–		•	–	–	•			92	L(a)	1556
	1b		•		•			–	–			•	•			•			•	–	–	–		•		•	•			74	L(a)	1558–62
	1c		•		•				n			•	•			•			•	n		n		•		•	•				L(a)	1562–76
	2	•			•			•			•		•		•	•		•				•	•		n			•			H	1576–83
	3	•			•			•			•			•			•	•			•		•		•			•			G	1567
John Legate	1	•			•			•			n		•		•	•		•				•	•		•			•			H	1590–99, 1604–10
	2	•			•			•		•				•			•	•				n	•		•			•			G	1593, 1599
	3		•	•					•	•				•		•			•			•		•		•	•				L(b)	1594, 1600–04
Cantrel Legge		•			•			•			•		•		•	•		•				•	•		•			•			H	1607–10
Humphrey Lownes	1	•			•			•			n		•		•	•		•				•	•		•			•			H	1604–08
	2		•				•	n	•	•			n	•		•			•			•		•		•	•				L(c)	1606–10
Thomas Marsh	1		•	•					•	•				•		•			•	•				•		•	•				L(b)	1567–79
	2		n				•	•		•				•		•			•			n	•			n			•		Gu	1577–87
Henry Middleton	1a		•	•					•	•				•		•			•	•				•		•	•				L(b)	1570–75
	1b		•	•					•	•				•		•			•			•		•		•	•	n			L(b)	1576–82
	2	•			•			•			•		•		•	•		•				•	•		•			•			H	1579–86
	3	•	•	•	•			•	•	•	•		•	•	•	•		•	•			•	•	•	•	•	•	•			H+L(b)	1579–81
Nicholas Okes	1	•			•			•		•		•	•		•	•		•				•	•		•			•			H	1606–07
	2		•		n				•	•				n		•			•			•		•		•			•		L(c)+[Gu]	1606–10
Thomas Orwin	1	•			•			•		•		•		•			•	•			•		•		•			•			G	1587–91
	2a		•		•				n			•	•			•			•			n		•		•	•				L(a)	1589–92
	2b		•		•				n			•	•			•	n		•		n	•	•	•	n	•	•				L(a)+G	1590–91
	3a		•	•					•	•				•		•			•			•		•		•	•				L(b)	1591–92
	3b		•	•	•				•	•		•	•	•		•	•		•		•	•	•	•	•	•	•				L(b)+(a)+G	1591
	4	•			•			•			•		•		•	•		•				•	•		•			•			H	1592–97
Thomas Purfoot	1	•			•			•		•				•			•	•		n	•		•		•			•			G	1569–82
	2	•	n		•			•			•		•		•	•		•				•	•		n		n	•			H	1582–1610
Robert Raworth			•				•	n	•	•				•		•			•			•		•		•	•				L(c)	1608
Richard Read	1	•			•			•			•		•		•	•		•				•	•		•			•			H	1600, 1602
	2		•	•	n			n	•	•			n	•		•			•			•		•		•	•	n			L(b)	1601

		1 g	2 g	1 i	2 i	3 i	4 i	1 k	2 k	1 o	2 o	3 o	1 p	2 p	q	1 s	2 s	1 v	2 v	1 w	2 w	3 w	1 x	2 x	1 y	2 y	1 M	2 M	3 M	mm	FACE	DATES
James Roberts	1		●	●	n				●	●				●		●			●			●		●		●	●	r.			L(b)	1593–1606
	2	●				●		●		●				●		●			●		●			●	●				●	76	Gu	1597, 1602
	3	●			●			●			●	●	●		●	●		●				●	●		●			●			H	1599
	4		●		●			●			●		●			●			●			n		●		●	●				L(a)	1604–05
George Robinson		●			●			●		●	●			●			●	●			●		●		●			●			G	1585–87
Robert Robinson	1	●			●			●		●	●			●			●	●			●		●		●			●			G	1585–87
	2	●			●			●			●		●	●	●	●	●	●			●	●	●		●			●			G+H	1587–88
	3	●			●			●		●			●		●	●		●				●	●		●			●			H	1588–97
Thomas Scarlet		●	n		●			●		●	●		●		●	●		●				●	●		●			●			H	1590–97
William Seres	1a		●	●					●	●				●		●			●		●			●		●	●				L(b)	1567–74
	1b		●				●		●	●				●		●			●		●			●		●			●		L(c)+[Gu]	1575–76
Peter Short		●			●			●			●		●		●	●		●				●	●		●			●			H(oo)	1590–1603
Valentine Simmes	1a		●	n	n				●	●				n		●			●			●		●		●	●				L(b)	1594–1606
	1b		●		n				●	●				●		●			●			●		●		●	●				L(c)	1606–07
Gabriel Simpson			●	●	n			n	●	●				●		●			●			●		●	●	●	●	●			L(b)	1595–1600
Thomas Snodham	1		●		n				●	●				●		●			●			●		●		●	●				L(c)	1603, 1609, 1610
	2	●			●				n	●			●				n		●		●			●		●		●			B	1609–10
G. & L. Snowden		●			●			●		●			●		●	●		●				●	●		●			●			H	1605–06
Simon Stafford		●	n		●		●	●	n	●	●	●	●	●	●	●			●			n		●	●		●	●			H+L(a)+(c)	1598–1610
William Stansby		●			●			●			●		●		●	●		●				●	●		●			●			H	1609–10
Henry Sutton		●			●			–	–		●			●		●			●	–	–	–	●		●		n				T	1557–59
Richard Tottel		●					n	●		●				●			●	●			●		●		●			●			G	1587–93
Thomas Vautrollier	1	●			●			●			●		●		●	●		●				n	●		●			●			H	1574–88
	2		●	n					●	●				●		●			●			●		●		●	●				L(b)	1587–88
Robert Waldegrave	1	●			●			●		●				●			●	●			●		●		●			●			G	1584–1600(?)
	2	●					●		n		●			●		●			●			n		●	●				●		Gu	1600(?)–03
Roger Ward	1		●	●					n	●				●		●			●			●		●		●	●				L(b)	1580–85
	2	●	●		●			●			●	●	●	●	●	●		●	●			n	●		●			●			H+L(a)	1589–92

		1 g	2 g	1 i	2 i	3 i	4 i	1 k	2 k	1 o	2 o	3 o	1 p	2 p	q	1 s	2 s	1 v	2 v	1 w	2 w	3 w	1 x	2 x	1 y	2 y	1 M	2 M	3 M	mm	FACE	DATES
Richard Watkins	1		•		•				n			•	•			•			•	–	–	–		•		•	•			75	L(a)	1561
	2		•	•					•	•				•		•			•	•		n		•		•	•				L(b)	1570–79, 1591, 1594, 1598
	3	•			n			•			•			•			•	•			•		•		•			•			G	1579–83
William White	1	•	•	•	•			•	•	•	•		•	•	•	•		•	•		n	•		•	•	•	•				L(b)+H(oo)	1598–1606
	2		•				•		•	•				•		•			•			•		•		•	•				L(c)	1607–10
Thomas Wight	1	•			•			•			•		•		•	•		•				n	•		•			•			H	1598–1601
	2		•	•					•	•				•		•			•			•		•		•	•				L(b)	1602–03
William Williamson			•	•					•	•				•		•			•	•				•		•	•				L(b)	1572–74
John Windet	1		•	•					•	•				•		•			•			•		•		•	•			85	L(b)	1584
	2a	•			•			•	n		•			•			•	•			•		•		•			•		85	G	1585–91
	2b	•			•			•			•			•			•	•			•		•		•			•			G	1600–06
	3		•		•			•				•	•			•			•			•		•		•	•				L(a)	1592–99
	4		•				•	n	•	•				•		•			•		n	•		•		•	•				L(c)	1606–07
	5	•	•		•		•	•	•	•	•			•		•	•	•	•		•	•	•	•	•	•	•	•			L(c)+G	1607–09
John Wolfe	1a	•			•			•	n		•			•			•	•			•		•		•			•		79	G	1581–91
	(?)1b	•			•			•	•		•			•			•	•			•	n	•		•			•		85	G	1591
	(?) 2		•		•			•			•	•	•			•			•			•		•		•	•				L(a)	1591
Reyner Wolfe	1a	•			•	•		•			•		•			•		•			n		•			•				85	Gra	1556–63
	1b	•			•	•		•			•		•			•		•			n		•			•				76	Gra	1564–73
Henry Wykes			•	•					•	•				•		•			•	•				•		•	•				L(b)	1569–71
Charles Yetsweirt			•	•	n				•	•			•	•		•			•			•		•		•	•				L(b)	1594–96

Table 2. Garamond

		1 g	2 g	1 i	2 i	3 i	4 i	1 k	2 k	1 o	2 o	3 o	1 p	2 p	q	1 s	2 s	1 v	2 v	1 w	2 w	3 w	1 x	2 x	1 y	2 y	1 M	2 M	3 M	mm	FACE	DATES
Christopher Barker	1	•					•	•			•			•			•	•			•		•		•			•			G	1576–77
Edmund Bollifant	EC1	•			•			•		•				•			•	n			•		n		•			•			G	1584–98
Robert Bourne		•			•			•	n		•			•			•	•			•	n	•		•			•		86	G	1592–93
Henry Bynneman	2	•			•			•			•			•			•	•			•		•		•			•			G	1567
Thomas Dawson	1	•			•			•		•	•			•			•	•			•		•		•			•			G	1577–87
John Day	2	•	n		•			•	n	•				•			•	•			•	n	•		•			•			G	1567–81
Arnold Hatfield	EC1	•			•			•		•				•			•	n			•		n		•			•			G	1584–88
John Jackson	EC1	•			•			•		•				•			•	n			•		n		•			•			G	1586–95
John Kingston	3	•			•			•			•			•			•	•			•		•		•			•			G	1567
John Legate	2	•			•			•		•				•			•	•				n	•		•			•			G	1593, 1599
Thomas Orwin	1	•			•			•		•		•		•			•	•			•		•		•			•			G	1587–91
Thomas Purfoot	1	•			•			•		•				•			•	•		n	•		•		•			•			G	1569–82
George Robinson		•			•			•		•	•			•			•	•			•		•		•			•			G	1585–87
Robert Robinson	1	•			•			•		•	•			•			•	•			•		•		•			•			G	1585–87
Richard Tottel		•					n	•		•				•			•	•			•		•		•			•			G	1587–93
Robert Waldegrave	1	•			•			•		•				•			•	•			•		•		•			•			G	1584–1600(?)
Richard Watkins	3	•			n			•			•			•			•	•			•		•		•			•			G	1579–83
John Windet	2a	•			•			•	n		•			•			•	•			•		•		•			•		85	G	1585–91
	2b	•			•			•			•			•			•	•			•		•		•			•			G	1600–06
John Wolfe	1a	•			•			•	n		•			•			•	•			•		•		•			•		79	G	1581–91
	(?)1b	•			•			•	•		•			•			•	•			•	n	•		•			•		85	G	1591

Table 3. Guyot

		1 g	2 g	1 i	2 i	3 i	4 i	1 k	2 k	1 o	2 o	3 o	1 p	2 p	q	1 s	2 s	1 v	2 v	1 w	2 w	3 w	1 x	2 x	1 y	2 y	1 M	2 M	3 M	mm	FACE	DATES
Edmund Bollifant	EC2	•					•		n		•			•		•			•			n		•	•				•		Gu	1600–02
Henry Bynneman	3	•			•			•		•				•		•			•		n			•	•				•		Gu	1569–78
Thomas Dawson	4	•					•		n		•			•		•			•			n		•	•				•		Gu	1604–
Henry Denham	2	•			•			•		•				•		•			•		•			•		n		•			Gu(?)	1567–72
Arnold Hatfield	EC2	•					•		n		•			•		•			•			n		•	•				•		Gu	1598–1602
Adam Islip	3	•					•		n		•			•		•			•			n		•	•				•		Gu	1602–04
Abel Jeffes	1	•					•	–	–		•			•		•			•	–	–	–		•	–	–			•		Gu	1585
Thomas Marsh	2		n				•	•		•				•		•			•			n	•			n			•		Gu	1577–87
James Roberts	2	•				•		•		•				•		•			•		•			•	•				•	76	Gu	1597, 1602
Robert Waldegrave	2	•					•		n		•			•		•			•			n		•	•				•		Gu	1600(?)–03

Table 4. Haultin

		1 g	2 g	1 i	2 i	3 i	4 i	1 k	2 k	1 o	2 o	3 o	1 p	2 p	q	1 s	2 s	1 v	2 v	1 w	2 w	3 w	1 x	2 x	1 y	2 y	1 M	2 M	3 M	mm	FACE	DATES
Edward Allde	4	•	n		•			•	n		•		•		•	•		•				•	•		•		n	•			H	1597–1604
Robert Barker		•			•			•		•			•		•	•		•				•	•		•			•			H	1600–10
Joseph Barnes	1	•			•			•			•		•		•	•		•				•	•		•			•			H	1585–91
George Bishop		•			•			•			•		•	n	•	•		•				•	•	n	•			•			H	1590–99
Richard Bradock		•			•			•	n		n		•		•	•		•				•	•		•			•			H	1597–1609
John Danter	2	•			•			•			•	n	•		•	•		•				n	•		•			•			H	1594, 1597
Henry Denham	3	•			•			•			•		•		•	•		•				•	•		•			•			H(oo)	1581–89
George Eld	1	•			•			•			•		•		•	•		•				•	•		•		n	•			H	1604–10
Richard Field	2	•			•			•			•		•		•	•		•				•	•		•			•			H	1598–1610
William Hall	2	•			•			•	n		•		•	n	•	•		•	n			•	•		•			•			H	1609–10
John Harrison III		•			•			•			•		•		•	•		•				•	•		•			•			H	1600–06
William Jaggard	1	•			•			•			•		•		•	•		•				•	•		•			•			H	1604–10
Thomas Judson		•			•			•			•		•		•	•		•				•	•		•			•			H	1598–99
William Kearney	1	•			•			•			•		•		•	•		•				•	•		•		n	•			H	1591–92
Felix Kingston	1	•			•			•			•		•		•	•		•				•	•		•			•			H	1597–1610
John Kingston	2	•			•			•			•		•		•	•		•				•	•		n			•			H	1576–83
John Legate	1	•			•			•			n		•		•	•		•				•	•		•			•			H	1590–99, 1604–10
Cantrel Legge		•			•			•			•		•		•	•		•				•	•		•			•			H	1607–10
Humphrey Lownes	1	•			•			•			n		•		•	•		•				•	•		•			•			H	1604–08
Henry Middleton	2	•			•			•			•		•		•	•		•				•	•		•			•			H	1579–86
Nicholas Okes	1	•			•			•		•		•	•		•	•		•				•	•		•			•			H	1606–07
Thomas Orwin	4	•			•			•			•		•		•	•		•				•	•		•			•			H	1592–97
Thomas Purfoot	2	•	n		•			•			•		•		•	•		•				•	•		n		n	•			H	1582–1610

		1 g	2 g	1 i	2 i	3 i	4 i	1 k	2 k	1 o	2 o	3 o	1 p	2 p	q	1 s	2 s	1 v	2 v	1 w	2 w	3 w	1 x	2 x	1 y	2 y	1 M	2 M	3 M	mm	FACE	DATES
Richard Read	1	•			•			•			•		•		•	•		•				•	•		•			•			H	1600, 1602
James Roberts	3	•			•			•			•	•	•		•	•		•				•	•		•			•			H	1599
Robert Robinson	3	•			•			•		•			•		•	•		•				•	•		•			•			H	1588–97
Thomas Scarlet		•	n		•			•		•	•		•		•	•		•				•	•		•			•			H	1590–97
Peter Short		•			•			•			•		•		•	•		•				•	•		•			•			H(oo)	1590–1603
G. & L. Snowden		•			•			•		•			•		•	•		•				•	•		•			•			H	1605–06
William Stansby		•			•			•			•		•		•	•		•				•	•		•			•			H	1609–10
Thomas Vautrollier	1	•			•			•			•		•		•	•		•				n	•		•			•			H	1574–88
Thomas Wight	1	•			•			•			•		•		•	•		•				n	•		•			•			H	1598–1601

Table 5. *Lyon* (*a*)

		1 g	2 g	1 i	2 i	3 i	4 i	1 k	2 k	1 o	2 o	3 o	1 p	2 p	q	1 s	2 s	1 v	2 v	1 w	2 w	3 w	1 x	2 x	1 y	2 y	1 M	2 M	3 M	mm	FACE	DATES
Edward Allde	3		•		•			•	n			•	•			•			•			•	n	•		•	•				L(a)	1591–96
Joseph Barnes	2		•		•			•				•	•			•			•			•	•	•		•	•				L(a)	1591–1610
Thomas Creede	2		•		•			•			•	•	•			•			•			n		•		•	•				L(a)	1594
John Danter	1a	n	•		•			•	n			•	n			•			•		•	n		•		•	•				L(a)	1591–97
Nicholas Hill			•		•				n			•	•			•			•	–	–	–		•		•	•			75	L(a)	1553
Adam Islip	1a		•		•			•				•	•			•			•			•		•		•	•				L(a)	1592–99
	1b		•		•			•				•	•			•			•			n		•		•	•			86	L(a)	1592–99
Abel Jeffes	3		•		•			•				•	•			•			•			•		•		•	•				L(a)	1591–98
Richard Jugge	1		•		•			n				•	•			•			•	–	–	–		•		•	•				L(a)	1561
John Kingston	1a		•		•			–	–			•	•			•			•	–	–	–		•	–	–	•			92	L(a)	1556
	1b		•		•			–	–			•	•			•			•	–	–	–		•		•	•			74	L(a)	1558–62
	1c		•		•				n			•	•			•			•	n	n			•		•	•				L(a)	1562–76
Thomas Orwin	2a		•		•				n			•	•			•			•			n		•		•	•				L(a)	1589–92
James Roberts	4		•		•			•			•		•			•			•			n		•		•	•				L(a)	1604–05
Richard Watkins	1		•		•				n			•	•			•			•	–	–	–		•		•	•			75	L(a)	1561
John Windet	3		•		•			•				•	•			•			•			•		•		•	•				L(a)	1592–99
John Wolfe	(?) 2		•		•			•			•	•	•			•			•			•		•		•	•				L(a)	1591

Table 6. *Lyon* (*b*)

		1 g	2 g	1 i	2 i	3 i	4 i	1 k	2 k	1 o	2 o	3 o	1 p	2 p	q	1 s	2 s	1 v	2 v	1 w	2 w	3 w	1 x	2 x	1 y	2 y	1 M	2 M	3 M	mm	FACE	DATES
Edward Allde	2		•	•				n	•	•				•		•			•			•	n	•		•	•				L(b)	1587–91
John Allde			•	•					•	•				•		•			•	n				•		•	•			78	L(b)	1569–80
John Awdeley			•	•					•	•				•		•			•	n				•		•	•			79	L(b)	1570–76
Henry Ballard	2		•	•	n				•	•			n	•		•			•			•		•		•	•				L(b)	1608
Henry Bynneman	1a		•	•					•	•				•		•			•	•				•		•	•				L(b)	1567–78
	1b		•	•					•	•				•		•			•			•		•		•	•			85	L(b)	1578–80
John Cawood			•	•					•	•				•		•			•	•				•		•	•				L(b)	1569–71
John Charlewood	1a		•	•					•	•				•		•			•	•	n	n		•		•	•				L(b)	1570–89
	1b		•	•					•	•				•		•			•			•		•		•	•				L(b)	1589–92
Thomas Creede	1		•	•	n				•	•				•		•			•			•		•		•	•				L(b)	1593–94
Thomas Dawson	2		•	•					•	•				•		•			•			•		•		•	•				L(b)	1587–88
John Day	1		•	•					•	•				•		•			•	n				•		•	•			85	L(b)	1558–71
Henry Denham	1a		•	•					•	•				•		•			•	–	–	–		•		•	•			85	L(b)	1565–68
	1b		•	•			n		•	•				•		•			•	•	n	n		•	n	•	•				L(b)	1568–80
Thomas East	1a		•	•					•	•				•		•			•	–	–	–		•		•	•			88	L(b)	1569–70
	1b		•	•					•	•				•		•			•	•				•		•	•				L(b)	1571–79
Richard Field	1		•	•					•	•				•		•			•			•		•		•	•				L(b)	1589–99
William Griffith			•	•					•	•				•		•			•	•				•		•	•				L(b)	1570–71
Thomas Hacket			•	•					•	•				•		•			•	n				•		•	•				L(b)	1574
Rowland Hall			•	•					•	•				•		•			•	–	–	–		•		•	•			92	L(b)	1563
Lucas Harrison			•	n					•	•				•		•			•			•		•		•	•				L(b)	1578
William How	1a		•	n					n	•				•		•			•	n				•		n	•				L(b)	1569–78
	1b		•	n					•	•				•		•			•			•		•		•	•				L(b)	1582–88
Hugh Jackson			•	•					•	•				•		•			•			n		•		•	•				L(b)	1576–94
Richard Jones	1		•	•					•	•				•		•			•	n	n	n		•		n	•				L(b)	1573–95
Richard Jugge	2		•	•					•	•				•		•			•	n				•		•	•				L(b)	1566(?)–79

		1 g	2 g	1 i	2 i	3 i	4 i	1 k	2 k	1 o	2 o	3 o	1 p	2 p	q	1 s	2 s	1 v	2 v	1 w	2 w	3 w	1 x	2 x	1 y	2 y	1 M	2 M	3 M	mm	FACE	DATES
William Kearney	2		•	•					•	•				•		•			•			•		•		•	n	•			L(b)	1591–92
John Legate	3		•	•					•	•				•		•			•			•		•		•	•				L(b)	1594, 1600–04
Thomas Marsh	1		•	•					•	•				•		•			•	•				•		•	•				L(b)	1567–79
Henry Middleton	1a		•	•					•	•				•		•			•	•				•		•	•				L(b)	1570–75
	1b		•	•					•	•				•		•			•			•		•		•	•	n			L(b)	1576–82
Thomas Orwin	3a		•	•					•	•				•		•			•			•		•		•	•				L(b)	1591–92
Richard Read	2		•	•	n			n	•	•			n	•		•			•			•		•		•	•	n			L(b)	1601
James Roberts	1		•	•	n				•	•				•		•			•			•		•		•	•	n			L(b)	1593–1606
William Seres	1a		•	•					•	•				•		•			•		•			•		•	•				L(b)	1567–74
Valentine Simmes	1a		•	n	n				•	•				n		•			•			•		•		•	•				L(b)	1594–1606
Gabriel Simpson			•	•	n			n	•	•				•		•			•			•		•	•	•	•	•			L(b)	1595–1600
Thomas Vautrollier	2		•	n					•	•				•		•			•			•		•		•	•				L(b)	1587–88
Roger Ward	1		•	•					n	•				•		•			•			•		•		•	•				L(b)	1580–85
Richard Watkins	2		•	•					•	•				•		•			•	•		n		•		•	•				L(b)	1570–79, 1591, 1594, 1598
Thomas Wight	2		•	•					•	•				•		•			•			•		•		•	•				L(b)	1602–03
William Williamson			•	•					•	•				•		•			•	•				•		•	•				L(b)	1572–74
John Windet	1		•	•					•	•				•		•			•			•		•		•	•			85	L(b)	1584
Henry Wykes			•	•					•	•				•		•			•	•				•		•	•				L(b)	1569–71
Charles Yetsweirt			•	•	n				•	•			•	•		•			•			•		•		•	•				L(b)	1594–96

Table 7. Lyon (c)

		1 g	2 g	1 i	2 i	3 i	4 i	1 k	2 k	1 o	2 o	3 o	1 p	2 p	q	1 s	2 s	1 v	2 v	1 w	2 w	3 w	1 x	2 x	1 y	2 y	1 M	2 M	3 M	mm	FACE	DATES
Edward Allde	1		•	n	•				•	•				•		•			•	•				•		•	•				L(c)	1584
	5		•				•	n	•	•			•	•		•			•			n		•		•	•				L(c)	1604–10
Henry Ballard	1		•		n				•	•				•		•			•			•		•		•	•				L(c)	1608
Thomas Creede	4		•		n				•	•				•		•			•			•		•		•	•				L(c)	1603–09
Thomas East	1c		•	n	n				•	•				•		•			•			•		•		•	•				L(c)	1580–1609
George Eld	2		•				•		•	•				•		•			•			•		•		•	•				L(c)	1605–09
Adam Islip	2		•		n				n	•				•		•			•			•		•		•	•				L(c)	1602–10
Humphrey Lownes	2		•				•	n	•	•			n	•		•			•			•		•		•	•				L(c)	1606–10
Robert Raworth			•				•	n	•	•				•		•			•			•		•		•	•				L(c)	1608
Valentine Simmes	1b		•		n				•	•				•		•			•			•		•		•	•				L(c)	1606–07
Thomas Snodham	1		•		n				•	•				•		•			•			•		•		•	•				L(c)	1603, 1609, 1610
William White	2		•				•		•	•				•		•			•			•		•		•	•				L(c)	1607–10
John Windet	4		•				•	n	•	•				•		•			•		n	•		•		•	•				L(c)	1606–07

Table 8. Le Bé, Grapheus, Tavernier

		1	2	1	2	3	4	1	2	1	2	3	1	2		1	2	1	2	1	2	3	1	2	1	2	1	2	3			
		g	g	i	i	i	i	k	k	o	o	o	p	p	q	s	s	v	v	w	w	w	x	x	y	y	M	M	M	mm	FACE	DATES
Le Bé																																
Thomas Creede	5	•			•			•	n	•	•			•		•	n		•		•		•			n		•			B	1609–
William Hall	1	•			•	n		n			n			•		•			•		•	n	•			•		•			B	1609–10
Felix Kingston	2	•					•		n		•		•			•			•			n		•	•			•			B(?)	1599–1607
Thomas Snodham	2	•			•				n	•			•				n		•		•			•		•		•			B	1609–10
Grapheus																																
Reyner Wolfe	1a	•			•	•		•			•		•			•		•			n		•			•				85	Gra	1556–63
	1b	•			•	•		•			•		•			•		•			n		•			•				76	Gra	1564–73
Tavernier																																
Henry Bynneman	4	•			•			•	n		•			•		•			•	–	–	–	•		•			•			T	1570–74
Henry Sutton		•			•			–	–		•			•		•			•	–	–	–	•		•		n				T	1557–59

Table 9. Mixtures

		1 g	2 g	1 i	2 i	3 i	4 i	1 k	2 k	1 o	2 o	3 o	1 p	2 p	q	1 s	2 s	1 v	2 v	1 w	2 w	3 w	1 x	2 x	1 y	2 y	1 M	2 M	3 M	mm	FACE	DATES
Christopher Barker	2	•			•		•	•			•		•	•	•	•	•	•			•	n	•		•			•			H+G	1578–87
Ralph Blower		n	•		•			n	•	•	n		n	•		•			•			•	n	•	n	•	•	n			L(c)+H	1603–07(?)
Edmund Bollifant	EC3	•				•		•		•				•		•		•			•			n	n		•				B(?)+[L(a)]	1602
Melchisidec Bradwood	EC3	•				•		•		•				•		•		•			•			n	n		•				B(?)+[L(a)]	1602–08
	EC4		•				•		•	•				•		•			•			•		•		•			n		L(c)+[Gu]	1608–
Henry Bynneman	1c		•	•					•	•				•		•			•			•		•		•		•		85	L(b)+[G]	1580–83
Thomas Creede	3	n	•	•	•			•	•	•	•	•	•	•		•			•			•		•		•	•				L(a)+L(b)	1594–1603
John Danter	1b	n	•		•			•			•	•	•	n		•			•		n	•	n	•	n		•				L(a)+H(?)	1592
Thomas Dawson	3	•	•	•	•			•	•	•	•			•		•	•	•	•		•	•	•	•	•	•	•	•			G+L(b)	1587–98
Arnold Hatfield	EC3	•				•		•		•				•		•		•			•			n	n		•				B(?)+[L(a)]	1602–07
William Jaggard	2	•	n		•			•			•	•	•	n	•	•		•	n			•	•	n	•			•			H+L(a)	1606
Abel Jeffes	2	•	n		•			•	n	•	•	•	•	•	•	•	n	•			•	•	•		•			•			H+L+G	1587–90
Richard Jones	2	•			•			•			•		•		•	•		•				•		•	•		n				H(oo)+[L(b)]	1595–97
Henry Middleton	3	•	•	•	•			•	•	•	•		•	•	•	•		•	•			•	•	•	•	•	•	•			H+L(b)	1579–81
Nicholas Okes	2		•		n				•	•				n		•			•			•		•		•			•		L(c)+[Gu]	1606–10
Thomas Orwin	2b		•		•				n			•	•			•	n		•		n	•	•	•	n	•	•				L(a)+G	1590–91
	3b		•	•	•				•	•		•	•	•		•	•		•		•	•	•	•	•	•	•				L(b)+(a)+G	1591
Robert Robinson	2	•			•			•			•		•	•	•	•	•	•			•	•	•		•			•			G+H	1587–88
William Seres	1b		•				•		•	•				•		•			•		•			•		•			•		L(c)+[Gu]	1575–76
Simon Stafford		•	n		•		•	•	n	•	•	•	•	•	•	•			•			n		•	•		•	•			H+L(a)+(c)	1598–1610
Roger Ward	2	•	•		•			•			•	•	•	•	•	•		•	•			n	•		•			•			H+L(a)	1589–92
William White	1	•	•	•	•			•	•	•	•		•	•	•	•		•	•		n	•		•	•	•	•				L(b)+H(oo)	1598–1606
John Windet	5	•	•		•		•	•	•	•	•			•		•	•	•	•		•	•	•	•	•	•	•	•			L(c)+G	1607–09

Plates

With five exceptions the plates are reproduced by permission of the Bodleian Library. The exceptions are plates 39, 73, 95, 120 and 121, which are reproduced by permission of the Syndics of Cambridge University Library. The Publishers gratefully acknowledge the help of these institutions and the assistance provided by their respective photographic departments.

he would rather doo him self, to haue as hee deserueth the glory of bothe: therfore I besech you to learne his minde heerin. And if he agre it pas in such sort: yet that he peruse it before the printing, and amend it if in any point I haue mistaken him. I pray you likewise to ask M Ferrers his iudgement heerin, and shew him that the cure of the great plague of M Streamers translatiō out of the Arabique, which he sent me from Margets, shalbe imprinted as soon as I may conueniētly. And if I shal perceiue by your triall that M. Streamer allow my endeuours in this kinde: I wil heer after (as Plato did by socrates) pē out such things of the rest of our Christmas cō municatiōs as shalbe to his great glory, and no lesse pleasure to all thē that desire such kindes of knowledge. in the mean vvhile i beseech you to accept my good wil and learn to beware the Cat. So shall you not only perform that i seek: but also please the almightie who alwayes preserue you

Amen.

Yours to his power. G. B.

I. E. ALLDE I Baldwin, W. *Beware the cat.* 1584
STC 1245 Huth 66 (BL) Sig. A3v

the riuers and flouds of this world are, or to haue knowledge, how embassages were sent, of Parlaments, of the managing and handling of affaires, or to vnderstand the voyages of armies, their order in ranging battailes, their encamping, their Stratagems, their beseegings, their expugnations & their victories, but rather to drawe and suck out of all these particular things, the sap, the sweete and marrow, reducing them into precepts, for the commoditie of great persons, that being otherwise busied, neither haue they time, neither can they well, continually apply thẽselues in reading of histories, which was the onely motiue that made me take in hand this book, wherinto if any prince or gouernour will looke, he may (as though it were in a bright christal glasse) incontinently beholde the substance that fully is contained, in the volumes of the most commendable auncient and moderne writers. And for so much as so worthie and noble food appertaines vnto Princes, and for that amongst Princes, your Emperiall Maiestie is of highest degree and dignitie : therfore comming toward your Maiestie with no lesse affection of minde, then that wherwithall I was enflamed, when I applyed my selfe about this profitable enterprise: I present the same most humbly at the feete of your Maiestie, to the intent, that with your sacred name, due & perfect honor may be giuen to this worke, since it shalbe vnder the protection of your Emperiall maiestie, who carying in his noble person, the greatnes and felicity of so many famous Emperours and Heroes, of that worthie house of *Austridge*, which through a long course of worlds, haue gouerned and shall gouern heerafter the sacred Empire, who being no lesse benigne and affable, then high in blood and honour: I assure my self, that he will not disdaine to look vpon the same, for although it be little in quantity, yet notwithstanding it is very great in qualitie, since it containes in it self a Quintesence of those thinges that haue been written for the profit and commoditie of men, gouernours and Princes. Venice the 24. of February, 1578.

The most humble and dutifull seruant of your Emperiall Maiestie, Francisco Sansouino.

The

2. E. ALLDE 2 Sansovino, F. *The quintessence of wit.* 1590
STC 21744 Malone 1012 Sig. A4v

tie of Sathan, who there more rageth
then in any place elſe, becauſe his kingdome is more neere to the ouerthrow
then where ignorance reignes, and the
kingdome of Chriſt is not preached at
all. Who although that they haue not
put foorth, nor publiſhed that mayne
poynt or Maxime of the profeſſed *A-
nabaptiſtes*, which is vtterly to denie
the lawefull eſſence or being of a Ma-
giſtrate, yet haue they daungerouſly
ſought, and ſtill doe ſeeke to infringe
the authoritie of the ſupreme Magi-
ſtrate, making more reckning of their
owne meetings in priuate, and their
ſubtill decrees made (as we ſay) vnder
a hedg, in euery aſſembly of their own,
then of any publique edict, law, or ordinance, made by publique & lawfull
Princes, Magiſtrates, Iudges, Miniſters, in a publique and nationall aſſembly lawfully, in the name of God met
and aſſembled for the redreſsing of
things amiſſe, either in Church or cō-
mon welth. By whō alſo it is to be feared, that that other point of the Ana-
baptiſti-

3. E. ALLDE 3 Cottesford, S. *A treatise against traitors*. 1592
STC 5840 Malone Q11 Sig. B5v

798. check the Beaſt, who by reaſon he was ſo wel guarded by his foreſaid head & champion *Charles*, eaſily neckt it. Notwithſtanding ſome 100. and 50. yeres after, this vlcer now growen to a riper head, vnder the practiſe of one *Alberique* and *Octauian* his ſonne, brake out a new, and charg'd the Beaſt in ſo ſharp a mãner, as without dout he had receaued the mate, had not his head in the midſt auoided it once againe, whoſe name was now chang'd frõ *Charles* the great, to *Otho* the great: who as being by oth deuoted, came to Rome, baniſht her new riſen Conſuls, hang'd her Tribuns, and mõuted her *Prefectus vrbis*, Mr. of miſrule, naked on an Aſs, crouned and attended through the citie with great deriſion; from thence committed to priſon, & ther execu-
967. ted with exquiſite torments. And by this means, the heat of this defection was ſo aſſwag'd, that it appered not for 7. yeres after: but then (vnder the leading of one *Cin-*
974. *cius*) flam'd out anew, in ſo furious a ſort, as it had doutles fyr'd the Beaſt out of al his holds, had not his middle head (*Otho* the ſecõd) haſted into Italy to quẽch the ſame: who (knowing how much it imported to

punish

4. E. ALLDE 4 L., T. *Babylon is fallen.* 1597
STC 15111 Mason A.A.128 Sig. C7v

The Phisick helps.

The roote of the Floure-delure, is only vsed in medicine, and is hot and dry of qualitie in the second degree: and it is very profitable against the cough, in extenuating those humours of the brest, which hardly are spit foorth: and it also purgeth the grosse flegmatick and chollericke humours, & taking sixe drams of the roots, with water and hony, and the same drunke, prouoketh sleepe, staieth the tearmes, & ceaseth the greefes of the body, and being drunke with Vinegar, doth help the diseases of the milt, the crampe, the colde shaking, which comes before the fit of an ague, and helpeth also the sheading of the Sperme: and drunk in wine prouoketh monthly courses, and the decoction thereof applyed to the womans priuie part, doth soften the hardnes thereof, and likewise open the stopping therof: & mixed with turpentine, by annointing, doth ease the greefes of the loynes and hips: and the pouder onely drawne vp into the nose, prouoketh sneezing, and cleanseth the head, and by chawing the roote in the mouth, dooth amend a stinking breath, and taketh away the strong sauour comming from the armhoales, and the greene fresh roote boyled, and the same laid plaisterwise, doth soften wens, & other hard impostumes.

And the pouder of the dry roote, mixed with honny, and the same thicke laid on Vlcers, dooth cleanse them: and the same aplied plaisterwise, doth draw out the bones in wounds and doth couer again the bare flesh, and the pouder of the root applied plaster-wise to the forhead, doth greatly help the paine & griefe of the head: also, the pouder of the root, mixt with the pouder of white Nosewort, and two parts of hony, the same annointed, dooth take away the pimples of the face, & all spots caused by the Sun, and against the dropsie, take a new laid Eg, pouring out the white, and to the yolk put so much of the iuice of the roote as was the white, after set the same egge a while in hot embers, which being sufficiently warm, sup off fasting in the morning, and the patient shall after send forth a merueilous aboundance of water betweene the skinne and the siege: and this hath bene often experienced.

5. E. ALLDE 5 Hill, T. *The arte of gardening.* 1608
STC 13497 Vet.A.2.e14 Sig. O3r

fly against God, secondly against holy men and against the trueth it self, and against holy things. They shalbe diso- bedient to their Fathers, to their mo- thers, to their magistrats, to their mai- sters, and to their teachers, beeing not onely vnthankful to God and to men: but also requiting good turnes vvith euil. They shalbe vvicked men, such as haue no fear nor reuerence, and such as impudētly run hedlōg vnto all kind of mischeuo^9 acts. They shalbe Astorgoi, vvithout any harty and feruent chari- tie, vvithout any zelus remorse of loue, godlines, and humanitie, not louing somuch as those that be neer vnto thē, as Fathers, mothers, Children, VViues and kinsfolkes. But bitter, cruel, and vngentle, endued vtterly vvith vvilde and vnciuil manners, vvho also haue not the common sence and remorse of nature, measuring all things by affecti- on, by couetousnes, by ambition, and greedy desire.

They shalbe vnmindeful of their co- uenāts, of their faith, of their bargaines, and of their promises, beeing vnfaith- ful and moste vain, and vtterly incon- stant and moste light persons, finally, backbiters

6. J. ALLDE Bullinger, H. *Of the end of the world*. 1580
STC 4070 Mason A.A.55 Sig. I3r

To the Chriſtian Reader.

WHere as ſome for the trial of
their wyttes, and proofe of
knowledge, are mooued to
pen their ſtudies & trauels,
which they do moſt exqui-
ſitely, and others for the benefit of their country, ſome
tyme of their own labours ſet forth bookes,
and ſome of other mens workes in our mother toung do open the meanyng, and all I
truſt to Gods glory, and the furtherance of
knowledge: Euen ſo I, not of my ſelfe moued, by any worthynes I know in my ſelfe,
neither to purchaſe prayſe of men (for this
my dede is nothing praiſe worthy to me, for
if ought be fauty, that is to me due, and if
any thing be to purpoſe, that was & is Gods
worke in me) haue laboured as farre as memorie might teache, neither addyng nor de-
miniſhing to or from the wordes I ſpake in
the pulpet, to write and pen ſomwhat for the
help of the poore. VVhich the rather I haue
done, for that then I was requyred by my
friend ſo to do. VVhich purpoſe or ſum of
matter, though of an other it might be more
excellently done, then of me it is in this treatiſe done: yet thinking that all men wil con-

A,ij ſider

7. J. AWDELEY Bedel, H. *A sermon exhorting to pitie the poore.* 1573
STC 1784 Mason C.C.34 Sig. A2r

ble for him, and what a do he had with himselfe to containe from floods of teares; especially because his eyes seeing them, and his hands holding them, and his heart taking delight and pleasure in them, his minde could not but discourse on this manner: And shall I within these few daies vtterly forsake these sweete babes, and leaue them to the wide and wicked world, as though they had neuer beene my children nor I their father? Yea happy had I bin if I had either neuer had them, or hauing them might enioy them. To be a father is a comfort, but a father of no children, and yet to haue children, that is a misery. And you poore Orphans, what shal become of you whē I am gone? your hap is hard euen to be fatherlesse, your father yet liuing: and what can your great birth now helpe you? for by my departure you shall lose all your honour, all your liuing and wealth, and all dignity whatsoeuer; which otherwise you had bin sure of: nay my departure shall not onely depriue you of al this, but lay you open to all infamy, reproch, and slander, and bring vpon you all kind of misery: and thus miserable man that I am, shall the time be cursed that euer they had me to their father. And what can your wofull mother doe when she looketh on you, but weepe and wring her hands, her griefe still increasing as she lookes vpon you? Yet thus must I leaue you al confounded together in heaps of griefe, weeping and wailing one with another, and I in the meane time weeping and wailing for you all. Many other griefes, temptations, and hinderances assaulted him, though they were not so weighty as these formerly named, yet which might haue beene able to haue hindred any mans departure, being in his case; as to leaue the company of so many gallant noblemen and gentlemen, his kinred and acquaintaince; to lose so honourable an office and place as he bare in the Emperours Court; to leaue for euer his natiue soile the delicate *Italy*; to depriue himselfe and his posterity of the noble tittle and rich liuing of a Marquesdome; to vndertake a most long and tedious iourney; to cast himselfe into exile, pouerty, shame, and many other miseries without hope

8. H. BALLARD I Balbani, N. *Newes from Italy*. 1608
STC 1233 4° E.6Th Sig. E4r

I thinke more worthy of my sisters loue.
But since the matter growes vnto this passe,
I must not seeme to crosse my Fathers will.
But when thou list to visit her by night,
My horses sadled, and the stable doore
Stands ready for thee, vse them at thy pleasure,
In honest mariage wed her frankly boy,
And if thou getst her lad, God giue thee ioy.

Moun. Then care away, let fates my fall pretend,
Backt with the fauours of so true a friend.

Fab. Let vs alone to bussell for the set,
For age and craft, with wit and Art haue met.
Ile make my spirits to dance such nightly Iigs
Along the way twixt this and Totnam crosse,
The Carriers Iades shall cast their heauie packs,
And the strong hedges scarse shall keepe them in:
The Milke-maides Cuts shall turne the wenches off,
And lay the Dossers tumbling in the dust:
The franke and merry London prentises,
That come for creame and lusty country cheere,
Shall lose their way, and scrambling in the ditches
All night, shall whoop and hollow, cry and call,
Yet none to other finde the way at all.

Mount. Pursue the proiect scholler, what we can do,
To helpe indeauour ioyne our liues thereto.

Enter Banks, Sir Iohn, and Smug.

Banks. Take me with you good Sir *Iohn*; a plague on thee *Smug*, and thou touchest liquor thou art founderd straight: what are your braines alwayes water-milles? must they euer runne round?

Smug. *Banks*, your ale is a Philistine fox, z'hart theres fire i'th taile: out; you are a rogue to charge vs with Mugs i'th rere-ward: a plague of this winde, O it tickles our Catastrophe.

Sir Io. Neighbour *Banks* of Waltham, and Goodman *Smug* the honest Smith of Edmonton, as I dwell betwixt you both at Enfield, I know the taste of both your ale houses, they are good both, smart both: Hem, Grasse and hay, we are all mortall, let's

9. H. BALLARD 2 *The merry devill of Edmonton.* 1608
STC 7493 Trinity College, Cambridge Sig. C1r

iudice to our fathers ſaid will, and for diuers other weightie and neceſſarie cauſes, wee could not any lōger forbeare for knowledge of the truth, & anſwering of ſuch reportes as haue bene vntruely bruted and ſpred abroad to the contrarie, openly to giue herewith a true teſtimonie of the ſaide matter, cauſing the ſaid Confeſsion as it was word for word written and inſerted in our fathers ſaid teſtament, to be publiſhed and printed: To the intent that the duetiful accompliſhment and fulfilling of his ſaid laſt and deare will, which is not onely committed to the charge of the Electour our ſaid lord & brother (although to him chiefly) but alſo to his ſubiectes, Counſellours, officers, and eſpecially to the vniuerſitie here, the Schole, and miniſters, & alſo to the whole poſteritie, & euery man in particular (as is expreſſely conteined in the ſaid teſtament) might be knowen vnto them and they thereby vnderſtande their duetie what they haue to do: and further euerie perſon whatſoeuer, be thereby aſſuredlie perſwaded in his conſcience, that our ſayd lord and father, in no other confeſsion nor in any erronious condemned opinion, but in a moſt Chriſtian confeſsion and acknowledging of the infallible and inuincible truth

us against Cesar, Hānibal against Scipio, had aboue al equality far greater armies then their enemies, by which thou hast reason to conclude with me, that against the anger of the soueraigne God, cānot preuaile most huge & mighty hosts. I marueile Popilio, that being great in birthe, valiaunt of stomache, welthy in goods, & mightie in estate & dignity, why thou bearest with such sorowe, the losse of this battel, seeing that in no worldly things fortune is more vncerteine & variable, then in the action of warre. It is tolde me, thou drawest to solitary corners, & sekest out shaded places, thou eschewest the cōuersatiō of mē, & complainest of the gods, which extreme perplexities since thou wert not wōt to suffer in others, much lesse oughtest thou to giue place in thy self: for that the valiāt mā loseth no reputatiō, for that fortune faileth him, but is the lesse esteemed of, if he want discretion to beare her mutability.

To assēble great armies, is the office of Princes, to leuy huge treasures, belongs to soueraigne Magistrats, to strike the enemie is the part of a couragious captaine: but to suffer infirmities & to dissēble mishaps, is a propertie duely annexed to noble & resolute mindes: so that one of the greatest vertues that worldly men cā expresse, in the common behauior of this life, is neither to rise proud by prosperitie, nor to fal into despaire by aduersitie. For fortune hauing a free wil, to come & go whē she list: the wise man ought not to be sorie to lose her, nor reioyce to hold her. Such as in their miserie shew heauie countenance, do wel proue, that they made accompt to bee alwayes in prosperitie, which is a great folly to thinke, & no lesse simplicitie to hope for: Seing the giftes & graces of Fortune haue no better thing more certain in them, then to be for the most part, in al things most vncertaine, according to the successe of the day, wherein thou gauest me battel: for there thou orderedst thy campe according to a wise captaine, madest choise of the place, in great policie, tookest aduantage of the sunne, as a leader of long experiēce, in consideration of which things thou hast cause to complaine against thy fortune, which fauored not thy vertue, & not blame thy discretion, wherein could be found no errour.

nûm, & Ænigmatum & Parabola-
rum, & Similitudinum plena erant:
atque per hæc docendi ratio, non
occultandi artificium quæſitum eſt;
rudibus ſcilicet tunc temporis hominum ingenijs, & ſubtilitatis, niſi
quæ ſub ſenſum cadebat, impatien-
tibus, & ferè incapacibus. Nam vt
Hieroglyphica Literis, ita *Parabolæ*
Argumentis erant antiquiora. Atq;
etiam nunc, ſi quis nouam in aliqui-
bus lucem humanis mentibus affun-
dere velit, idq; non incommodè &
aſperè, prorſus eâdem viâ inſiſten-
dum eſt, & ad ſimilitudinum auxilia
confugiendum. Quare quæ dicta
ſunt, ita claudemus. *Sapientia* Priſci
Sæculi, aut magna, aut fœlix fuit:
Magna, ſi de induſtriâ excogitata eſt
Figura ſiue Tropus: Fœlix, ſi homines aliud agentes, materiam &
occaſionem tantæ contemplatio-
num dignitati præbuere. Operam
autem noſtram (ſi quid in eâ ſit,
quod iuuet) in neutrâ re malè collo-
catam cenſebimus. Aut enim Anti-
quitatem illuſtrabimus, aut res ipſas.
Neque

12. R. BARKER Bacon, F. *De sapientia veterum liber*. 1609
STC 1127 Arch G.f15(3) Sig. A12r

good wil manifoldly extended to my father, who long ſince departed this mortality, had not at all ſtretched to me his ſon, but had with him alone both lived & died. Yet might not I, without ſome skar of impiety, commit that ever the memory of that ſhould die in me, the profit & pleaſure wherof I knew in him ſo long to liue. But ſeeing it hath further alſo, as I lately was given to vnderſtand, ſo pleaſed your Honour, that this happy courſe of your favour ſhould not beginne & end in one, but ſhould continue & lineally rũ on: & that the force & vertue therof ſhould paſſe continuately frõ the root vnto the branches: much more blameable verily would bee my ſilent forgetfulneſſe, & double would the fault be, where duty doublely is required. In which cõſideratiõs, if I ſhould haue made any diſtruſt of your good acceptation, or ſhould any way haue with-drawen this ſmal preſent, by miſdoubting the welcome it ſhoulde receiue at your Honours hands: I might haue been moſt iuſtly arraigned & condemned of an vndutiful & vngrateful cogitation, being without al either color of excuſe, or ſhadow of pretence to free and acquite me from it. And that eſpecially, ſeeing the authour, whom I interprete, & the matter which hee conteineth, are both of that qualitie, as, if I ſtoode to waite and expect a fit time, and a worthy perſon for them, noe time might ſeeme fitter than this, for which I ſhould reſerue thẽ, noe perſonne worthier than your ſelfe, to whom I might preſent them.

For this being the time, and theſe the evil daies, wherein

13. J. BARNES I Ursinus, Z. *The summe of Christian religion.* 1591
STC 24534 8° Z.573.Th. Sig. ¶ 2v

IOHN CASE D. OF PHYSICKE TO HIS FRIENDE R. H. OF NEW COLLEDGE.

WHEN I first heard (learned and kinde friende M. *Haydocke*) of your purpose in setting forth a large Booke concerning the Arte of Painting, two thinges caused me much to marvaile; first how you could winne time, and weane your selfe from *Hippocrates* to *Apelles*; and then what matter you could yeelde vs from a Painters pot and pencell: But after reading a few lines of the worke, I utterly chaunged my minde, and beganne contrariwise to wonder, how so excellent a Booke coulde bee compiled vpon so meane a subiect; Meane I say in name, but not indeede: meane as we call a Gnatt, in whose life, parts, forme, voice and motion, Nature hath bestowed her best arte, and left vnto vs wonders to beholde. What shall I say more? One shaddow of man, one image of his partes, in this Booke, sheweth vs better vse. For if *Hippocrates* will reade an Anatomie, heere-hence he may learne exact and true proportion of humane Bodies; if *Dioscorides* will make an Herball, here he may haue skill to set forth hearbes, plantes, and fruites, in most liuely colours. *Geometritians* heere-hence for Buylding may take their perfect Modelles. *Cosmographers* may finde good arte to make their Mappes and Tables. *Historians* cannot heere want a pencell to over-shaddow mens famous Actes, Persons, and Morall pictures. *Princes* may heere learne to builde Engines of warre, and ornamentes of peace. For (*Vitruvius* who writeth of Building to *Augustus* the Emperour) saith, that all kinde of warlike Engines were first invented by Kings and Captaines, who were skilfull in the Arte of Painting and Caruing. One thing more I adde aboue all the rest (my good friende M. *Haydocke*) that in reading your booke I finde therein two notable images of Natural and Morall Philosophie, the one so shaddowed with preceptes of Nature, the other so garnished with the best colours of Vertues; that in mine opinion, I neuer found more vse of Philosophie, in any booke I ever read of the like theame and subiect. And truely had I not read this your Auctor and Translation, I had not fully vnderstoode what *Aristotle* meante in the sixth booke of his Ethickes, to call *Phidias* and *Polycletus* most wise men; as though any parte of wisedome did consist in Caruing and Painting; which now I see to be true; and more-ouer must needes confesse the same, because God himselfe filled *Bezaleel* the sonne of *Vri*, *with an excellent spirit of Wisedome and vnderstanding, to finde out curious workes, to worke in Golde, Siluer, and Brasse, and in Grauing stones to set them, and in Caruing of wood, euen to make any manner of fine woorke*. In like manner hee indued the heart of *Aholiab with Wisedome* (as the Texte saith) *to worke all manner of cunning in embrodred and needle-worke*. And this he did for the making of his Arke, his Tabernacle, his Mercy-seate, his glorious Temple, which were the wonders of the Wordle, and only rare monumentes of

Exod. cap. 35. vers. 31.

* j. this

14. J. BARNES 2 Lomazzo, G. P. *A tracte containing the artes of curious painting*. 1598
STC 16698 Douce L.460 Sig. *1r

is, he exhorted them all with purpose of heart to cleaue to the Lord: in which speech there are euident markes of affectionate words and perswasions vsed by *Barnabas*, which name if it doe signifie the sonne of consolation as *S.Luke* interpreteth the same, euill shoulde hee deserue it, if he did neither comfort, exhort, nor apply, but onley barely teach. *Act.4.36.*

Of *Apollos* the Scriptures giue testimonie that he was an eloquent man, & mightie in the Scriptures, & that he proued with great vehemency that Iesus was the Christ: but meane scholers can tel, that there is small eloquence in teaching the first rudiments and principles of any science, and that the ende of eloquence is to perswade, and to mooue. which if the disciplinarians can doe without exhortation or application, they must sure doe it by miracle, or like the loadestone by some secret naturall qualitie. Further, if the Scriptures bee not for refutation onely, but for exhortation also, and many other purposes: and if also they profite not without application no more then if *Tho. Cartw.* should haue a sore finger, and keepe the plaster in his sachell: then must it follow that *Apollos* eyther was mightie but in some part and vse of Scripture, & that he taught to small purpose & profit of his hearers, or that with his teaching, he ioyned application, & exhortation which the wordes (*with great vehemencie*) doe also declare. For obseruing decencie, vehemencie cannot be vsed in short conclusions, nor in deliuerie of generall rules, but in forcible and earnest perswasion or exhortation. Moreouer, as the Apostle taketh planting to himselfe: so he giueth watring to *Apollos*, which requireth some more labour, affection and perswasion, then is vsuall in bare and ordinarie teaching. And if as ancient writers affirme, *Apollos* succeeded *Paul* in the ministerie at *Corinth*, or as a certaine doctor affirmeth, baptized, which he proueth in that he watred: then must he do the office of the pastor, not onely of doctor, at the least he must passe the boundes of bare teaching. *Act.18.* *1.Cor.1.*

Let vs descend to speake of the doctors of schooles, and we shall further perceiue, that it is a strange deuise to tie them to bare teaching, without exhortation and application. *Origens* lectures whom the disciplinarians transforme into a bare teaching doctor, were full of exhortations and applications. The man is by the iudgement of all learned, most eloquent: I appeale to *Th.Cartw.* himselfe, whether being doctor, or, that I displease him not, professor of Diuinitie, he did not often slippe aside into exhortation; and whether hee thinke it the part of a doctor, to leaue the place he handleth, without making

15. G. BISHOP Sutcliffe, M. *A treatise of ecclesiasticall discipline.* 1590
STC 23471 G. Pamph. 1327(1) Sig. E3r

A Dedicatorie poem to the Triumphs of our moſt dreade and Soueraigne Lorde, King Iames.

HONOR attend thy gratious Maieſtie,
Bliſſe be her Partner, in thy Soueraigntie:
Though Dayes are yet young, olde Ioyes wil haſten on,
When fearefull times, are dateles, deade and gone.
Thy gouerning hand, that neuer yet knew other,
Then a Rulers equall ſuckt from thy faire Mother.
Whoſe carefull thoughtes, in thee by Gods commaunde,
Haſt from thy Childe-hoode, helde a happie hande.
By which fayre hand, Gods grace hath led thee hither,
To plant thy peace, plenty and grace together:
So as our Tryumphs, glorious be in ſhowe,
So Tryumph-like, Ioy may with quiet goe.
That both in one, and one both wayes may be,
A double Ioy, in this Solempnitie.
So Tryumph ſings. this ſong of Ioy and Mirth,
King IAMES live happie, happieſt on the Earth:
That God all ſeeing, may ſo bleſſe thy Lande,
That ſeeing all, may all thy evils withſtande.

Death Spurneth,
Life ſtarteth:
By Eliza.
Life returneth,
Death departeth:
By K. Ia:

A 2 The

16. R. BLOWER Dugdale, G. *The time triumphant.* 1604
STC 7292 4° G.8.Art.BS Sig. A2r

their predecessors had neither gold nor silver, possessions, riches, goods, nor revenues: and why then should they being in gifts and paines inferior unto them, have greater preferments in the world then they had? If they have a messe of pottage and a canvas dublet, may it not content them? Surelie these advancements which they have, do greatlie hinder and hurt them.

Even as though one should saie unto you, my brethren of the poorer sort: these gentlemen and wealthier sort of the laitie do greatly abuse you: the children of God (you know) are heires of the world, and these things which the wicked have they enjoy by usurpation. The earth is the Lords and the fulnes thereof. You have an equall portion with the best in the kingdome of God: and will you suffer this unequall distribution of these worldlie benefits? Consider how in the apostles time the faithfull had all things common. They came and laid their goodes at the Apostles feet, and division was therof made according to everie mans necessitie. You can not but groane under the heavie burden which is laid upon you. Your landlords do wring and grinde your faces for the maintenance of their pride in apparell, their excesse in diet, their unnecessarie pleasures, as gaming, keeping of haukes & dogs, The Anabaptists.

and

17. E. BOLLIFANT EC I Bancroft, R. *A sermon preached at Paules Crosse.* 1588
STC 1347 8° T100.Th Sig. C5r

easily answered, and let those men assure themselues that in action nothing is more dangerous then an ouerweening conceit of their owne wisdome. For it is not inough, barely to say, that the Grand seignior will be superior in sea forces, but wise men must weigh, whether it lie in his power so to do, or no. For although the Turke be Lord of a larger sea coast then the king, yet can he not compare with his Maiestie, either in furniture or mariners. Along all the coast of Africke he hath not an harbour, where he can builde or keepe a couple of gallies, except Algier and Tripolie. In the Euxine sea what place of name is there besides Capha & Trapezond? What better report can we giue to the coast of Asia? More implemēts then a spacious sea-coast are incident to this busines: he must haue plenty of timber & cordage; he must be furnished with a people practised in sea affaires, able to endure the labour & working of the waters; delighting in traffique & nauigation; cheerfull in tempests & rough weather, which dare dwell as it were amongst perils, & expose their liues to a thousand dangers: as for the Turkish subiects the better part neuer saw sea, & those that haue vsed it, are not to be cōpared to the Biskains, Catalonians, Portugals, & Genowais; (I adde this people for their many good seruices done at sea in the behalfe of this crowne.) To conclude, in two things the king excelleth the Turke; the first is, that although the Turke can command more men, yet the best and greater part of them being Christians, he dare hardly trust against vs; the second is, that the sea coasts of the king are neerer conioyned, then those of the Turke, and in that regard are sooner assembled and prouided. By this commoditie, experience hath prooued, that the Easterne nauies haue beene often ouerthrowen by the Western, the Southern by the Northern, the Carthaginian by the Romaine, the Asian by the Grecian. *Octauius Cæsar* with the nauie of Italy defeated the fleete of Ægypt; and in our times the Armada of the Christians, the fleete of the Turkes. The Turkes themselues confesse, that in sea-fights the Christians excell, and are vnwilling to deale with those forces. As often as *Charles* the fift rigged foorth his nauie, it was so puissant, that the Turke neuer durst leaue the harbour. In his iourney of Algier he rigged

18. E. BOLLIFANT EC2 Botero, G. *The world.* 1601
STC 3399 Tanner 201 Sig. G2r

The sixt Booke.

19. E. BOLLIFANT EC3 Warner, W. *Albions England*. 1602
STC 25083 Malone 673 Sig. A6r

2. Our daily bread is communicating bread. 45. b.
3. To walke before God in the trueth of the ſatisfaction of Gods iuſtice. 51. a.
4. To purge a cleere conſcience. 51. b
5. The pages *65. 66, 67.* are ſo penned, as the Reader cannot knowe what was my meaning.

Now, conſidering by this vngodly practiſe, Chriſtian and well diſpoſed people are much abuſed, to omit the iniurie done to my ſelfe: I thought it my dutie to make a redreſſe by publiſhing this treatiſe according as the pointes therin were deliuered: otherwiſe I was not willing to haue ſet downe anie thing in way of Expoſition of the Lordes praier: becauſe it is alreadie ſufficiently performed by others.

An

20. R. BOURNE Perkins, W. *An exposition of the Lords prayer.* 1592
STC 19700 8° M.39.Th BS Sig. A4v

thelries: the pure chastitie of his vndoubted Church hath inuited and drawne me to her communion. I will now swallow no more of those bitter-sweete baites, which haue so long time abused my taste, as now appeareth by this contrarie heauenly sauour. I desire in the company of the Children of God, to feede on liuing bread in the house of the Lord. The Onions, Leekes and Garlike of *Ægypt*, haue seemed most odious and stinking to me, since I tasted of the celestiall *Manna*, which the heauens haue rained downe vpon vs. Too long haue I suckt the putrified and venemous blood, issuing from the impure dugges of that cruell woman, made drunke with the bloode of the Martyres, *Apoc.* 17.6. High time was it therefore, to relish now (henceforward) the sweete milke, distilling from the pure pappes of our dearest mother. Too long time hath the deadly cup of abhominations, deliuered daily abroad by that horrid strumpet, beene ouerlauishly quaffed on: now therefore it behooueth the more carefully, to experiment the sweete liquour of life, in the Cuppe presented to vs by the modest spouse of Iesus Christ.

Hauing then hitherto borne the heauie burden, which the tyranny of Antichriste charged my shoulders withall, I holde it reasonable, since it hath pleased God so gratiously to deliuer me: that all the rest of my life should be imployed thus, to lay my neck vnder the sweete and pleasing yoake, of the iust rule and gouernment, belonging to my legitimate and Soueraigne king.

And my tongue also, which heretofore hath beene loose, & vnbound to blasphemies, as also the preaching of dreames and lyes: shall henceforth doe his office, in singing the maruels of my God, to blesse his holie name, in the congregation of his Saints, to preach his worde, for the edification of his Church, (if it stand with his good pleasure, to render mee worthy and capable thereof) and also to giue him thankes, for that it hath pleased him (after hee gaue me knowledge of his trueth) to deliuer me out of the denne of Lyons, & lodge mee in the fold among his owne flocks. Moreouer, to craue pardon of him, for my hainous transgressions committed, in that since the time

In locis ignotis Ecclesiæ.

Hugolinus Camerarius Sancti Edwardi Confessoris.
Edwinus Abbas tempore Sancti Edwardi,
Dominus Galfridus Mandeuile,&
Domina Athelarda vxor eius.
Galfridus Mandeuile Iunior,
Dominus Iacobus Berners Miles.
Dominus Oliuerns de Durdens, frater Regis Henr.3.
Petrus Calhan Ciuis.
Thomas Peuerell Subprior.
Sulcardus Monachus,& Cronographus:
Domina Æleonora Comitissa de Barra, filia Regis Edwardi 1.
Richardus Harounden Abbas.
Guilielmus Stoner Miles.
Guilielmus Atclyffe Secretarius Regis Edwardi.4.
Domina Katharina filia Ducissæ Norfolciæ nupta Edwardo Aylmer.
Walterus Hungerford filius Edwardi Hungerford Militis.
Dominus Salesbury Miles.
Guilielmus Hauerell.
Thomas Bounflower,& Philippa vxor.
Thomas Romayne.
Iohannes Alyngreth.
Rogerus Braharsen.
Dominus Richardus Rous Miles.
Galfridus Haspall.
Iohannes Shorditche Miles & Helena vxor eius.
Iacobus Palmer clericus,& Iohanna soror eius.
Iohannes Blockely.

22. M. BRADWOOD ECI Camden, W. *Reges, reginae, nobiles et alij . . .* 1603
STC 4519 Douce WW.108 Sig. L2r

a line vnto him, which he taking hold of may dragge him
out; ſo except the grace of
God deſcend vpon thee,
thou canſt neuer get out of
the pit of ſinne; but yet thou
muſt know that this grace of
God, is alwaies ready to help
thee, and to draw thee foorth
of the pit, doe thou only take
hold of the mercy of God
when it is offered, and applie
thy will vnto his will, and all
ſhall be well.

It is not therefore in him
that willeth, nor in him that
runneth, but in God that
ſheweth mercy, who like a
carefull nurſe directeth and
beareth vp her little infant,
vntill it bee able to goe of it
ſelfe; So the Lord (who can
denie himſelfe to none) in

23. M. BRADWOOD EG2 Lennard, S. *An exhortatory instruction.* 1609
STC 15460 Dulwich College Sig. M2r

48. *shops be equal now, because I alleaged S. Cyprians and S. Hie-* Answered in
Dorman in *romes iudgement, that by Gods law originally all Bishops were* this booke fol.
his Disproufe *equall. This most false surmise he repeteth in aboue a score of* 320.&c.
Fol.3.b.16.a *places of his boke: vsing the like in a great number of suche o-*
33.b.51.b. *ther, wherby chiefly his volume hath growne. These being once*
52,55.a.65. *or twise answered I do after omit.*
72.74.b.81
84.a.85.a. 49 *And as he repeteth very often that, which he had no cause* 49.
86.b. 97.a. *once to name, so that, which he list not answer, he omitteth vn-* Fol.41.b. 42.
130.b. 131. *der the colour that it is impertinent or vnnecessary matter:* &.c.54. 61.
161.b. 181. *though himselfe was the first mouer thereof.* a.86.278.a.
205.b.&c.in 50 *This being the substance of his boke he hath adorned and* 279.a.&c.
multis locis. *garnished with his Rhetoricall floures of leud scoffes and fond* 50.
tales framed vpon his owne fingers ends. As of the worship
Dorman in his Disproufe fol.92.b that I had, vvhen being prolocutour in the Conuocation house, I wold as it is reported, first haue passed by the house, that they should all be taken for heretikes, that vvould not agree to a law, that should be afterward made. *And when* I thought to conclude (being earnest to haue my wise deuise take place) vpon the silence that then was in the house (euery man being astonied at so folish a demaũd) by this Maxime in the law: *Qui tacet consentire videtur*, He that holdeth his peace seemeth to consent, where a vvise man, and a great Lawyer telling me, that in making of lavves the consent must be expressed, and not presumed: I sate downe in my place, as wise as before I stode vp.

These are this Bachelers words: and he is in hand herewith once or twise againe, as with a notable matter, being in dede such as was neuer spokẽ, thought, ne wrought, that I know of, but by M. Dorman himself: for surely I neuer heard of it, before I read it in his boke. Of the same sort is this his report. (Afterward in his Disprouse fol. 178.a)

Dor.207.b. That I so good a mannes body, and so valiant a captaine, as full oftentimes I haue at Paules crosse shevved my selfe to be, vvhen that coragious stomake of mine hath prouoked the Papists to mete with me vvhen they durst, whose daggers vvere as sharpe as theirs I tolde them: vvhen I offered my selfe vvith a small company, but yet so, that they vvere

of

24. H. BYNNEMAN 1a Nowell, A. *A confutation.* 1567
STC 18739 Ms. Tanner 230 Sig. **4r

The Boyes ſpeech at Maiſter Peckes dore.

Great things were meant to welcome thee (ô Queene,)
If want of time had not cut off the ſame:
Great was our wiſh, but ſmall is that was ſeene,
For vs to ſhew, before ſo great a Dame.
Great hope we haue it pleaſd our Princes eye,
Great were the harmes that elſe our paynes ſhould reape:
Our grace or foyle, doth in your iudgement lie,
If you miſlike, our griefes do grow on heape:
If for ſmall things, we do great fauour find,
Great is the ioy, that *Norwich* feeles this day:
If well we waid the greatneſſe of your mind,
Few words would ſerue, we had but ſmall to ſay.
But knowing that your goodneſſe takes things well
That well are meant, we boldly did proceede:
And ſo good Queene, both welcome and farewell,
Thine owne we are, in heart, in word, and deede.

The Boy thereupon flang vp his Garlande, and the Queenes Highneſſe ſayd, This Deuice is fine.

Then the noyſe of Muſicke beganne agayne, to heare the which, the Quéene stayed a good while, and after departed to the Cathedrall Churche, whiche was not farre from thence. And the nexte day after, which was Sunday, when Princes commonly come not abroade (and tyme is occupyed wyth Sermons, and laudable exerciſes) I was to watch a conuenient ſeaſon, where and how might be vttered the things that were prepared for paſtime. And ſo vpon Monday before ſupper, I made a Deuice, as though MERCVRIE had bin ſente from the Gods, to requeſt the Quéene to come abroade, and beholde what was deuiſed for hir welcome, the whole matter whereof doth follow.

The

25. H. BYNNEMAN 1b Churchyard, T. *A discourse.* 1578
STC 5226 Tanner 745 Sig. C1v

the eare.

Vn buffet & dressoir, *a cubbard, a dresser.*

Vn buffet d'or & d'argent, c'est à dire, la vaisselle qu'il fault pour le service de la table, *a cubbard of plate.*

Busle, *a beast called a Buffe.*

Bugler comme font les boeufs, *to loowe, to bellowe.*

Buglement, *a loowing.*

De la Buglosse, *Buglosse.*

Buie, *a pitcher.*

Vne buire à mettre l'huile, *an oyle glasse, a vyole.*

Vne buire, ou buirette, *a cruet.*

Buisart sorte d'oiseau, *a Bussarde, a Bittour.*

Vn Buscher, *a pyle of wood.*

Buisson, *a thorne or bryar.*

Bulle, *a Bull.*

Vn Buletin, pour estre franc du port, *a bill, a cocket.*

Buquer à l'huis, *to knocke at the doore.*

Vn habillement de Bureau, ou autre drap meslangé de petit pris, dont les serfs & menu peuple souloit estre accoustré, *a coate of chaungeable colours for seruauntes slighte rugge, or pampilion.*

Mettre vn proces sur le Bureau, *a cause ready to be iudged.*

Mettre l'afaire sur le bureau, *to examine a matter.*

Vn Burin, *a grauing sticke.*

But, *a scoupe, a but, a pray, or bootie,*

Butiner, *to bootie, or pray.*

Herbe qui se nomme Butoesne, *Betony.*

Buvetter, Buvette, Buvage, *seeke* Boire.

Buyele, *the Diall of Marriners.*

Buyzart, *seeke* Buisart.

C. ante A.

CA & là, *hither and thither.* Courir ça & là, *to runne hither and thither.*

Cabane, *a cotage.*

Caberet, *a tauern or vitling house.*

Cabaretier, *he that keepeth a vitling house.*

Herbé qu'on appelle Cabaret, *an hearbe called Haselwort.*

Vn Cabas de figues, *a fraile of figs.*

Caba\ssetCabasset, *a helmet or heade peece.*

Cabinet, *a Coffer, a Wardrobe.*

Le Cabinet d'vne femme, toutes sortes d'ornements, joyaux & affiquets qu'elle à pour s'accouïnter, & attifer, *a womans casket.*

Les Cabinets des femmes, *womēs caskets.*

Caboche, *the head.*

Cabochon de pierre precieuse, quand la pierre est taillée en bosse, *the bosse or rysing of a pretious stone, the hood of a foole.*

Choux Cabus, *Cabiges.*

Cacher, *to hide, to conuey awaye.*

Caché, *hidden.*

26. H. BYNNEMAN IC Desainliens, C. *The treasurie of the French tong.* 1580
STC 6761 Douce H.H. 276 Sig. F3r

ters. But as this scholer would nedes be like his maister in this point, so woulde I that he had resembled him also in reporting of my wordes wholly, as his master hath delt with the Apologie: but there is very little of my booke to to be seene in M. Dormans Chapters, and so litle that the Reder can in very few places understand what I said, or what of mine M. Dor. impugneth, in which obscuritie and darke dealing, he putteth (as it may seme) his chiefe confidence. Surely by such dealing he hath driuen me to much labor in the rehersing both of his former sayinges, and of mine owne: which though it be tedious both to me and to the good Reder, yet is it for perspicuities sake, most necessary for such as would understande whereabout M. Dorman goeth, and what he intendeth. And here to beginne with that necessarie repetition: the sentence of S. Austen about the which M. Dorman bestoweth this first Chapter, is this. *Si quaeras quibus fructibus. &c.* If thou demaundest (he speaketh to Petilian the Heretike) by what fruites I know you to be rather the rauening wolues, I obiect to you the fault of schism, which thou wilt deny, but I will out of hand proue, for thou doest not communicate with all nations, *nor* with those Churches founded by the Apostles labour. This sentence M. Dorman alleageth in the first frent of his booke, minding to abuse the simple and unlearned therewith, as being of it self plain against us, which opinion I labored to remoue from them by my answer thereto in my booke to be sene. But M. Dor. here somtime chargeth me that I haue left this sentence vnanswered, sometime that I goe out of the way, and slily slippe from S. Austens interpretation unto mine own. But may it please the good Reder to resort to my booke, he shal finde my direct answer to S. Austens wordes of the schisme, that they touche not us, but the papists themselues, beginning at these wordes: Now concerning the schisme which M. Dorman shoteth

Dorman.

M. Dorman doth falsifie S. Austens copulatiue in translating it *nor*.

Post Praefa. b. 3.

teth

27. H. BYNNEMAN 2 Nowell, A. *A confutation.* 1567
STC 18739 Tanner 230 Sig. O1v

king of Emulation spared not to touche the worthy *Scipio* with most vntrue surmyses? Yea *Themistocles* when he had deliuered al Greece from the huge host of *Xerxes*, was yet by his vnkinde citizens of Athens expulsed from his owne, and constrained to seeke fauour in the sight of his late professed enemie. But the Magnanimitie of their mindes was such, as neither could aduersytie ouercome them, nor yet the iniurious dealing of other men coulde kindle in their brestes any least sparke of desire, to seeke any vnhonorable reuenge.

I haue loytred (my lorde) I confesse, I haue lien streaking me (like a lubber) when the sunne did shine, and now I striue al in vaine to loade the carte when it raineth. I regarded not my comelynes in the Maymoone of my youth, and yet now I stand prinking me in the glasse, when the crowes foote is growen vnder mine eye. But what?

Aristotle spent his youth very ryotously, & *Plato* (by your leaue) in twenty of his youthful yeares, was no lesse addicted to delight in amorous verse, than hee was after in his age painful to write good precepts of moral Phylosophy. VVhat shoulde I speake of Cato, who was olde before he learned latine letters, and yet became one of the greatest Oratours of his time? These examples are sufficient to proue that by industrie and diligence any perfection may be attained, and by true Magnanimitie all aduersities are easye to be endured. And to that ende (my verie good lorde) I do here presume thus rudely to rehearse them. For as I can be content to confesse the lightnesse wherewith I haue bene (in times past) worthie to be burdened, so would I be gladde, if nowe when I am otherwise bent, my better endeuors might be accepted. But (alas my lorde) I am not onely enforced stil to carie on my shoulders the crosse of my carelesnesse, but therewithall I am also put to the plonge, too prouide (euen nowe) weapons wherewith I maye defende all heauy frownes, deepe suspects, and dangerous detractions. And I finde my selfe so feeble, and so vnable to endure that combat, as (were not the cordialles before rehearsed) I should either cast downe mine armoure and hide myselfe like a recreant, or else (of a malicious stubbornesse) should busie my braines with some Stratagem for to execute an enuious reuenge vpon mine aduersaries.

But neither wil Magnanimitie suffer me to become vnhonest, nor yet can Industrie see me sinke in idlenesse.

For I haue learned in sacred scriptures to heape coles vppon the heade of mine enemie, by honest dealing: and our sauiour himselfe hath encoraged me, saying that I shal lacke neither workes nor seruice, although it were noone dayes before I came into the Market place.

These things I say (my singular good lorde) do renewe in my troubled minde the same affection which first moued me to honor you, nothing doubting but that your fauo-

28. H. BYNNEMAN 3 Gascoigne, G. *The steele glas*. 1576
STC 11645 Malone 791 Sig. A2v

the vvhich (ouer & besides the fitnesse and aptnesse of the phrases, and the maiestie of the sentences therein conteyned) is hidden vnder the barke of the vvords therof, a diuine preeminence and authoritie mixed vvith a certaine quickenesse of speeche to reproue vice (yea ready to applye the cauterie, and to pull vp the same by the rootes) vvhere the offences appeare to be inueterate and incurable, alvvayes obseruing suche a modestie and reuerence tovvards Princes and Magistrates, as it shoulde seeme rather to be much comfort to their harts, thā any vvays offensiue or greuous. And bicause the vvel doings of the good and vertuous, and the disorder of the euil & vvicked might appeare to al posteritie, that they may lerne therby to folovv the one, & to leue the other, this author in this his said discourse (most gracious princesse) hath set forth as it vver to the eie, hovv that many being descended of base & vnknovvn bloud, through their vertue, great valiantnesse and vvorthie acts, haue of a very smal beginning, ben aduanced to this noble estate of kings and princes, vvho after they had atchieued the place of rule and gouernement, by continuing their noblenesse and vvorthinesse, in ordering and vsing their authoritie vvel and prudently, haue merited immortall fame and prayse: and hovv that some others doing the contrary, vvere (by the iust iudgement of God) shamefully ouerthrovvn and cast dovvn from high estate and degree, to great vvretchednesse and miserie, to their great reproche and ignomie for euer: by vvhich exāples the good may lerne to encrease in vertue and noblenesse, and the vicious and insolent see the frutes of their vvickednesse, and perceyue hovv that naughtie dooings haue alvvayes naughtie endes. And in the *treatise of Peace and Warre*, (most noble Princesse) added to this sayd Author by the translater therof out of the Latin into the french tong, there is at large set foorth the benefits and commodities of the one, and the discommodities and enormities of the other: vvhereby all Kings and Princes may rather be moued to embrace and maynteyne peace and quietnesse (as things moste necessarie for all common vvealths) than any vvays be inclined to vvarre and crueltie (moste pernicious and hurtfull) vvhiche

bringeth

29. H. BYNNEMAN 4 Chelidonius *Of the institution of . . . princes.* 1571
STC 5113 Tanner 273(2) Sig. A3r

ecclesiasticall ministers, whose greatnes after the doctrine and example of our sauiour, should cheefely stand in humbling of them selues: and that the byshop of Rome being by the order of Gods worde none other then the bishop of that one see and diocesse, and neuer yet well able to gouerne the same, dyd by intollerable ambition chalenge not onlye to be the head of all the Churche dispersed throughout the worlde, but also to be Lorde of all the kyngdomes of the worlde, as is expressly set foorth in the booke of his owne Canon lawes, moste contrary to the doctrine and example of our sauiour Christe, whose Vicar, and of his holye Apostles, namely Peter, whose successour he pretendeth to be: after this ambition entred, & this chalenge once made by the Byshop of Rome, he became at once the spoyler and destroyer both of the Churche, whiche is the kyngdome of our sauiour Christe, and of the Christian Empyre, and all Christian kyngdomes, as an vniuersall tyraunt ouer all. And whereas before that chalenge made, there was great amitie and loue amongst the Christians of al countreys, hereupon began emulation, and muche hatred betweene the Byshop of Rome and his cleargie and freendes on the one part, and the Grecian cleargie and Christians of the east on the other part, for that they refused to acknowledge any suche supreme auctoritie of the Byshop of Rome ouer them: the Byshop of Rome for this cause amongst other, not onlye namyng them,

Mat.18 a.4. &.20.d.28. Luk.9.f.48. &.22.c.27.

Sext. decree lib.3.tit.16. cap.vnico. &.lib.5.tit. 9.cap.5.in glossa.

30. J. CAWOOD *An homilie agaynst disobedience.* 1571
STC 13680.6 Wood 633(1) Sig. H2r

tions which I by toſſing, tumbling, and ruffling diuers auc-thors to and fro, collected and gathered. Therfore they re-maine in mine owne hands, and I intend to preſerue them vntill ſuch time as I haue tranſlated Virgils Georgikes in-to Engliſhe (which I meane to do, by gods aſſiſtance, at my conuenient leaſure when I haue cleered my hands of other exerciſes, and as I feele my minde diſcharged of clogging cares) then to broche them that the liquor of the ſame may runne abroade for euery young ſcholer to taſte and ſuppe. VVherefore it remaineth that ſuch whoſe chaunce it is to ſee, and reade this tranſlation, & to confer it with the La-tine, to increaſe their knowledge in that whereof they are ignorant, that ſuch I ſay cōtent themſelues with this hand gripe of notes, yet my wil, my wit, & my worke wreſtled to haue them fully ſatiſfied. To conclude, this booke, not ſo poliſhed as I wiſhed, I vndertoke to dedicate to your wor-ſhippe: if a reaſon of this my preſumption be demanded, truly, I can render none: And yet certaine motiōs of mind vrged me to offer theſe fewe floures and fruites of my la-bour (hope of a courteous acceptation emboldening me therin) vnto your hands. I would they deſerued dedication to ſo good, ſo godly, & ſo vertuous a gentleman (I ſpeake of mine owne trauaile, for the Poets verſe no doubt, hath many a worthie patrone,) yet hope is mine ancor, that for Virgils ſake, (whom Cicero aduaunced with this *Hemiſti-chion, Magnæ ſpes altera Romæ*) mine attēpt ſhalbe thought the more cōmendable, mine endeuour the more approue-able, finally, this pamphlet the more acceptable. Thus as hauing bynne ouertedious, and boldly ſtraining courteſie with your worſhip, I thinke it more then time to make an end, beſeeching God to giue you the wealth of Callicrates, the health of Xenophilus, the long life of Argantonius, & (that I may ſpeake like a Chriſtian) to bleſſe you with all earthly proſperitie in this tranſitorie tabernacle, and to crowne and beautifie you with heauenly felicitie, in the glorious, triumphant, and euerlaſting Ieruſalem.

Your worſhippes ſuppliant
Abraham Fleming.

31. J. CHARLEWOOD 1a Virgilius Maro, P. *The bucolikes.* 1575
STC 24816 C.C.28.Jur Sig. A3v

who beeing credited with the ſtocke of the poore, pertaining to the Bride-well houſe of *Canterburie* to ſette men a work, was compelled to keepe it to himſelfe, becauſe no poore folkes of the houſhold of Faith could be found in all that Cittie. There ſhall you ſee the life and learning of a Paſtor of your Church, which expounding the Articles of our Beliefe in *Deuon-ſhire,* when he came to handle the deſcending into Hell, wrote a Latine Letter to a neighbour Miniſter of his to craue his aduiſe, and rapt it out luſtilie, *Si tu non vis venire mihi, ego volo venire tibi:* and ſo by the leakes that remaine in his Latine, made more worke for the Tinker, than euer your Father made for the Cooper. I will leape ouer one of your Brother Preachers in *North-hampton-ſhire,* which is as good a Hound for his ſent to ſmell a feaſt as euer man ſawe. *Paſquill* met him betweene *Bifield* and *Fawſeley,* with a little Hatte like a Sawcer vppon hys crowne, a Filch-man in his hande, a ſwapping Ale-dagger at his back, containing by eſtimation, ſome two or three poundes of yron in the hyltes and chape, and a Bandogge by his ſide, to commaund fortie foote of grounde whereſoeuer he goes, that neuer a Begger come neere him to craue an Almes. O how my Palfrey fetcht me vppe the Curuetto, and daunced the Goates iumpe, when I ranne the ring round about him to retriue him: it ſhould ſeeme by the manages my beaſt made, that hee knewe his Maiſter had a ſpeciall peece of ſeruice in hande. You ſhall haue a goodly bande of theſe men in the volume of the Saints. *Paſquill* is nowe gone ouer-ſea to commit it to the Preſſe, and it is his pleaſure (becauſe it is the firſt opening of his ſhop) to giue you a taſte of his Wares before you buy them, like a franck Merchant.

In the mean ſeaſon, ſweet *Martin Iunior,* play thou the knaue kindly as thou haſt begun, and waxe as olde in iniquitie as thy father. Downe with learning and Vniuerſities, I can bring you a Free-maſon out of *Kent,* that gaue ouer his occupation twentie yeeres agoe. He wil make a good Deacon for your purpoſe, I haue taken ſome tryall of his gifts, hee preacheth very pretilie ouer a Ioynd-ſtoole. Theſe Biſhops are ſomewhat too well

32. J. CHARLEWOOD 1b Pasquill *A countercuffe.* 1589
STC 19456 4º M.42.Th Sig. A3r

Occhi. My Lord.

Sel. Lo flie boy to my father *Baiazet*,
And tell him *Selim* hi obedient sonne,
Desires to speake with him and kisse his hands,
Tell him I long to see his gratious face,
And that I come with all my chiualrie,
To chase the Christians from his Seigniorie:
In any wise say I must speake with him.

Exit Occhiali.

Now *Sinam* if I speed.

Sinam. What then my Lord?

Sel. What then? why *Sinam* thou art nothing woorth,
I will endeuour to persuade him man,
To giue the Empire ouer vnto me,
Perhaps I shall attaine it at his hands:
If I cannot, this right hand is resolu'd,
To end the period with a fatall stabbe.

Sin. My gratious Lord, giue *Sinam* leaue to speake,
If you resolue to worke your fathers death,
You venture life: thinke you the Ianissaries
Will suffer you to kill him in their sight,
And let you passe free without punishment?

Sel. If I resolue? as sure as heauen is heauen,
I meane to see him dead, or my selfe King:
As for the *Bassaes* they are all my friends,
And I am sure would pawne their dearest blood,
That *Selim* might be Emperour of Turkes.

Sin. Yet *Acomat* and *Corcut* both suruiue,
To be reuenged for their fathers death.

Sel. *Sinam* if they or twentie such as they,
Had twentie seuerall Armies in the field,
If *Selimus* were once your Emperour,
Ide dart abroad the thunderbolts of warre,
And mow their hartlesse squadrons to the ground.

Sin. Oh yet my Lord after your highnesse death,
There is a hell and a reuenging God.

Sel. Tush

33. T. CREEDE I Greene, R. *The first part of . . . Selimus.* 1594
STC 12310a Malone 226(3) Sig. B4v

Least these small sparkles grow to such a flame,
As shall consume thee and thy houses name.
Alasse I spare when all my store is gone,
And thrust my sickle where the corne is reapt,
In vaine I send for the phisition,
When on the patient is his graue dust heapt.
In vaine, now all his veines in venome sleept
Breake out in blisters that will poyson vs,
VVe seeke to giue him an Antidotus.
He that will stop the brooke, must then begin
VVhen sommers heate hath dried vp his spring,
And when his pittering streames are low & thin,
For let the winter aide vnto him bring,
He growes to be of watry flouds the King.
And though you dam him vp with loftie rankes,
Yet will he quickly ouerflow his bankes.
Messenger, go and tell yoong *Selimus*,
We giue to him all great *Samandria*,
Bordring on *Bulgrade* of *Hungaria*,
Where he may plague those Christian runnages,
And salue the wounds that they haue giuen our states,
Cherseo. Go and prouide a gift,
A royall present for my *Selimus*,
And tell him messenger another time
He shall haue talke inough with *Baiazet*.

Exeunt Cherseoli and *Occhiali*.

And now what counsell giues *Mustaffa* to vs?
I feare this hastie reckoning will vndo vs.
Must. Make haste my Lord from *Andrinople* walles,
And let vs flie to faire *Bizantium*,
Least if your sonne before you take the towne,
He may with little labour winne the crowne.
Baia. Then do so good *Mustaffa*, call our gard,
And gather all our warlike Ianissaries,
Our chiefest ayd is swift celeritie,
Then let our winged coursers tread the winde,

34. T. CREEDE 2 Greene, R. *The first part of . . . Selimus*. 1594
STC 12310a Malone 226(3) Sig. C2r

And *Belierbey* of faire *Natalia*.
Now *Acomat*, thou monster of the world,
Why stoup'st thou not with reuerence to thy king?
Aco. *Selim* if thou haue gotten victorie,
Then vse it to thy contentation.
If I had conquer'd, know assuredly
I would haue said as much and more to thee.
Know I disdaine them as I do thy selfe,
And scorne to stoupe or bend my Lordly knee,
To such a tyrant as is *Selimus*.
Thou slew'st my Queene without regard or care,
Of loue or dutie, or thine owne good name.
Then *Selim* take that which thy hap doth giue,
Disgra'st, displai'st, I longer loath to liue.
Seli. Then *Sinam* strangle him: now he is dead,
Who doth remaine to trouble *Selimus*?
Now am I King alone and none but I.
For since my fathers death vntill this time,
I neuer wanted some competitors.
Now as the weerie wandring traueller
That hath his steppes guided through many lands,
Through boiling soile of *Affrica* and *Ind*,
When he returnes vnto his natiue home:
Sits downe among his friends, and with delight
Declares the trauels he hath ouerpast.
So maist thou *Selimus*, for thou hast trode
The monster-garden paths, that lead to crownes.
Ha, ha, I smile to thinke how *Selimus*
Like the Ægyptian *Ibis* hath expelled
Those swarming armies of swift-winged snakes,
That sought to ouerrun my territories,
When soultring heat the earths green childrẽ spoiles
From foorth the fennes of venemous *Affrica*,
The generation of those flying snakes,
Do band themselues in troupes, and take their way
To *Nilus* bounds: but those industrious birds,

last king of the Britaines.

Warwicke that raisde the race of *Mortimer*,
Whose eyes did see too soone, thy death saies so:
The downfall of immortall *Lancaster*,
'Twas he that did, what could not *Warwicke* doo?
Make Kings and Queenes to loue and feare him too.
'Twas that great Peere, who with one warlike hand,
Crown'd and vncrown'd two kings who rulde the land.

Thus while these Royall but disloyall Peeres,
Maugre reuenge to him that knew not feare,
Vnnumbred bands of men and swarmes appeares
In North and South, East, West, yea euery where
They throw away their Coats, and Corslets weare.
Wiues, maides, and Orphants eyes are stuft with teares,
And cannot see the Spades transform'd to Speares.

The Shepheards hooke is made a souldiers pike,
Whose weather-beaten hands must learne aright
His speare to traile, and with his sword to strike
Vpon the plumed beauer of a knight,
None must be sparde by warres impartiall might.
If euery souldier were a King, what then?
Princes should die as fast as other men.

The Senator must leaue his skarlet gowne,
And keepe him in some Turret of defence:
When warres once flourish, Iustice must goe downe,
Lawes to correct, is lawlesse warres pretence,
Valure doth greeue to see ill gotten pence.
To see a man without deserts to rise,
Makes warre such men, not Iustice to despise.

F You

36. T. CREEDE 4 Harbert, W. *A prophesie of Cadwallader.* 1604
STC 12752 Douce Add. 38 Sig. F1r

to crie alarum and bid battell and defiance against the truth: to distresse, and as much as in them lieth, to extirpate and roote out the Gospell: in a word, to exployte all the feates, play all the casts of *Machiauil*, be the imitation of our blessed Sauiour; which your own hearts will witnesse, were no point his fashions, no prints of his foot-steps: so as they deserue to bee called by the name of Iebusites, rather then Iesuites. Now then by the way, tell me, good Christians, all passion and parcialitie laide aside, all faction & affection put apart, must it not needes be a holie Procession, where such Diuels as these carrie the Crosse? A sweete and blessed Hierarchie, where such Regents bankerupt of the true feare of God, destitute of common honestie among men, raigne and rule the roast? A right Catholike church, which first was planted, and euer since hath beene watered, managed and maintained by such false Apostles, such lying Merchants, and counterfeit hypocrites as these?

The web of Popery is spun vpon the distaffe, and wouen in the loome of lies.

As for the Religion professed in the Papacie, howsoeuer it be disguised with the Maske of Catholicisme, what is it else in grosse for the realtie of it selfe, the vizard discouered and plucked off, but a lumpe of *lyes*, errours and heresies? Their worshipping of Images, their Church seruice in a straunge tongue, their Masse, their Sacrifice propitiatorie for quicke and dead, their Transubstantiation, their reall presence, their Demi-Communion administred but in one kinde, their eleuation and adoration of the Eucharist, their auricular confession, their freedome of will, their pardons, their pilgrimages, their Purgatorie, their inforcement of single life to the Cleargie, their meritoriousnesse of workes, their inuocation of Saints, their Popes supremacie: These with infinite other Articles of the

Romish

37. T. CREEDE 5 Ingmethorpe, T. *A sermon.* 1609
STC 14087 Tanner 842(3) Sig. B4v

red by Phœbus, when in the face of heauen, they both were taken in an yron net: wherein hir wrong to Vulcan was apparant; and since that, many other escapes considered. But lastly and most especially, her publike adulterie she hath committed with that base monster Contempt they haue all consented, and to this decree firmed; that no more shall Venus possesse the title of a Goddesse, but be vtterly excluded the compasse of heauen: and it shalbe taken as great indignitie to the Gods to giue Venus any other title than the detested name of lust, or strumpet Venus: And whosoeuer shall adore Contempt or intertaine him, shalbe reputed an enemie to the Gods. More, it is decreed that warre shalbe raysed against Boœtia, and victorie shall not fall on their side, till the Cabbin of Contempt be consumde with fire. Giuen at Olimpus by Iupiter and the celestiall Synode.

Ru: Ill tidings for my Lady these.
Ina: Ill newes pore babe for thee.
Mer: VVhat who are these?
I take yee to bee two of Venus virgins, are yee not?
Ru: Faith she is a pure virgin indeed,
For the childe she had by Venus chaplin,
Is a big boy and followes the Father.
Ina: And so are you a maide too, are ye not?
For the girle you had by Mars his Captaine,
Shees dead, and troubles not the Mother.
Mer: then I perceiue ye be both maids for the most part.
Ru. well for our maidenheads it skill not much.
For in the world I know are many such.
Ina: I Mercurie I pray let that goe,
wee are faire Venus maides, no more but so.
And in our Ladies cause we doe intreate
to know, if that be true thou didst proclaime?
Or was it spoken but of pollicie,
To fright vs whome thou knewst to be her maides.
Mer: As true as neither of you both are maides
So true it is, that I haue vttered.
The sentence is set downe, *Venus* exilde,

And

38. J. DANTER 1a Wilson, R. *The coblers prophesie.* 1597
STC 25781 Malone 802 Sig. E4v

which compasseth vs about, or through the il quallity of other thinges, which violently breake in vppon vs; or through some wicked disposition of the bowels or other humours. The heate of the aire, not onely of that which outwardly compasseth vs about, but also that which wee draw into our bodies by breathing, inflameth first the lunges, then the hart, & all the spirits, so far till often times a feuer is kindled, and caused thorow the same. Thorow which distemperature of the spirits, needs must the strength of the body languish & becom enfeebled: yea by this excessiue heat of the air, the spirits are not only subiect to alteration of temperament, but besides they are also thereby greatly wasted & diminished. Euen so in like maner, immoderat cold outwardly, & the same receiued inwardly into the body by breathing, weakneth the spirits, & inward heat: yea & sotime altogether put out, and extinguish the same. The aire venemous & pestilent, drawen into the bodie with an infection quite ouerturneth the spirits of life and of nature: wherof ensueth grieuous sicknesses to the body, no little decay of bodily strength, yea life it selfe is taken away by the sodaine disease, commonly called the plague.

Now much more apparantly are the spirites infected with bitings of Scorpions, mad

39. J. DANTER 1b Gyer, N. *The English phlebotomy.* 1592
STC 12561 Cambridge U.L. Sig. K4r

From whence ye came to bide the doome of law,
Speake, will ye liue and serue as true men should?

All: I, I, I.

Raph: I am sure ye take me for none of theyr number.

Sat: No Raph, thou shalt be still with mee,
I haue an hoast of worthie souldiers
Readie to march, to them now will I goe,
Heauens and good fortune quell our furious foe.

Sound drums, *Exeunt omnes.*

Enter Contempt, Venus following him, hee pushing her from him twice or thrice.

Cont; Awaie thou strumpet, scandall of the world,
Cause of my sorrow, author of thy shame,
Follow me not, but wander where thou wilt,
In vncouth places loathed of the light,
Fit shroude to hide thy lustfull bodie in,
Whose faire's distaind with foule adulterous sin.

Ven: Ah my Content, proue not so much vnkind,
To flie and leaue thy loue alone behind,
I will go with thee into hollow caues,
To desart to the dens of furious beasts,
I will descend with thee vnto the graue;
Looke on me loue let me some comfort haue.

Contempt still turnes from Venus.

What not a word to comfort me in wo?
No looke to giue my dying heart some life?
Nothing but frownes, but lowres, but scornes, disdaines?
Woe to my pleasures that haue brought these paines.
Haue I for this set light the God of warre,
Against whose frownes nor death nor heauen can stande,
Haue I for this procurde the angrie Gods
To make me exile from all blessednes,
Haue I for this lost honor and renowme,
Become a scandall to the vulgar world,

40. J. DANTER 2 Wilson, R. *The coblers prophesie.* 1597
STC 25781 Malone 802 Sig. F4v

holy ghoſte, and is no fiction of the *Rabines*, as are manye things in thoſe Thalmudician bookes, and may in my iudgement, be cõfirmed by the anſweare of *Vriel* the Angell vnto the demaunds of Eſdras, although *Hierome*, and thoſe which followe him, doubt hereof. But *Theodore Bibliander* in the explication of *Eſdras* his dreame, doth ſay, that *Hierome* did rather imitate the raſhnes of the Iewes, than probable reaſon. And proueth by many moſte plaine arguments, this fourth booke to be *Eſdras* owne booke, Prophetical, & diuine: and ſaith: That marueill it is not though this diuine booke (bycauſe it moſte plainly telleth of the raigne, and cheifeſt, lawfull, and euerlaſting kindome of Ieſus Chriſt, and alſo of the refuſall of the Iewes, and conuerſion of the *Iſraelites* vnto Chriſt the Lorde) be deſpiſed of the blinded ſynagog of the *Iewes*, which do wilfully ſet themſelues againſt their ſauiour: And alſo addeth that this booke is yet extant in the Hebrue tongue, and was tranſlated out of the ſame. To this Eſdras (demaunding of *Vriell* the Angell, whether the time paſt, be greater than the time that is to come, or whether that which is to come, exceede the tyme paſt?) the Angell doth anſweare by two ſimilitudes. And doth ſhewe vnto him firſt a burning fornace, and afterwarde, a watrie cloude, and ſaith, Marke whether the fire do ouercome the ſmoke, and the ſhowre the drops? or otherwiſe? To whom Eſdras ſayth: I ſee Lord, that a very great ſmoke doth paſſe away, I ſee alſo a great ſhowre to come powring downe: but afterwarde I perceiue the flame to ouercome the ſmoke, & the drops the ſhowr. Then ſaith the Angel. Now iudge of the continuance of the world. Euen as firſt the ſmoke vanquiſhed the fire, and the drops the ſhowre: ſo the yeeres of the tyme paſt, ſhall exceede the tyme which is to come. But nowe, according to the computation of yeeres, it is euident that

4. Eſdras. 4.

The iudgement of Bibliander concerning the fourth booke of Eſdras.

The anſweare of Vriell to Eſdras.

41. T. DAWSON I Geveren, S. *Of the ende of this world.* 1577
STC 11803a.7 4° E.5Th BS Sig. A2r

fuiſſe infixſũ, nullum periculũ infeſtius, nullũ malũ calamitoſius, nullum venenum tetrius aut virulentius, eidem vnquam contingiſſe, quàm cùm relicto patrum ſalutari conſilio ac ſapiente procax audaxque iuuenilis ardor, omnia noua nouato ignorantiæ ritu docere non erubuit. O præclarã maiorũ peritiã, & in omni facultate eximiam certitudinem, cuius radius clarus ille quidem & luminoſus aditum mihi aperuit ad artem hanc Laconica breuitate deſcribendam, animumque dedit non verecundandi, non dubitandi non mordacis linguæ telum venenatum formidandi nondum incæptum opus abijciendi, ſed aquas licet profundiſsimas, artemque ipſam (Neptuno duce) animo forti ac conſtanti aggrediendi. Eoque magis quòd omnes natandi vias, omnes varietates, omnes huius artis concluſiones claris in aquis nonnunquàm ſum expertus, nihil noſtri ſequaſes moniturus, cuius priùs, præcedens non fuerim particeps & præmonſtrator peritus. Quod vero ſimplici natione vel prona vel ſupina, vel vrinante non contẽtus, vlteriores gradus agilitatis (filum orationis vnà producens) pluresque deſcripſerim: id & huius facultatis alumnus generoſè in profundis geſtiens, & ipſa ars) quæ certam ſibi vndique omni moleſtiæ diluendæ, omni periculo amouendo, omni denique anxietati abſtergendæ, amoliendæque viam præmuniuit (non modo poſtulat, verum etiam efflagitat. Cùmque hominũ inclinatio tam diuerſa ſit & multiplex, natura tã diſsidens ac omninò diſſentanea, cunctaque ſub ancipiti pendent mortalia caſu, & euentu librantur nonnunquam inopinato: multæ aquæ, & ſpacioſus amnis amplam nobis artem, certiſque regulis ad ſalutarem vſque vitæ humanæ concluſionem deductam ac diriuatam ſuppeditauere. Quæ etſi ſub humili orationis amictu, paucíſque regulis conciſè pertractatis & contextè, compareat: tumida tamen fouet vbera, multoque ſcientiæ laſte diſtenta: inſtitutionẽ breuem, veram, dilucidam, cuiuſque natationis, cuiuſque facilitatis & gratiæ, cuiuſque euaſionis, ſiue ludas in aquis, ſoluſque te oblectes ſiue cum altero contendas, ſiuè immaniſsimas beſtias adoriare, ſiue ſerpentum aconita venenoſa diffugias, ſiue merſo lintre, ſubſidente equo, periclitante teipſo, emergere ſtudeas, clara quaſi luce ſoleque meridiano exhibet, habens in ſummo aquarum diſcrimine præſens ſemper auxilium: generi quod det humano & dat nulla ſcientia largiùs, nulla citiùs, nulla ſalutarius. Quòd ſi nuper enatæ facultatis huius, aut ſaltem calamo noſtro ab

42. T. DAWSON 2 Digby, E. *De arte natandi.* 1587
STC 6839 B.22.11.Linc Sig. A3r

vsed a very strange practise, that few Princes would haue done in their greatest extremities. He resigned his kingdome to one *Velica Knez Simeon*, the Emperours sonne of *Cazan*: as though hee meant to draw himselfe from al publike doings to a quiet priuat life. Towards the end of the yeere, hee caused this newe King to call in all Charters graunted to Bishoprickes, and Monasteries, which they had enioyed manie hundred yeeres before. Which were all cancelled. This done (as in dislike of the fact and of the misgouernment of the newe King) hee resumed his scepter, and so was content (as in fauour to the Church and religious men) that thev should renew their charters, & take them of himselfe: reseruing and annexing to the Crowne so much of their lands, as himselfe thought good.

A strange practise to get money.

By this practise hee wrung from the Bishoprickes, and Monasteries (besides the landes which he annexed to the Crowne) an huge masse of money. From some 40, from some 50, from some an hundred thousande rubbels. And this aswell for the increase of his treasurie, as to abate the ill opinion of his harde gouernment, by a shewe of woorse in an other man. Wherein his strange spirite is to bee noted: that beyng hated of his subiectes, (as himselfe knew wel

43. T. DAWSON 3 Fletcher, G. *Of the Russe common wealth.* 1591
STC 11056 8° F.12.Art Seld Sig. G3r

postea tam præfidentis & prefractæ temeretatis & violatæ diuinæ prouidentiæ penas luit. *Salomoni* autem coronato & Regnum occupanti sic applausum est ab omnibus vt terra illorum clamoribus resonaret. Sic Regibus & Principibus diuina prouidentia sancitis & ascitis affatim & effuse omnium ordinum homines congratulantur. Illa hominum tibi subditorum tuorum (præclarissime Rex) corda tetigit, voluntates impulit, affectus inflammauit. Illa tantas occursationes acclamationes & applausus tibi ex omnibus regni huius territorijs longe lateq; in tuo ad hoc regnum accessu excitauit. Illa te ad hoc regnū ab ipsis incunabulis progenuit, aluit, prouexit, et illud tibi tranquillum & securum hæreditariam in possessionem tradidit & ceu clarissima *Helice* diuinis & luculentis testimonijs omnium animis ac studijs præluxit. Dei nimirum accersitu M. V. in Angliam venisse, horum regnorum hæreditatem creuisse, ecclesiæ & reipublicæ vniuersæ procurationem & propugnationem suscepisse, patriæ nostræ parentem esse: loco indulgentissimæ matris demortuæ esse cæpisse. Vidisti regio in aduentu non solum vias subditorum tuorum agminibus constipatas, sed gratulationibus & applausibus vndiquaque resonantes. Quid viarum memorem celebritatem, & quæ propatulis in locis gesta sunt? Certè intimis ex visceribus & præcordijs profusam tum nobilium tum plebeiorum in M. V. singularem amorem & charitatem 1.Reg.1.

ritatem

44. T. DAWSON 4 Reniger, M. *Syntagma hortationum.* 1604
STC 20887 8° R.68.Th Sig. A7r

the horrible and moſt hurtful hereſies,hatched by the deuel, in the neſt of mans mind,and vttered by the tōg and pen of buſy bodies,ſealed vp to ſerue Satan in this kind of miniſte- ry.Such wer in our ancettors dais, the Nycolaitans, the Ce- rinthians,Arrians,Macedonians,Pelagians, Eutychians, Eu- nomians,Neſtorians and ſuch other. And in theſe our latter daies,the old feſtred ſores newly broken out,as the Anabap- tiſtes,the freewillers, or rather frowardewillers,the iuſticia- ries.&c,and others that be new,as Adiaphoriſtes Oſiandri- niſts,Maioraniſts,Papiſts,with infinit other ſwarms of gods enemies,by whom our aduerſari Satan ſeketh to diſturb the true vnitie of Chriſtes church,to choke the good corn of late ſown in gods field,and to dim that excellent lighte,whiche according to his ſecreate counſell and decree, he determined ſhuld ſhine to the vnſpeakeable cōfort of his elect,in theſe our dais. Among theſe vgglie monſters and brodes of the de- uils brotherhead,hath of late krept out(I cā not tel whether by wil or ignorance)certen πολιςϕθάρματα which haue called into queſtion among vs ſuch thinges, as good ſubiectes be- fore neuer doubted of,whether it wer lawful for women,in- heritours of kingdoms,to gouern and guid the ſame,or no. Although this error may appeare,not to touch ſo neare the ſoule and ſaluacion of man,as ſome of the fornamed do:yet conſidering that the quiet of common weales is the nurſe of religion and bulwark of good and faithful men:and that the apoſtle pronounceth againſt the rebellious vtter damnaciō: VVe can not think it to be a trifle to diſturbe the common ordres of pollicies,to ſondre the mindes of ſubiectes,by new inuented contrauerſies,and briefly to make men to muſe,of that they neuer before miſtruſted. Vvherfor chaunſing vp- on a boke,about a yere paſt,intitled the firſt blaſt, cōteining new broched doctrine to diſproue the regiment of women: After I had red it,I wiſhed that ſome notable learned man, wold haue anſwered it,that,like as thoſe which be ſtonge of burne, vnto whom Ælfricke wryteth the first of the epistles we here speake of. Elfleda a Nunne of Romesey, and Wulhilda Abbesse of Barkyng, lyued in the dayes of king Edgar. And laste of all Wlfritha K.Edgars cōcubyne. All these I say with some other more, be canonized for sainctes of this age in which Ælfricke him self liued in great fame & credite. Also Leofricke and Wulfsine, whom we haue shewed to haue been the geuers of those Cannon bookes wherin be seene Ælfrickes epistles be reuerenced for moste holy men and saintes of their churches. And these ij. liued byshops in the comming in of the Conquerour. Thus doe some men now a dayes not onely dissent in doctrine from their owne church, but also from that age of their

of their churche which they haue thought moste holy, and judged a most excellēt paterne to be folowed. Wherfore what may we nowe thinke of that great cōsent, wherof the Romanistes haue long made vaunte, to witte, their doctrine to haue cōtinued many hundred yeares as it were lincked together with a continuall chaine, wherof hath been no breche at any time. Truely this their so great affirmation hath vttered vnto vs no truth, as good christian reader thou mayest well iudge by dulye weighing of this which hath been spoken, and by the reading also of that which here followeth, wherunto I now leaue thee.

Trusting that after thou hast well weighed this matter of such manner of the being of Christes body in the sacramēt,

46. J. DAY 2 Aelfric *A testimonie of antiquitie*. 1567
STC 159 8º T.28.Th Seld Sig. A2r

grace to haue brideled you, ere this, vvith shorter raynes, ye had not bene at this day, so headstrong as ye are. Many hundreths of you (repenting your rebellious hearts) had bene cōuerted to Christ, and by seueritie learned that, vvhiche clemencie shal neuer teach you. Novv is your insolēce grovven to such excesse, that ye abuse al other, and your selues to: that ye think men dare not for feare do that, vvhich for tēder hart and pitie they do not: that ye thinke vvith hipocrisie to deceiue God, and vvith flatterie the vvorld. Ye threaten kindnesse on the Queenes maiestie, saying that hir noble personage in al princely prowesse (for so ye terme it) and hir good affection to the crosse (vvhich is the matter ye treate of) moued you so presūptuously to aduenture, so adventerously to presume (I shoulde say) as to recommend your Treatise to hir highnesse. In dede vve haue a most noble Princesse (God for his mercy prosper hir, lōg to raigne ouer vs in despite of your malice, & increase of our ioy) such a one as is beautified vvith rare giftes of nature, in vvisdome maruellous, in vertue singuler. Provvesse she leaueth to the other sexe. Subiectes she hath ynovve to practise it. As for hir priuate doings, neyther are they to be dravven as a president for all: nor any ought to creepe into the Princes bosome, of euery facte to iudge an affection. This can the vvorlde vvell vvitnesse vvith me, that neyther hir grace and vvisedome, hath such affiaunce in the Crosse, as you doe fondly teach: neyther takes it expedient, hir subiectes should haue that, vvhich she hir selfe (she thinketh) may keepe vvithout offence. For the multitude is easyly through ignoraunce abused: hir Maiestie to vvell instructed for hir ovvne persone, to fal into Popish error and Idolatrie. Novv for that vvhich follovveth, if ye vvere so good a subiecte, as you oughte, and framed your selfe to lyue according to the lavves, ye should see and consider, hovve good order is taken by Publique authoritie, not Priuy suggestions, that Roodes and Images should be remoued, according to Gods lavve, out of churches, chappels, and oratories: and not so despitefully Folio.1.b.

B.j. throvven

47. H. DENHAM 1a Calfhill, J. *An aunswere to the treatise.* 1565
STC 4368 A.3.14.Linc Sig. B1r

acquaintaunce. And thus we are come to the.7.yeare of his bi-
shoprike of Antioche, in which time he yet neuer came at Antioche. Nowe the yeare of our Lord 46. the.4 of Claudius he
goeth from Antioche to Rome, and there is bishop.25.yeares,
2.months.8.dayes, from the.16 of Ianuary, to the.24 of March.
Suche accompt I trow they make, that tell vs how many mile it
is to heauen. But be it so, he is gone out of the prisone in Ieru-
salem.2000.mile of to Rome to be made bishop. If the story of
dame Ioane were so incredible as this, maister Harding vvith
some countenaunce might haue written against it. But let vs go
foreward. In the yeare of our Lorde.48. notwithstanding this *Act.15.7.*
posting to Rome, he is yet at Ierusalem. *And from hẽceforth *Orosius.lib.7*
that he ment not to goe to Rome, but kepe his promise that he *cap.6.*
would continue among the Iewes, we haue this profe. First his *Suetonius.*
othe where Iames, Peter, and Iohn doe sweare vnto Paule, and *Nauclerus.*
Barnabas, that they would execute their Apostleships among *Gal.2.9.
the Iewes. Which sure Peter woulde not haue done, if he had
thought to haue gone to Rome, and all the Papists in the world
shall neuer be able to ansvver it, iangle hovv they vvil, that Peter vvas bishop of Rome. He vvas not, he ment it not, he kept
his promisse. Paule calleth him the Apostle of circumcision. Gal.2.11.
He vvas aftervvarde among the Ievves at Antioche, he vvry- Gal.2.7.
teth his Epistle to the Ievves, that vvere straungers, and scatte- 1.Peter.1.1.
red abroade in Asia, euen as Iames dothe to the tvvelue Tribes Iacob.1.1.
scattered among the nations, and Iohn to them that had heard 1.Ioh.2.24.
and seene from the beginning, vvhich vvere the Ievves. Thus
did those Apostles minde their promise, though vve talke of
bishopprikes, vve knovve not vvhat. But bicause there are yet
three and twenty yeares behinde, let vs as vve may, examine
them by the scriptures. In the Actes vve read, that Priscilla and Act.18.2.
Aquila, and all the residue of the Ievves vvere banished out of *Orosius.lib.7*
Rome. But this vvas done the.9.yeare of Claudius. *Anno Do-* *cap.6.*
mini.51. When now Peter should haue bene more than.5.yeare *Suetonius.*
bishop in Rome. Thus yll may this fable agree vvith the scrip- *Nauclerus,*
tures of God. But let vs examine it further. *& alij.*

48. H. DENHAM 1b Dering, E. *A sparing restraint.* 1568
STC 6725 Tanner 255 Sig. *4r

hoate, nor colde, I will ſpue thée out of my mouth, sayth the Lord? This hobbing was the cauſe that you fell agayne to your vomit. And this rouing euer ſince, made your ſhoting vncertaine. You could not ſée the marke, that M. Juell ſhootes at, the vale of colde deuotion was before your eyes. You looked euen now like an Eagle, in the poore mans queſtion. But nowe you haue oyled your blere eyes, that you can not ſée Chriſt. God lighten your eyes, that you ſléepe not ſtyll in death. You ſtoode without (you ſay) and ſhot ſmaller game, in déede you ſhot ſuch game, as was not worth your labour. At the imaginations of mans brayne you roued ſo muche vncertainly, that you ſhoote yet now beating the ayre. Therfore haue you eyes, and ſée not. &c. There be manye ſuche hobbers now adayes. God giue vs grace to beware by your example, and to take héede of ſuch cold play.

¶ As for your reſpectes, to ſaye truely I neuer knew. what they were. At the gaming of your Goſpell, you ſhote, to ſtrike downe the true, and reall body of Chriſt, out of the bleſſed ſacrament of the aulter, with certaine phraſes of ſpechwith, telling the people of your tropes, and figures, with comparing the Euchariſt to the baptiſme, with making the preſẽce of Chriſt, like in both. You bend your force to ſtrike away the eternall, and ſinguler ſacrifice of the church, with ſuch a ſort, and forme, as I hetherto neuer vſed, and yet thinke to be very ſtraunge, as for example with teaching as you do, that *miſſa* ſignifieth not the maſſe, but your Cõmuniõ, that Euchariſtia is to be taken not for the ſacrament conſecrate, but for common bread, wherewith one Biſhop did preſent another. That Melchiſedech, and Malachias ſignified the ſacrifice of your cõmunion, wherat the people lift vp their handes, and hartes, as you ſay, vnto heauen, praieth, and ſacrificeth togither, reioyſing in the

Hardyng.

49. H. DENHAM 2 Dering, E. *A sparing restraint.* 1568.
STC 6725 Tanner 255 Sig. H4r

of corruption, to put on the ſpirit the cauſe of ſanctification : forſaking ignorance wherein ſhe was blind, to come to knowledge, whereby ſhe may ſee : remoouing ſuperſtition, wherewith ſhe was ſmothered, to imbrace true religion, wherewith ſhe may reuiue.

The fruit of this Treatiſe (good Reader) is thine amendment : this onelie had, the writer is ſatiſfied. This good Ladie thought no ſhame to deteſt hir ſinne, to obteine remiſſion ; no vilenes, to become nothing ; to be a member of him, which is all things in all ; no follie to forget the wiſedome of the world, to learne the ſimplicitie of the Goſpell at the laſt ; no diſpleaſantneſſe to ſubmit hir ſelfe to the ſchoole of the croſſe, the learning of the *Crucifix*, the booke of our redemption ; the verie abſolute librarie of Gods mercie and wiſedome. This waie thought ſhe hir honour increaſed, and hir ſtate permanent, to make hir earthlie honour heauenlie, and neglect the tranſitorie for the euerlaſting.

Of this I would thee warned, that the profit may enſue. Theſe great myſteries and graces be not well perceiued, except they be ſurelie ſtudied ; neither be they perfectlie ſtudied, except they be diligentlie practiſed ; neither profitablie practiſed, without amendment. See and learne hereby what ſhe hath doone, then maiſt thou practiſe, and amend that thou canſt doo : ſo ſhalt thou practiſe with eaſe, hauing a guide, and amend with profit, hauing a zeale. It is eaſier to ſee theſe, than to learne : begin at the eaſieſt to come to the harder ; ſee thou hir confeſſion, that thou maieſt learne hir repentance ; practiſe hir perſeuerance, that thou maieſt haue like amendment ; deſpiſe thy ſelfe in eſchewing vice, that thou maieſt pleaſe God in asking grace : let not ſhame hinder the confeſſion, which hindered not the offenſe. Be thou ſure if we knowledge our ſinnes, God is faithfull to forgiue vs, and to clenſe vs from all vnrighteouſnes. Obeie the Prophets ſaieng ; *Declare thy waies to the Lord.*

Thus far thou maiſt learne to knowe thy ſelfe ; next this be thou as diligent to releeue thy ſelfe in Gods mercie, as thou haſt beene to reueale thy ſelfe in thine owne repentance. For God hath concluded all things vnder ſinne, bicauſe he would haue mercie vpon all, who hath alſo borne our ſinnes in his bodie vpon the tree, that we ſhould be deliuered from ſinne, and ſhould liue vnto righteouſnes, by whoſe ſtripes we be healed. Here is our anchor ; here is our

ſhepheard ;

50. H. DENHAM 3 Bentley, T. *The monument of matrones.* 1582
STC 1892 4° C.38.Jur Sig. H6r

¶TO THE RIGHT HONORABLE
and my very good lord, ſyr Thomas
Sackuyle knight, lord Buckhurſt:
Thomas Vnderdovvn vviſheth
continuall health, vvith
encreaſe of Ho-
nor.

IN addreſsing of my booke (right honorable, & my very good lord) it is neceſſary, that the geuer thereof should conſider, vvhether the gyfte be a preſent meete for the patron or not, leaſt in preſuming ouerbouldly to offer the ſame, he purchaſe great dyſpleaſure in ſtead of deſyred fauor. VVhich conſideration debated ſo long of this voorke in my braine, that I determyned it a thinge ouerbaſe to be profered to your excellent honor: not for the vnvvorthineſſe of the vvorke vvhich is very vvytty, but for the ſimpleneſſe of the tranſlation vvhich ill beſemeth the ſame: yet I vvas comforted

A.ii. againe,

51. T. EAST 1a *Ouid his inuectiue against Ibis*. 1569
STC 18949 Wood 87 Sig. A2r

the meanes how to auoyde the crooked by pathes which leade vnto destruction. So that the offences ones auoyded, and the mynde fully bent to goe forthwardes in godlynesse, it shalbe hard to withdraw vs from performance of our possible duties. Vnto these three parts thus collected & ordred, I haue thought good to adde an olde letter which teacheth *Remedies against the bitternes of Death*. Being perticulerly and yet (in myne opinion) eloquently and well wrytten by the originall aucthour. Yea & very meete to be redde as the present tyme requireth. All which to gether drawing to a reasonable vollume, I haue now finished and publyshed in print. And aswell bicause I thought the light of the aucthors ouer bright a Candle to be hydden vnder a busshell, as also for that I would make the worlde wytnesse how deepe my graue freendes aduise dyd sinke into my memorye, but especially to leaue some pawne of thankfulnesse in your honorable handes, vntyll I may with greater deserte dyscharge some parte of such infinite dewties as I owe vnto your Lordshippe: I presume ryght humbly to dedicate my trauayle herein vnto your patronage & noble name. Euen so beseching the same to pardone myne imperfections, if any (through ignoraunce and not for lacke of zeale) haue passed my penne throughout this worke. And much the rather for that in deede I haue bothe vsed the conference, and abyd the correction of learned Deuines, to make it the more worthy of so honorable a patrone. How so euer it be, my wyll and desire are very earnest to please and profyt all true christians in generallitie, and to purchase the continuance of your comfortable fauour in perticularitie. In full hope whereof I seace any further to trouble your good Lordshippe, but shall neuer cease to beseech the almightie that he vouchsafe longe to vpholde the prosperous pyllers of your estate to his pleasure. From my lodging where I finished this trauayle in weake plight for health as your good L: well knoweth this second daye of *Maye*. 1576.

¶ *Your Lordshippes right humble and faithful seruaunt. George Gascoigne.*

52. T. EAST 1b Gascoigne, G. *The droomme of doomes day.* 1576
STC 11641 Malone 590 Sig. **3v

TO THE FAMOUS and most reuerend Father in God, Edmond by the permission of God, Archbishop of Canterbury, Primate, and Metropolitane of all England.

ARTAXERXES king of Persia, (right reuerend & worthy) as Plutarch writing of the auncient & notable sayings of kings, Princes, & Capitaines, doth witnesse, esteemed so highly the good will of those that did freely offer him presents in token of their obedience and duetifull loue, that at a certeine time, when a poore man, who liued by the sweate of his browes, and had nothing otherwise to present him withall, offered him water which he tooke vp out of the riuer with his handes, hee receiued the same of him ioyously, and with a smiling countenaunce, measuring the gift according to the zealous intent of the giuer, and not after the value of the gift or present offered. Euen so I with the sayd poore man, which am neither indued with any of Crœsus riches, Platoes skill, nor Tullies eloquence, am bold (yet presuming vpon your good graces like clemēcie) who deme it, I doubt not, no lesse part of magnanimitie and heroicall vertue, to accept louingly small presents, then to giue great, to offer vnto you this simple present: crauing, that albeit on my part I deserue none or very smal praise, who haue but only collected out of other the Sermons of Barnardine Occhine, these certein of Faith, Hope, and Charitie, and transl[a]ted them out of the Italian, into our maternall tongue: yet that for the works sake, both bicause that of the said argumēt, there is none other, or those very rare workes extant before this, and also bicause that in these sayd Sermons, is very

53. T. EAST IC Ochino, B. *Certain godly sermons.* 1580
STC 18769 Vet.A.1.e17 Sig. A2r

een what please the heauens to send vs; so the Sunne stand not still; and the Moone keepe her vsuall returnes; and make vp dayes, moneths, and yea res.

Quick. And you haue good securitie?

Secu. I mary *Francke*, that's the speciall point.

Quick. And yet forsooth wee must haue Trades to liue withall; For wee cannot stand without legges, nor flye without wings; and a number of such skurvie phrases. No, I say still; hee that has wit, let him liue by his wit: hee that has none, let him be a Trades-man.

Secu. Witty Maister *Francis*!
Tis pittie any Trade should dull that quicke braine of yours. Doe but bring Knight *Petronell* into my Parchment Toyles once, and you shall neuer neede to toyle in any trade, a my credit! You know his wiues Land?

Quick-siluer. Euen to a foote Sir, I haue beene often there: a pretie fine Seate, good Land, all intire within it selfe.

Secu. Well wooded?

Quick. Two hundered pounds woorth of wood readye to fell. And a fine sweete house that stands iust in the midst an't, like a Pricke in the midst of a Circle; would I were your Farmer, for a hundred pound a yeere.

Secu. Excellent M. *Francis*; how I do long to doe thee good: *How I doe hunger, and thirst to haue the honour to inrich thee?* I, euen to die, that thou mightest inherite my liuing: *euen hunger and thirst*, -for a my Religion, M. *Francis.* And so tell Knight *Petronell* I doe it to doe him a pleasure.

Quickesiluer. Marry Dad, his horses are now comming vp, to beare downe his Ladie, wilt thou lend him thy stable to set 'hem in?

Secur. Faith M. *Francis*, I would be lothe to lend my Stable out of dores, in a greater matter I will pleasure him, but not in this.

Quick. A pox of your hunger and thirst. Well Dad, let him haue money: All he could any way get, is bestowed on a Ship, now bound for *Virginia*: the frame of which voiage is so closely conuaide, that his new Ladie nor any of her friendes know it. Notwithstanding, as soone as his Ladyes hand is gotten to the

sale

54. G. ELD 1 Chapman, G. *Eastward Hoe.* 1605
STC 4971 Malone 765 Sig. C2v

ſale of her inheritance, and you haue furniſht him with money, he will inſtantly hoyſt Saile, and away.

Secur. Now a Franck gale of winde goe with him, Maiſter *Franke*, we haue too few ſuch knight aduenturers: who would not ſell away competent certainties, to purchaſe (with any danger) excellent vncertainties? your true knight venturer euer does it. Let his wife ſeale to day, he ſhall haue his money to day.

Qui. To morrow ſhe ſhall, Dad, before ſhe goes into the coũtry, to worke her to which actiõ, with the more engines, I purpoſe preſently to preferre my ſweete *Sinne* here, to the place of her Gentlewoman; whom you (for the more credit) ſhall preſent as your friends daughter, a Gentlewoman of the countrie, new come vp with a will for a while to learne faſhions forſooth, and be toward ſome Ladie; and ſhe ſhall buzz prettie deuiſes into her Ladies eare; feeding her humors ſo ſeruiceablie (as the manner of ſuch as ſhe is you know.)

Secur. True good Maiſter *Fraunces.*

Enter Sindefie.

Quic. That ſhe ſhall keepe her Port open to any thing ſhe commends to her.

Secur. A'my religion, a moſt faſhionable proiect; as good ſhe ſpoile the Lady, as the Lady ſpoile her; for tis three to one of one ſide: ſweete miſtreſſe *Sinne*, how are you bound to maiſter *Frances*! I doe not doubt to ſee you ſhortly wedde one of the head men of our cittie.

Sinne. But ſweete *Franke*, when ſhall my father *Securitie* preſent me?

Quic. With all feſtination; I haue broken the Ice to it already; and will preſently to the Knights houſe, whether, my good old Dad, let me pray thee with all formallitie to man her.

Secur. Commaund me Maiſter *Frances*; *I doe hunger and thirſt to doe thee ſeruice.* Come ſweete Miſtreſſe *Sinne*, take leaue of my *Wynnifride*, and we will inſtantly meete *francke* Maiſter *Frances* at your Ladies.

Enter Winnifride aboue.

Win. Where is my *Cu* there? *Cu*?

Secur. I *Winnie.*

Win. Wilt thou come in, ſweete *Cu*?

55. G. ELD 2 Chapman, G. *Eastward Hoe.* 1605
STC 4971 Malone 765 Sig. C3r

albeit it were rooted out,this subsidie would neuerthesse be leuied, vnder colour of preseruing the Church from like inconueniences. Neither is there any remedy whereby to eschue this consequence, but by taking part against the League, which doth exact these reuenues : that is, by declaring them selues seruauntes to the king, and enemies to the League , and taking to the support of their estate , such persons as regard not the Pope, who hath layd this burthen vpon them . Moreouer I doubt not but the Clergie are faithfull to the King, but neuerthelesse the League is a cõspiracie of the Pope against the crowne of Fraunce: but all that are of the League,are not of the cõspiracie, neither do they vnderstand the purpose thereof: and the Pope made it not to Reforme the time of Philip the Faire, when he caused the kinges owne children to conspire against their father : but it is an old practise of the Popes, to shuffle the French kinges cardes, and to seeke reuenge of the Pragmaticall Sanction, as well against the king as against the Clergie, but he is glad to take the cause of Reformation for a cloake, to the end vnder pretence thereof, to doe that which otherwise would be very hard for him to doe.

But I pray yon,what cause haue they to obey a forrein Franciscan Frier,rather then some one of the French Clergie?For the Pope hath bene a poore Mõkish deuill,that hath cast his coate to catch the Papacie,and would now gladly vncrowne the king to make him a Monke.There be amõg the French Clergy many Princes, Lordes and men of accompt, whom we might better obey then a Franciscane at Rome:howbeit if we must needs obey a Franciscan,are there not enough in Fraunce, that do better deserue it then he, who was neuer created Pope but vpon fauour ,rather then the worthinesse in him? But in case a Romish Franciscan were fitter to gouerne the French Clergie, yet were it requisite he were brought into France, so to spare both labour and cost, and to be nearer his flocke, for it is neuer the propertie of a good shepheard, to lye farre from his fold : but now a dayes we make such shepheardes,as doe neuer visite their flockes,yea that neuer see the flockes,that they entitle them selues shepheardes of.

56. R. FIELD I Frégeville, J. de *The reformed politique.* 1589
STC 11372 4° L.90.Art Sig. G2r

They wold faine haue laid the tempest, that thus readily loose the wares, and cast out their verie tackling into the sea, but the sea will not be satisfied, the waters must wash the sinner, or there is no safetie, nay the danger is greater, the sea continually more & more troublesome, vexing them. But *Ionah* was no sooner cast into the sea but all was quiet, the windes are calme, and the sea ceaseth from her raging: ô that iustice were executed, and he that troubleth the ship were in the sea. He that troubleth, not he that against all reason is thought to trouble. Then should all be safe, yea peraduenture *Ionah* to. *Ionah.*1.11 15.

And they cast the wares that were in the ship into the sea.

Obserue here that oftētimes manie are punished for one mans sin, as all the host of Israell were punished for the sin of *Achan*, & here al the mariners & owners of ship or wares for *Ionahs* sin, &c. To the end that men may learne thereby to admonish one another when they see them do amisse, with loue: & not to say with *Cain*: Am I the keeper of my brother? for he that is not careful to keepe his brother frō sin, is not careful to keep himself either from sin or from sorrow: therfore let vs take heed that a wicked one be nor found amōgst vs vnadmonished. I wold there were not many worse then *Ionah* amongst vs. Will you know what I think of you? I thinke you are worse then Infidels, Turks or Pagans, that in this wonderfull yeare of wonderfull mercies, are not thankful, beleeue not in God, trust not in him, glorifie not his name: but like *Pharaohs* sorcerers, who seeing the great workes of God which *Moses* wrought passing their skill, confessed, saying: *Surely this is the finger of God*: for you cōfesse that it is the great work of God (as must needs) but where are the fruits it hath brought forth in you? The Captaine saith, I haue done nothing, the souldier saith, I stirred not, but the Lord sent out a mighty tēpest vpon them, & after that they escaped our hād s, the Lord stretched out his mightie arme against them, & *Pharao* is drowned in the sea, so that he neuer attained the land of promise which he gaped for, and made full accoūt to possesse. Further, herein we may note, that extremitie is Gods oportunitie: for when the wind had almost ouerturned all, & the waters had almost drowned al, & destructiō had almost deuoured all, thē, & not afore, was Gods oportunitie, to set forth his glorie. First they vsed prayer vnto the diuine powers for

*Ios.*7.5.12. Many punished for ones sin, therefore suffer sin in none. *Gen.*4.9. *Exod.*8.19. Mans extremitie Gods oportunity.

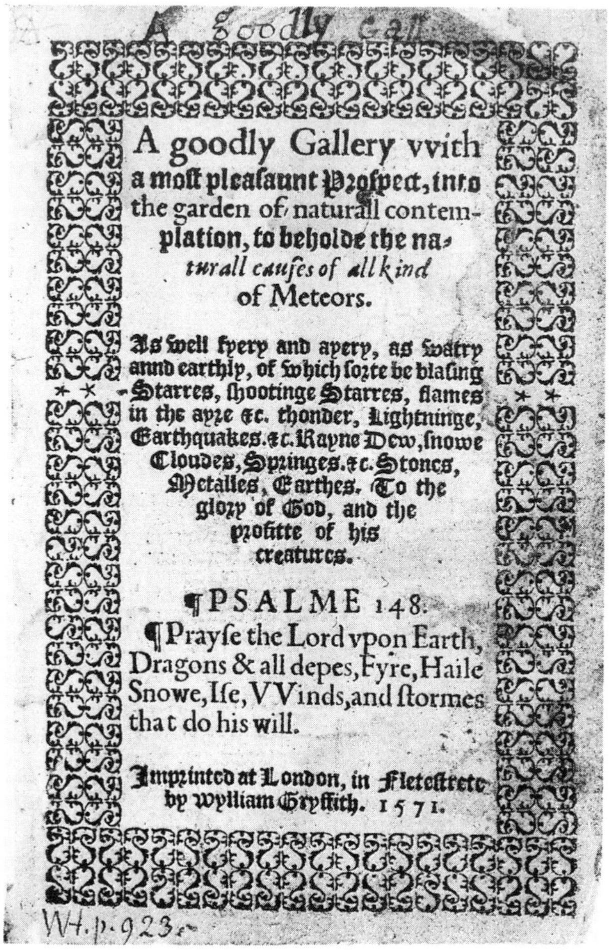

A goodly Gallery vvith a most pleasaunt Prospect, into the garden of naturall contemplation, to beholde the naturall causes of all kind of Meteors.

As well fyery and ayery, as watry annd earthly, of which sorte be blasing Starres, shooting Starres, flames in the ayre &c. thonder, Lightninge, Earthquakes. &c. Rayne Dew, snowe Cloudes, Springes. &c. Stones, Metalles, Earthes. To the glory of God, and the profitte of his creatures.

¶ PSALME 148.

¶ Prayse the Lord vpon Earth, Dragons & all depes, Fyre, Haile Snowe, Ise, VVinds, and stormes that do his will.

Imprinted at London, in Fletestrete by Wylliam Gryffith. 1571.

58. W. GRIFFITH Fulke, W. *A goodly gallery.* 1571
STC 11436 Mason C.C.59 TP

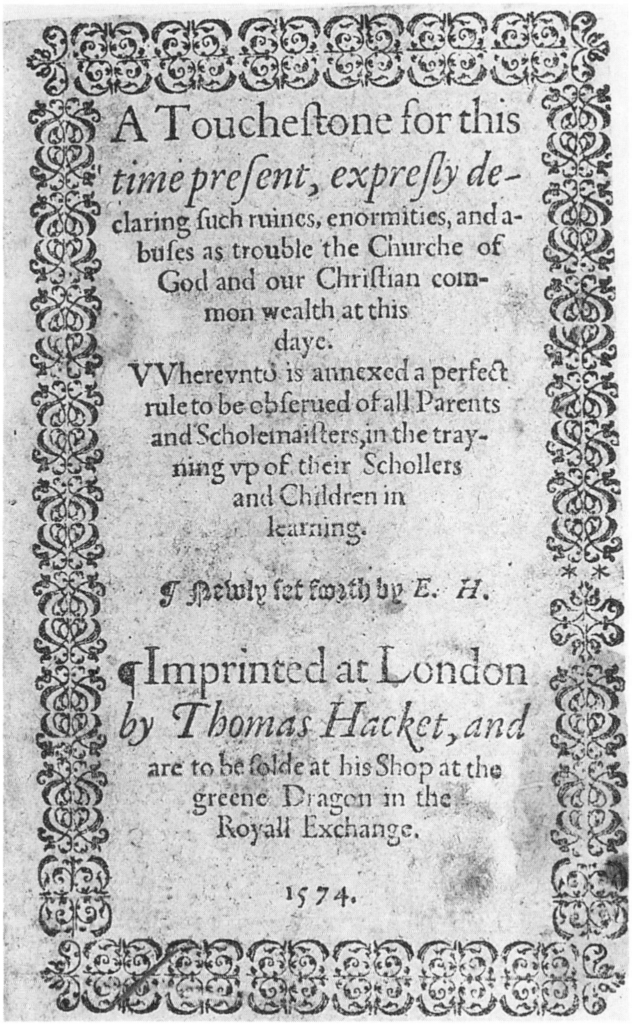

A Toucheſtone for this *time preſent, expreſly de*-claring ſuch ruines, enormities, and a-buſes as trouble the Churche of God and our Chriſtian com-mon wealth at this daye.

VVherevnto is annexed a perfect rule to be obſerued of all Parents and Scholemaiſters, in the tray-ning vp of their Schollers and Children in learning.

¶ Newly ſet forth by *E. H.*

¶ Imprinted at London *by Thomas Hacket, and* are to be ſolde at his Shop at the greene Dragon in the Royall Exchange.

1574.

59. T. HACKET Hake, E. *A touchestone.* 1574
STC 12609 Malone 456 TP

be tvvo principall enemies . The one is the Chirurgian himſelfe, vvho neither knovveth nor yet laboureth to learne his arte, but being inflamed vvith the loue of turpe lucrũ, rudely and blyndely exerciſeth his arte. The other enemie is the Pacient vvho hath need of Chirurgeries ayde. For he vvill haue in lyke eſtimation, a Cobler, a Ioyner, a Minſtraile, a vvoman, yea a Horſeleache, that he vvill an expert Chirurgian, yea and revvard them as vvell, if it be not better. The remedies for one of theſe miſchiefes you haue, I hope, in tyme prouided. I meane in ſetting out your Enchiridion. For there ſhall thoſe that in deed are licenſed to exerciſe Chirurgerie, finde no ſmale portiõ of this art compendiouſly and faythfully gathered together. V Vherefore leauing other their authours in vvhich many errours are hidden, I doe exhort them that bothe for the fame of Chirurgerie, vvhich they ought to their vttermoſte to maintaine: and alſo for their ovvne gaine and profite they vvill not only read this Enchiridion: but read and read it againe, not leauing vntill they be made vvell acquaynted vvith the ſame. And if any places do remaine obſcure and darke: they yet haue you the authour to reſort vnto, vvho vvill as gladly I am

A.iij. ſure

60. R. HALL Gale, T. *Certaine workes of chirurgerie.* 1563
STC 11529 Vet. A.1f.5 Sig. A3r

TO HIS WORSHIPFVL, WORthy and ſingular good friend Maſter *T. I.* theſe faithfull commendations.

(*.*.)

SIr,a farre greater happines then I of late haue had, either leiſure to hope for, or means to expect; I commend to your good ſelfe,& the frends of our acquaintance. Being certified by my affection, that your gentle nature, doth commiſerat the miſſortunes hath befalne me, and therein as a friend, doth ſhare with mee in ſorrow: I ſhall as ſoone as occaſion will ſuffer me, make haſt to *London*, to bee counſelled by your aduiſe, touching thoſe things in particular, that mainly concerne my eſtate: Nor make I any doubt, but before the receipt hereof, you haue heard of my miſhap, from the report of ſome of my men who I hope, are ariued by paſſage, by the way of *Holland*: therefore I omit herein to trouble you with the maner of my firſt taking by the *Turkes*, whoſe gouernours, I meane *Maſters* & *Pilates*, are all Engliſhmen, not onely *Pirates*, but mearely reprobates, and whoſe ſucceſſe at Seas is ſo great, that it is moſt lamentable to report, how many Ships of *London*, and other parts of England haue beene taken and made prey vnto them: without the help of which Engliſh, the *Turks* by no means could haue gouerned and conducted them through their vnskilfulnes and inſufficiencie in the art of *Nauigation*: yet of late to my wofull experience, I can witnes, they haue beene ſo readied by the inſtruction of our apoſtate countrimen, [I meane of *Ward* and others, who haue beene their commanders] to tackle their Ships, to man and mannage a fight, that if it doe not pleaſe God to moue the heart of his Maieſtie, and other Chriſtian Princes, and

A 2 ſtates,

61. W. HALL I Barker, A. *A . . . report of . . . Captaine Ward.* 1609
STC 1417 4° L.70.Art Sig. A2r

THis required the Kings Atturney Generall, ordained that his Maieſties Edict now read, ſhould bee regiſtred in the Court Rolles, that recourſe might be had thereto when need required, and to bee publiſhed with ſound of trumpet thorow all the ſtreets and corners of this City, where Proclamations are accuſtomed to be made, and ſent with all diligence, at the charges of the Notarie, to euery particular Court, there to bee likewiſe read, publiſhed, and regiſtred; whereof the Officers ſhall certifie the Kings Atturney. It is enioined, and We enioine, all perſons of what eſtate and condition ſoeuer they bee, to obey it, vpon paine as aforeſaid. Made this 11. of Iuly, *1609.*

THis preſent Proclamation hath beene read and publiſhed the Court being aſſembled, and beſides thorow all the ſtreets of this Towne of *Poictiers*, by me *Steuen Renier* Sergeant Royall, hauing with mee *Peter Pareau* Crier, and Trumpetter ordinarie of this City. Made this 11. of Iuly, *1609.*

Signed Renier and Pareau.

62. W. HALL 2 Henry IV (of France) *An edict . . . concerning . . . combats.* 1609
STC 13123 Pamph.c.7(1) Sig. B4v

the waxe from their hiues, and offered them for the soules Purgatorie.
in Purgatorie. But who eateth and drinketh the same? not the soules; but the Preists, and Friars, their concubines and children. A poore old woman watched early and late to spinne, and ad farthing to farthing, for a Masse to be said for the soule of her husband, brother or son: she forbare to eate, and gaue it vnto knaues. All these visions or apparitions they made by the Arte of the deuill. Iudge (Lord) thine owne cause: deliuer the poore people from the handes of these Inchaunters, false prophets and deceiuers. Open thine eies (ô Spaine) and see, beleeue him that with great loue doth aduise thee. Behold whether this that I say be true or no: *Iohn* 20. of poyson (as some Anno 1009.
say) in the 1009. yeare died. & *Don Fernando* 1. then reigned in Poyson.
Castile & Leons. *Sergius* 4. a Roman by the accustomed waies Sergius 4. an
in his time had the Bishopdome: albeit *Platina* and *Estella*, the inchanter.
Popes parasites, affirme him to haue bene a holy man. The Sun Prognostications.
in his time was darkened, the Moone in shew like bloud, famin & pestilence were in Italy, & the water of a certaine fountaine in *Lorena* was turned into bloud. All these were prognostications & most certain signs of Gods wrath, for the idolatry which then reigned. *Sergius* died in the 1012. yeare. *Benedict* 7. or 8. son Anno 1012.
of *Gregorie* Bishop of Porta, a lay man, by the aid of his nephew Benedict 8. an
Theophilact, a great inchanter, and disciple of *Syluester* 2. which inchanter.
learned his nigromancy in Seuill (as in his life before we haue declared) was made Pope. This *Theophilact* proued very expert in his art: so that sacrificing to the diuel in woods & moũtaines, he caused by his sorcery (saith Cardinal *Benon*) that women en- Theophilact.
amored of him, left their houses & followed him: such a one as an inchanter.
he was, he was afterwad Pope. Whilest *Henrie Banare* the Emperour liued, this *Benedict* was Pope quietly; but the Emperour once dead, the Cardinals dispoped him, & placed another in his room, but afterward appeased with mony, which *Benedict* gaue them, they inthronized him againe, & cast out the Antipope. This was the 19 Sisme. Of this *Benedict* reporteth *Pet. Damianus*. The 19. Sisme.
& the same also reciteth *Antoninus*, Frier *Iohn de Pineda par.* 3. Anno 1024.
lib. 19. *cap.* 17. ¶. 3. & others, that a horseman on a blacke horse (after his death) appeared to a Bishop his verie friend. The Bishop appalled with the vision, demaunded, saying:

63. J. HARRISON III Valera, C. de *Two treatises*. 1600
STC 24581 4° V.3.Th Sig. E6r

Albeit the time would not permit me to speake the laste day of the thirde verse, but forced mée to reserue it vnto this day, and to ioyne it with this matter that now you haue heard (of not making to our selues any grauen image:) yet that whiche time hath now knitte together, is by the iudgement of diuerse godlie and learned men, not to bée sundered at all. For they take that (of hauing the Lorde our God) which hath already béene declared, to be the firste commandement, and this Scripture that now I haue read, conteyned in these foure verses, to be the seconde.

Of this iudgement was that learned father Peter Martyr, whose wordes are these in his Commentarie vpon the Romanes. I suppose the firste commandement to be that which is set before the rest in steade of a proheme (I am the Lord thy God which haue brought thee out of the land of Aegypt.) For in these wordes are wee commaunded to accompt him for the true God. And that wee should not thinke that he is to be worshipped together with other gods, streight way is added the second precept, wherein we are prohibited to worship straunge gods, and grauen thinges and images. And if a man will more narrowly consider the thinge, hee shall see that together with this firste commaundement is offered vnto vs the Gospell, for in it God promiseth that he will bee our God. These are the wordes of Peter Martyr. Rom. 7.

Of this iudgemente in like manner was that learned and godlie man M. Bucer, as appeareth in his exposition vpon the 14. Psalme, where hée hath these wordes. The firste thinge of all in the matter of our saluation, is to beleeue in one Lorde our God, from whome as the fathers had their deliueraunce

64. L. HARRISON Knewstub, W. *Lectures of*. 1578
STC 15043 Antiq e.E.1578.1 Sig. B2r

What auaileth the shipmaister after the ship is sunke; what do weapons auaile after the battell is done; what pleasure after men are dead: likewise what auaileth the godlie instructor when the sicke is heauie and bereft of his senses; or to vnlocke his conscience, when the key of his toong is lost?

Let vs not deceiue our selues, thinking in age to amend, and to make restitution at our death: for it is not the point of wise men, nor of good Christians to desire so much time to offend, and yet will neuer spie any time to amend.

Would to God that the third part of time which men do occupie in sinne were imploied about the meditation of death; and the cares which they haue to accomplish their fleshlie lusts were spent in bewailing their filthie sinnes.

All worldlings do willingly sinne vpon hope onely in age to amend, and at death to repent: but they that in this hope sinne, what certaintie haue they of amendement, and assurance to haue long warning ere they die, sith in number there are more yoong than old which die?

The omnipotencie of the diuine mercie considered the space of an hower sufficeth, yea too much to repent vs of our wicked life: but yet I counsell all, sith the sinner for his repentance taketh but one hower, that it be not the hower too late. Repentance.

The sighes and repentance which proceedeth from the bottom of the hart, do penetrate the high heauens: but those which come of necessitie do not pearce the seeling of the house. Repentance.

What wrong doth God offer vnto vs when he calleth vs away: seeing from an olde decaied house he is to change vs to a new builded pallace? The benefite of death.

What other thing is the graue but a strong fort, wherin we shut our selues from the assalts of life, and broiles The graue.

of

65. A. HATFIELD ECI Paulet, W. *The lord marques idlenes*. 1586
STC 19485 Crynes 905 Sig. D4r

went alone, for that in his voiage there is signified this onely *Contemplation* of these paines and rewardes which in another world are reserued for good or guiltie soules. Moreouer, the operation of the *Vnderstanding speculatiue*, which is the working of one only power, is commodiously figured vnto vs by the action of one alone: but the *Operation Politicall*, which proceedeth together from the other powers of the minde (which are as citizens vnited in one commonwealth) cannot so commodiously be shadowed of *Action*, wherein many together and to one end working, doe not concurre. To these reasons, and to these examples I hauing regarde, haue made the *Allegorie* of my *Poem* such, as now shall be manifested.

The *Army* compounded of diuers Princes, and of other Christian souldiers, signifieth *Man*, compounded of soule and bodie, and of a soule not simple, but diuided into many and diuers powers. *Ierusalem* the strong citie placed in a rough and hilly countrey, whereunto as to the last ende, are directed all the enterprises of the faithfull armie, doth here signifie the *Ciuill happines*, which may come to a Christian man (as hereafter shall be declared) which is a good, verie difficult to attaine vnto, and situated vpon the top of the Alpine and wearisome hill of virtue; and vnto this are turned (as vnto the last marke) all the Actions of the politicke man. *Godfrey*, which of all the assembly is chosen Chieftaine, stands for *Vnderstanding*, & particularly for that vnderstanding, which considereth not the things necessarie, but the mutable and which may diuersly happen, & those by the wil of God. And of *Princes* he is chosẽ Captaine of this enterprise, because vnderstanding is of God, and of Nature made Lord ouer the other virtues of the soule and bodie, and commaunds these, one with ciuill power, the other with roiall command. *Rinaldo, Tancredie*, and the other Princes are in liew of the other powers of the soule; and the *Bodie* here becomes notified by the souldiers lesse noble. And because that through the imperfection of humaine nature, and by the deceits of his enemy, man attaines not this felicitie without many inward difficulties, and without finding by the way many outward impediments, all these are noted vnto vs by Poeticall figures. As the death of *Syrenus*, and his companions, not being ioined to the campe, but slaine farre off, may here shew the losses, which a ciuill man hath of his friends, followers, and other externall goods, instruments of vertue, & aids to the attaining of true felicitie. The armies of Affricke, Asia, and vnluckly battels, are none other than his enemies, his losses, and the accidents of contrarie fortune. But comming to the inward impediments, loue, which maketh *Tancredie* and the other woorthies to dote, and disioine them from *Godfrey*, and the disdaine which enticeth *Rinaldo* from the enterprise, doe signifie the conflict and rebellion which the *Concupiscent* and *Irefull* powers, doe make with the *Reasonable*. The *Diuels* which doe consult to hinder the conquest of *Ierusalem*, are both a figure, and a thing figured, and doe here represent the verie same euils, which doe oppose themselues against our ciuill happines, so that it may not be to vs a ladder of Christian blessednes. The two Magitians *Ismen* and *Armida*, seruants of the diuell, which indeuour to remooue the Christians from making war, are

66. A. HATFIELD EC2 Tasso, T. *Godfrey of Bulloigne*. 1600
STC 23698 Antiq d.E.1600/2 Sig. A3r

ſhall make you a place to keepe birdes in, of the ſame bredth with the porch, and as high as you will, the loweſt part of it ſhall ſerue for birds to keepe themſelues ſafe in, when either the raine or too much heate of the ſunne ſhall annoy them. One of the ſides of your barne, all along for the ſpace of three baies ſhall ſerue to put your rie and wheate in, and the other ſide for aſmuch length ſhall containe your pulſe or March corne: the middle part is that which is of the bredth of the porch, with his roofe aboue.

A hanging houſe for to keepe neceſſarie tooles for huſbandrie in.

And betwixt the ſheepe-cotes and ſwine-ſties, right ouer againſt the porch of the barne, you ſhall make a place of a competent height in manner of an appentice to ſet your ploughes, great carts, draies, tumbrels, waines, and other inſtruments and furniture for husbandry, if you pleaſe not rather to make the ground worke of your place to keepe and nouriſh byrds in, to ſerue for theſe purpoſes, when as your authoritie wil not beare you out to build a douehouſe on the ground, bicauſe you hold not in fee farme, or coppie hold.

Gardens and their partitions.

Vnder or vpon the ſide of your turne ſtaires according to the bredth of the bodie of your houſe, your farmer ſhall haue a way into the gardens: but you your ſelfe ſhall haue your way in by another winding ſtaire, which you ſhall make to deſcend from aboue, from your alley that is ouer them: the one of which gardens, as that one the right hand ſhall be for pot-herbes, and the other for quarters and pulſe, together with a place for Bee-hyues.

At the end of a great ally which you ſhall make from your winding ſtaire to the wall of your orchard, running betwixt the two gardens, without any manner of partition, except two hedges of quickſet, ſhall be your orchard ſeparated from your other gardens, by a wall continuing al along the two ſides of the incloſure of your place. And in the middeſt of the ſaid great ally, there ſhalbe wels to water by pipes and ſpouts, ſo much as is needfull in the gardens, if it like you not better to conuey ſome fountaine that way, or elſe to ſeeke for the heads of ſome ſprings, or elſe to make a ceſterne wel mortered to receiue and keepe raine water.

Feeding or paſture ground.

The Orchard ſhall make the fence on the ſide toward your houſe, and by it you ſhall make your waie into your feeding or paſture grounds, lying along by the ſides of ſome greene and flouriſhing water bankes, along the ſides of which brooke as alſo about your ponds of ſalt and freſhwater fiſh, you ſhall plant willowes.

The two nurceries for pippins and ſtockes.

Where you enter into your orchard out of your garden, you ſhall on the one ſide make a nurcerie for ſeedes and kernels, and one the other ſide for ſtockes and plants, and in the midſt the rankes of remooued and grafted trees, and at the end belowe you ſhall plant by ridges your Oſiers, which may for their better proſpering take the benefite of the coolenes and moiſture of ſome ſmall brooke.

The

67. A. HATFIELD EC3 Estienne & Liebault *Maison rustique*. 1606
STC 10548 Vet.A.2.e193 Sig. C5r

LIBELLVS ELEGAN
tissimus qui inscribitur Cato
de preceptis vitæ com-
munis.

CVM ANI-
maduerterē, quā
plurimos homi-
nes grauiter er-
rare in uia mo-
rum, succurren-
dum & consu-
lendum eorum
opinioni fore
existimaui, ma-
xime ut gloriose viuerent, & honorē con-
tingerent. Nunc te fili charissime docebo,
quo pacto mores animi tui componas. I-
gitur precepta mea ita legas, vt intelligas.
Legere enim et nō intelligere, negligere est

Itaq; Deo supplica. Parentes ama.
Cognatos cole. Magistrum metue.

The fyrst reuerence is to God, the next
to the father and mother, the thyrde to
the rest of thy kynsfolke. We make sup-
plication vnto God with our prayers
and sacrifices. We loue oure Parentes
whyle we obserue and obey them. We
embrace oure kynsfolke with offices of
humanitie and with vsynge their com-

Gradus pi
etatis.

A.iij. panye

68. N. HILL Cato, D. *Catonis disticha moralia.* 1553
STC 4844 Douce C.93 Sig. A3r

readines to make aunſwere to all thoſe which demaund a reaſon of their hope: ſo it appeareth therby, that the duety of a true Chriſtian, is to haue readye, & with him, ſome briefe reſolution and ſum of the principall poinctes of his religion, and alſo ſome principall reaſons, whereby he may on the one part confirme & ſtrengthen himſelfe therein, and on the other part, repell accordinge to his calling, the enemyes of the truth, and be readye to communicate his ſpirituall riches with all men. VVhereupon, I beinge already of that mind, and beſide the ſame being required to render a reaſon of my faith, by a perſonage whom next vnto God I am moſt bound to obey: I haue of late compoſed & made this treatiſe, which I haue entituled a confeſſion of the faith, wherin I haue comprehended after the beſt order I could, thoſe things which I haue learned in the Chriſtian religion by the reading of the Bible, with the conference of the moſt faithfull Expoſitours. At the firſt I made this but for mine owne vſe, & to ſatiſfie him who required it of me. But ſince, partly by the aduiſe of certaine good and learned men, and alſo beynge

moued

69. W. HOW 1a Bèze, T. de *A briefe and pithie sum.* 1572
STC 2010 Tanner 76 Sig. B5r

To the gentle and courteous *Readers*.

MEruayle not, gentle Readers, nor be not mooued, that I haue raſhly attempted to ſet vpon the reſidue of *Virgil*, after M. *Phaër*. The manifold examples that commonly are alleaged, to deterre men from finiſhing ſuch workes as haue bin left vnperfect by notable Artificers in all ſciences, could not make me afraid: howbeit perchance they may be laid in my diſh. I know there be many younge Gentlemen, and others, whoſe gift this way, ſo much excelleth my poore abilitie: that there is no compariſon betweene them. But peraduenture either they lacke good wil, which I aſſure you aboundeth in mee for my ſimple skill, or els leaſure, wherof I haue more at this preſent then I would gladly wiſh: or els they pinch curteſie like women, and one looketh vpon another who ſhall begin. But I, who haue bin brought vp in the *Vniuerſitie*, and meetly trained in other places, haue learned it to be good maners to be doing with that which is before mee. Wherin, though I be vpbraided of ſome for ouer raſhe, ſaucineſſe: what remedy? I truſt I haue attained to the Poetes meaning, though my verſe be far from fineſſe. And I know that it is an eaſier matter to finde fault withall, then to mend it. For in other Poemes and Dities of pleaſure, it is of leſſe difficultie to bring a mans owne ſenſe to his owne Rime: then in this kinde of tranſlation to enforce his Rime to the neceſsitie of another mans meaninge. Which they can not wel iudge of, that neuer came where it grew. And wheras there is now made an acceſsion of *Maphæus* xiij. Booke, for that the ſame Auctour iudged *Virgils* cõceit not to be perfected in the former xij. I haue not done it vpõ occaſion of any dreame as *Gawin Dowglas* did it into the Scottiſh, but mooued with the worthines of the worke, and the neerenes of the argument, verſe and ſtile vnto *Virgil*, wherin as I iudge, the writer hath declared himſelf an happie imitatour. Crauing for my good meaning and traueill but only freendly acceptance, wherby ye ſhall binde mee, as occaſion ſhalbe offred to attempt greater matters, aſwell for profit as pleaſure, if God prolong my daies with happie ſucceſſe. And to the end ye may be aſſured where my poore tranſlation enſueth M. *Phaërs*, I haue cauſed the Printer to ſet this note in the margine, within a few leaues after the beginninge of the tenth booke, wherof I thought it good not to leaue ye vnadmoniſhed.

And ſo fare ye well hartily, moſt freendly Readers.

Thomas Twyne.

70. W. HOW 1b Virgilius Maro, P. *The .xiii. bookes of Æneidos*. 1584
STC 24802 Tanner 791 Sig. π 3v

had denied : then began hee to remember himselfe, and consider that thinges were amisse. But was it the turning backe of his face, that wrought this in *Peter*? No, for then it might haue conuerted *Iudas*, (a) whome he looked vpon when he betraied him: but it was his grace and holie spirite, which did mercifullie fall downe into his heart, when the cocke did crow. And Iesus looked back, whereby wee see plainly, that it is not outward ministerie of the word of God, onely that bringeth saluation vnto mankinde: for *Paule* planteth, *Appollo* (b) watereth, but God giueth the increase. And this is the reason, that so many heare the word, and so few profite therein: because it belongeth to the Lord to shew (c) mercie to whome he will shew mercie. And therefore when the Gospell was preached to them of Antioche, by S. *Paule*: it is said, that so many as were (d) ordained to saluation, beleeued : so that if thou hearing, or reading Gods word, doest desire that it may woorke to thy saluation, pray earnestlie vnto the Lord, that it would please him of his infinit mercie to look back vpon thee with the eies of his grace, & so framing thy selfe in a true faith, & a single hart; to apply it vnto that end wherefore it is giuen thee: thou shalt surely feele in thy soule,

a Luke 22. 47.
b 1. Cor. 3. 6
c Exod. 33 19. Rom. 9. 5.
d Act. 13. 4

all godlines and vertue: & that is the cause that many (of whome wee may read) who hauing once tasted of the sweet woord of God, and after peruerted from the same, haue become the greatest enemies that euer the Church of God hath had at anie time: and therefore the Lord God (as he is most carefull for his children) maketh hast to deliuer *Peter* quicklie. This crowing of the Cocke was the same vnto *Peter*, that the preaching of Gods Ministers is vnto vs. (For God dooth not alwaies vse his ordinarie meanes) so that whensoeuer wee haue the woord of God preached, at what time soeuer wee heare our sinnes laid open before vs and rebuked: we must think with our selues that God dooth with vs as he did to *Peter*: namely, vseth means to cal vs from sin, & bring vs to repentance & amendment of life. This means the Lord vseth generally vnto all (for his Gospell must bee preached throughout the whole world, for a witnes vnto all nations) and yet we know, though many be called, yet few are chosen. Therefore it behoueth vs to know whether the Cocke doe crow vnto vs, to our saluation or no, and the first triall consisteth in this, that the Cocke of Gods word croweth

Heb.6.5.
Saul, Iulian the apostata, and all heretikes.
Mat.24.14.
20.16.

72. A. ISLIP 1b Udall, J. *Certaine sermons*. 1596
STC 24491 Vet.A.1.f15 Sig. F2r

1. Sobrietie in moderating not onely the inward fancies & affections, but also the outward sences.

serue perpetually the vertue of sobrietie, not onely in respect of gouerning their inward affections and fancies, but also in restraining the pleasures of their outward sences, especially of the sight and tast. Of sight, by restraining their eyes from beholding the objects of lust; such as are louely or lasciuious persons, wanton pictures, louebookes, obscene enterludes, and such like. For by the sence of sight, concupiscence is ordinarily conueyed to the heart: for as the old saying is, ἐκ τοῦ ὁρᾷν γίνεται τὸ ἐρᾷν, of looking comes louing. And therefore as wee must pray

Psal. 119.37. *Iob.* 31.1. *Eccles.* 9.8,9.

with *Dauid*, that the Lord would turne away our eyes, that they behold not vanitie; so must we with *Iob* make a couenant with our eyes: that as the sonne of Syrach aduiseth, we should turne them away from a beautifull woman, and not to eye the beautie of others: for by the beautie of women many haue beene seduced, and thereby loue is kindled as it were a fire.

2. Temperancie in diet.

Of tast, by temperancie in diet, that neither in respect of the quantitie they exceed by gluttonie or drunkennesse, nor in respect of the qualitie they affect such meats or drinkes as are fit to prouoke lust. And if they find not this sobrietie and abstinence to be sufficient for this purpose, then are they so oft as their health will beare, and their necessitie require, by fasting to chastise and subdue their bodies. And because continencie is not a thing in our owne power, but

Mat. 19.11. 1. *Cor.* 7.7. 3. Prayer. 4. Vigilancie. 1. *Pet.* 4.7. 1. *Thess.* 5.6. 5. Diligence & painefulnesse.

the free gift of God, we are therefore with our fasting to joyne earnest prayer for the same. And to our fasting and prayer we must joyne vigilancie and watchfulnesse, that as the Apostle exhorteth, wee may bee sober, and watch vnto prayer: and thereunto must wee adde painefulnesse in our calling, or in some honest labour.

Auoiding contrariwise intemperancie in diet. *Hieronym.*

4. For the greatest enemie to chastitie, and chiefest prouoker of lust, is excesse in meat and drinke: *Ciborum saturitas est seminarium libidinis*, fulnesse of meat is the seminarie of lust: for the ouerplus of our nourishment is the matter of generation, which aboundeth where nou-

rishment

73. A. ISLIP 2 Downame, G. *The Christians sanctuarie.* 1604
STC 7113 Cambridge U.L. Sig. B2v

ſignifieth the Church militant vpon earth, the holy Mountaine, the Church triumphant in heauen. By ſoiourning in the Tabernacle, is vnderſtood the ſhort and tranſitorie abode of Chriſtians, as it were pilgrims in the earth, as in a ſtrange land: by dwelling in the Mountaine of God, is ſignified their perpetuall and eternall reſt in heauen, as in their owne countrey. Wherein the Prophet alludeth vnto that materiall Tabernacle, which was called the Tabernacle of the aſſembly or congregation, and to the mount Moriah, where the Temple was placed: the one whereof was a type of the Church militant vpon earth, the other was a figure of the Church triumphant in heauen. I am not ignorant, that both members are by ſome expounded of the Church militant, and by others of the Church triumphant: but I follow that expoſition which ſeemeth beſt to agree with the words and meaning of the holy ghoſt. For the varietie of phraſe plainely argueth diuerſitie of matter: ſoiourning in Gods Tabernacle, being much different from dwelling in the Mountaine of his holineſſe. And the concluſion of the anſwere in the laſt words of the Pſalme, which without doubt doth render the true meaning of the queſtion, belongeth both to this life and to that which is to come. *He that doth theſe things, ſhall not be remooued for euer:* that is, he ſhall neither fall away from the grace of God in this life, nor bee excluded out of Gods glorious preſence in the life to come. The ſence therefore and meaning of the queſtion is this, Lord, thou ſearcher and trier of the hearts and raines of men, who art acquainted with all ſecrets, and beſt knoweſt who are thine, for as much as there is ſo much vnſoundneſſe and hypocriſie among them that profeſſe thy name, and frequent the places of thy worſhip, that many deceiue others with a counterfeit ſhew, and ſome beguile them ſelues with a falſe opinion of religion, declare, I beſeech thee, vnto thy Church ſome

1.Cor.3.1.

2.Tim.2.19.

To the Right Honorable, and moſt *vertuous Lady, the Lady Marye* Counteſſe of Pembrooke.

THE LITTLE POET ACCIVS NOT knowing which way to couer the ſmaleneſſe of hys perſon, which was ſomewhat leſſe then the meane, thought beſt to haue a great picture drawne for hys Counterfeyte: This Poet no doubt had ſome meaning in this deuiſe, for pictures often go there, where the perſon whom they repreſent are not admitted: And it might be that ſtrangers ſeeing the great ſhape, would imagine Accius to be a tall man. Tewcer a cunning Archer, but a faynte harted Souldiour, then wanted no courage when he was cloſe couered with the Target of his brother Aiax. Vliſſes, whoſe rype wyt made full amends for his weake body, thought no aduenture dangerous, though neuer ſo perillous, if he were protected with the ſhield of Pallas. So I right Noble Ladye knowing my abilitie to wryte, to bee farre leſſe then the perſon of Accius, and ſo more lykely to incurre more rebukes: my courage therfore more faynte then eyther Tewcers, or Vliſſes, and ſo more needing ſome ſtrong defence, haue aduentured to place in the forefrunt of this little treatiſe, the tytle of your name, as a great portrature to a little body, as a ſure ſhield to a weake Warriour, as a ſafe defence againſt any danger. For as they which ſhould ſee the picture of Accius, would imagine it to aunſwere his perſon: ſo if the Reader hereof, behold your name in the fyrſt leafe, he will deeme the whole Booke the more fruitfull, and the framer therof the more skilfull: but if he ſhall once perceyue your Honor to be Patroneſſe to this labour, he will eyther loue it, bicauſe he doth honor you, or wil not dare to reproch it, bicauſe he perceyueth you are as ready, and knoweth you are as able to defend it, as eyther Aiax was to garde Tewcer, or Pallas to guyde Vliſſes. I cannot right vertuous Ladye, imagine there was anye greater cauſe that might induce Accius to frame ſo bigge a picture: or cauſe Aiax to ſhielde Tewcer: or mooue Pallas to regarde the ſafety of Vliſſes: then my ſelfe

75. H. JACKSON Howell, T. *Howell his devises.* 1581
STC 13875 Malone 342 Sig. A3r

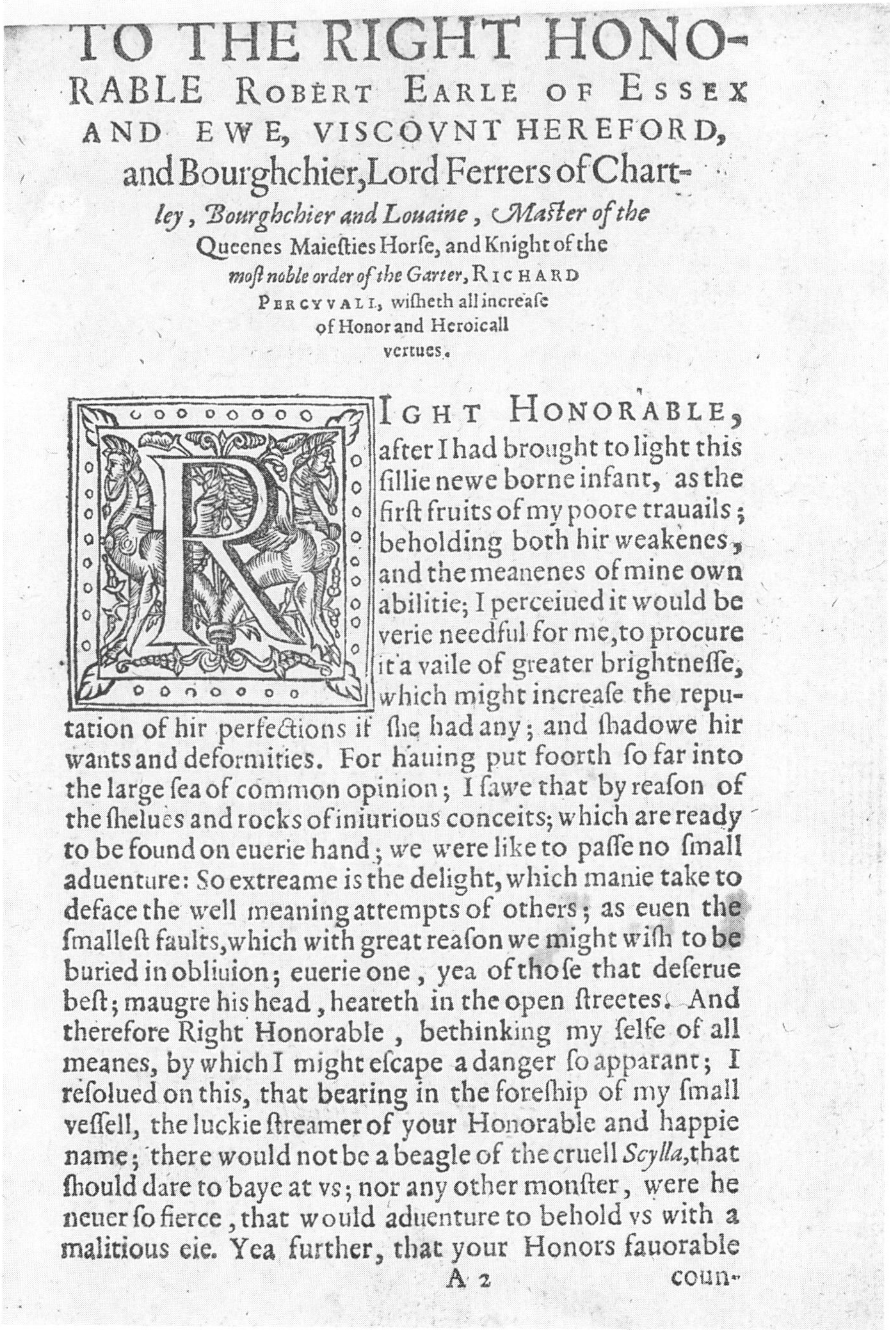

TO THE RIGHT HONO-
RABLE ROBERT EARLE OF ESSEX
AND EWE, VISCOVNT HEREFORD,
and Bourghchier, Lord Ferrers of Chart-
ley, Bourghchier and Louaine, Maſter of the
Queenes Maieſties Horſe, and Knight of the
moſt noble order of the Garter, RICHARD
PERCYVALL, wiſheth all increaſe
of Honor and Heroicall
vertues.

RIGHT HONORABLE, after I had brought to light this ſillie newe borne infant, as the firſt fruits of my poore trauails; beholding both hir weakenes, and the meanenes of mine own abilitie; I perceiued it would be verie needful for me, to procure it a vaile of greater brightneſſe, which might increaſe the reputation of hir perfections if ſhe had any; and ſhadowe hir wants and deformities. For hauing put foorth ſo far into the large ſea of common opinion; I ſawe that by reaſon of the ſhelues and rocks of iniurious conceits; which are ready to be found on euerie hand; we were like to paſſe no ſmall aduenture: So extreame is the delight, which manie take to deface the well meaning attempts of others; as euen the ſmalleſt faults, which with great reaſon we might wiſh to be buried in obliuion; euerie one, yea of thoſe that deſerue beſt; maugre his head, heareth in the open ſtreetes. And therefore Right Honorable, bethinking my ſelfe of all meanes, by which I might eſcape a danger ſo apparant; I reſolued on this, that bearing in the foreſhip of my ſmall veſſell, the luckie ſtreamer of your Honorable and happie name; there would not be a beagle of the cruell *Scylla*, that ſhould dare to baye at vs; nor any other monſter, were he neuer ſo fierce, that would aduenture to behold vs with a malitious eie. Yea further, that your Honors fauorable

A 2 coun-

76. J. JACKSON Percyvall, R. *Bibliotheca Hispanica.* 1591
STC 19619 Douce PP.200 Sig. A2r

earth is blessed this day. *Happie O King are thy people, and happie are thy Subiects or Seruants.* It is not my meaning, nor is it fit, to make a panegericall Oration in this place at large, therein to recount and amplifie also those manifold blessings, which by the meanes of our SALOMON, we doe now enioy. Yet the more to stirre vs vp to magnifie and blesse Gods glorious name, and if it be possible, more also, to loue and honour that Sacred Maiesty whom God hath chosen to be his royall Instrument, whereby so many and great blessings are deriued vnto vs; I may not omit to mention some few which are most eminent, commending the rest to your priuate & Religious consideration.

The first is our long tranquility and happie peace, with all the blessings and blessed fruites of peace. A blessing which God began to bestow on this land, at the ioyful entrance of our late Soueraigne QVEENE ELIZABETH, whose Sacred spirite doth now rest and raigne with the Lord, but her memory shall bee blessed and eternized in the world for euer; when all those venomous [k] and Viperous tongues (set on fire by hell) which now in vaine bark against her, and seeke to staine her spotlesse honour, shall rot, and be euen as the dung vpon the earth. Hauing enioyed long and happy peace, vnder her long and happy raigne, it was expected by the Agents and vassals of Antichrist, that the day which ended her life, should haue ended all our comforts, and beene to vs a dismall day, a day of murthers and massacres, a day of warres, of tumult, and of vtter desolation; one of their owne false Prophets [l] with a lying spirit in his mouth, foretelling of that day, *Catholici quidem dimicabunt*, at that day they will fight it out indeed.

[k] *Pars* in his answere to the Apol.

[l] *West. de trip. homin. offic. lib.* 3. *pag.* 435.

Behold, hee that sits in heauen laught them to scorne, the Lorde had them in derision. Himselfe placed in his owne Throne, after *David, Saloman*; *A* [m] *man of rest and peace, for God hath giuen him, and in him to vs, rest and peace from all his, and our Enemies, round about.* And loe, this is now more then the fiftieth yeare, wherein the people of this land

[m] 1. Chron. 22. 9.

77. W. JAGGARD I Crakanthorp, R. *A sermon, at the . . . inauguration of King James.* 1609
STC 5979 4° F.34.Th Sig. B4r

the word of God. To conclude these reasons, it is Antichrist, who, contrary to the doctrine of christ, contrary to the institution of the supper, contrary to the practise of the Apostles, and contrary to the vse of the former churches, hath excluded the people languishing and thirsting after the blood of christ, as the dry earth for the sweete shewers of raine, from taking the cup of the lord, and left them a dry cōmunion to eat the bread of the sacrament alone. Hauing considered the truth of God by sundry reasons, grounded in the scripture, that the people haue good interest and title in the cup, denied vnto them: let vs answer the [c] obiections of the aduersaries, made against the former doctrine. First, they pretend, that christ administred it to the apostles only, and not to any of the people: & consequently the institution for taking the cup can be no general cōmaundement for al men: thus [d] the *Rhemistes* reason. I answer, first it may be doubted and disputed, whether onely the Apostles were present at his last Supper. For seeing diuerse were added vnto the church, and professed the faith of christ, seeing he had other disciples beside the twelue, seeing many Godly men and women followed him to see his miracles, and to hear the gracious words that proceeded out of his mouth: why should we think that none of them were admitted to his table, who had often heard his preaching, and depended vpon him in their liuing. Again, the passeouer was celebrated in ẏ house, [e] of a faithful man, as may be collected by sundry circumstances: now thē, either the lord Iesus annexed that famely vnto his, as the law in one case appointed, or else we shall haue two passe-ouers at one time in one house, which hath no warrant of scripture, no colour of truth, no probability of reason. We read in the institution & celebration of the passe-ouer of ioyning house to house, [f] and taking his neighbor next vnto him in case of the insufficiency of one houshold to eate the lambe: but we neuer read of killing two lambes, and keeping two passeouers vnder one roofe. Besides, the smal remnant of the faithful among the *Iewes*, would no doubt rightly and religiously obserue the passe-ouer after the example of their lord

and

c Obiections for taking the cup from the people of god

d *rhem. test.* vpon *Math.* xxvi, & Mar. 14

e Math, xxvi. 17, 18

f Exod, xii, 4.

78. W. JAGGARD 2 Attersoll, W. *The badges of Christianity*. 1606
STC 889 Vet.A2e.256 Sig. T5r

andum & reformandum saniorem & tutiorem rationem.

Deinde, quòd mulcta illa pecuniaria vel in releuamen pauperũ eiusdẽ Parœciæ, vel in alios pios vsus erogetur, idque ecclesiæ solẽniter & fideliter approbetur & innotescat.

Quòd si verò crimen fuerit notorium ac publicum, Reus ipse vel in propria sua persona publicè in Ecclesia pœnitentiam suam minimè fictam profitendo, læsæ Ecclesiæ satisfaciet, vel Ecclesiæ minister in præsentia ipsius Rei, palam è suggestu, eius submissionem, & pœnitentiæ suæ coram Ordinario suo peractionem, atque etiam in veræ suæ resipiscentiæ testimonium quantam pecuniarum summam in vsus supradictos erogandam reddiderit, denuntiabit.

De moderandis quibusdam indulgentiis, pro celebratione Matrimonii *absque trinundina denuntiatione, quam Bannos vocant Matrimoniales.*

QVandoquidem honestæ, claræ ac illustris conditionis homines, siue vrgente aliqua necessitate, siue aliis non contemnendis rationibus, Matrimonium aliquando celebrandi causas habere possunt, facultate sibi de Bannis matrimonialibus aut non omninò, aut semel iterúmue denuntiandis indulta, sine aliquo graui scandalo seu detrimento: Idcircò ad euitanda generaliter quæ hæc in parte notantur incõmoda, visum est caueri ne vllæ facultates siue indulgentiæ de celebrãdo absque Bannis Matrimonio cõcedantur, nisi idonea cautio priùs sub hisce conditionibus ineatur: nimirum, Primò, quòd nullũ postea constabit impedimentum Præcontractus, Consanguinitatis, Affinitatis, vel vllius alterius legitimæ causæ cuiuscunque ratione. Secundò, quòd eo tempore quo eiusmodi facultas siue indulgentia concedetur, nulla controuersia, lis seu querela mota est, vel dependet coram aliquo Iudice Ecclesiastico aut Ciuili, de eiuscemodi legitimo impedimento Matrimonii inter huiusmodi personas contrahendi aut contracti. Ac tertiò,

79. A. JEFFES I *Articuli per archiepiscopum.* 1585(?)
STC 4584 Wood D.25 Sig. A3r

Phylomene.

IN ſweete Aprill the meſſenger to Maie,
When honie drops doo melt in golden
ſhowres,
When euery bird records hir louers lay,
And weſterne winds do foſter forth our
floures,
Late in an euen I walked out alone
To heare the deſcant of the Nightingale,
And as I ſtoode I heard her make great mone,
Waimenting much, and thus ſhe told her tale.
These thriftles birds quoth ſhe which ſpend the day,
In needleſſe notes, and chaunt withouten skill,
Are coſtly kept, and finely fed alway
With daintie foode whereof they feede their fill.
But I which ſpend the darke and dreadfull night
In watch and ward, when thoſe birds take their reſt,
Forpine my ſelfe that louers might delight
To heare the notes which breake out of my breaſt.
I lead a life to pleaſe the louers minde,
And though God wot my foode be light of charge,
Yet ſeelie ſoule that can no fauour finde,
I beg my bread, and ſeeke for ſeedes at large.
The Throſtle ſhe which makes the wood to ring
With ſhriching loud that lothſome is to heare,
Is coſtly kept in cage: O woondrous thing,
The Mauis eke whoſe notes are nothing cleare,
Now in good ſooth quoth ſhe ſometimes I weepe
To ſee Tom Tittimouſe ſo much ſet by.
The Finch which ſingeth neuer a note but peepe,
Is fed as well, nay better farre than I.
The Lennet and the Larke they ſing aloft,
And counted are as lords in high degree.
The brandlet ſaith for ſinging ſweete and ſoft
In her conceit there is none ſuch as ſhe.
Canara birds come in to beare the bell,

And

80. A. JEFFES 2 Gascoigne, G. *The whole woorkes*. 1587
STC 11638 Malone 589 Sig. Y6r

To the right honorable my ſingular good Lorde Sir *Nicholas Bacon* Knight, Lorde Keeper *of the Great Seale of England.*

CAlling to memorie right Honourable, and my ſingular good Lorde, the great fauour your Lordſhip bare my Father in his life time, and the conference it pleaſed your honour to vſe with him touching the Sciences Mathematicall, eſpecially in Geometricall menſurations, peruſing alſo of late certaine volumes that he in his youthe time long ſithens had compiled in the Engliſh tongue, among other I found this *Geometricall Practiſe*, which my Father (if God had ſpared him life) minded to haue preſented your Honoure withall, but vntimely Death preuenting his determination, I thought it my part to accompliſh the ſame, aſwell for the ſatiſfaction of his deſire, as alſo to ſhew my ſelfe not vnmindefull of ſo many good turnes as your honor from time to time moſt aboundantly hath beſtowed on me, hauing therfore ſupplied ſuch partes of this Treatiſe as were leaſt obſcure or vnperfect, adioyning therevnto a Diſcourſe Geometricall of the fiue regulare or Platonicall bodyes, contayning ſundry Theoricall and practicall propoſitions of the manifolde proportions ariſing by mutuall conference of theſe Solides *Inſcripton*, *Circumſcription* or *Tranſformation*, and now at the laſt fully finiſhed the ſame, I am bolde to exhibite and dedicate it to your Honor, as an eternall memoriall of your Lordſhips great fauoure towardes the furtherance of learning, and a publike teſtimonie of my bounden duetie: hoping your Honor will rather reſpect the good will wherewith it is preſented, than the worthineſſe of the preſent, not agreeable I confeſſe to the excellent knowledge wherewith your Lordſhippe is indued, euen in the verye Fountaines themſelues whence theſe concluſions as ſprings or branches are deriued. And yet ſuch as I nothing doubt your Honor will both accept in good parte, and alſo at vacant leyſure from affaires of more importance, delite your ſelfe withall, the rather for that it containeth ſundry ſuch new inuented *Theoremes*, and other ſtrange concluſions, as no Geometers haue hitherto, in any language publiſhed. Whereby your Lordſhip ſhall not only incourage me heereafter to attempt greater matters, but alſo as it were with a ſoueraigne medicine preuent the poiſoned infection of enuious backbiting toongs: for as the veritie of theſe experiments and rules ſhall neuer be impugned, being ſo firmely grounded, garded, and defended with Geometricall Demonſtration: againſt whoſe puiſſance no ſubtile Sophiſtrie or craftie coloured arguments can preuaile, ſo thinke I there is none ſo impudently malitious, as wil or dare reproue them for vaine or improfitable, when they ſhall perceiue your Lordſhip (whoſe learned iudgement, grauitie and wiſedome, is ſufficiently knowne to the world) doth allow and accepte them as fragrant floures, ſelect and gathered out of the pleaſant gardines Mathematicall, meete to delite any noble, free, or well diſpoſed minde, and profitable frutes ſeruing moſt commodiouſly to ſundry neceſſary vſes in a publike weale, and ſuch as ſhall thereby receiue pleaſure or commoditie, muſt of dutie yeeld condigne thankes vnto your Lorſhip, vnder whoſe protection and patronage I haue not feared to ſend abroade (as a wandring pilgrime) this Orphane and fatherleſſe childe, the which as I perceiue of your Honor fauorably accepted, ſo meane I, God ſparing life, to imploy no ſmall portion of this my ſhorte and tranſitorie time in ſtoring our natiue tongue with Mathematicall demonſtrations, and ſome ſuch other rare experiments and practicall concluſions, as no forraine Realme hath hitherto beene, I ſuppoſe, partaker of. In the meane time I leaue longer to detaine your honour with my rude and homely tale, from more ſeriouſe and waightie affaires, committing your Lordſhip to the tuition of the Almightie, who graunt you a long healthfull honourable life, accompanied with perfect felicitie.

Your Honours moſt bounden
Thomas Digges.

81. A. JEFFES 3 Digges, L. *A practical treatise.* 1591
STC 6859 H.4.20.Art Sig. A3r

Enter the three Lordes and their pages: Firſt, Pollicie with his page Wit before him, bearing a ſhield: the ympreze, a Tortoys, the word, *Prouidens ſecurus*. Next Pompe, with his page Wealth bearing his ſhield, the word, *Glorie ſauns peere*: the ympreze a Lillie. Laſt, Pleaſure, his page Wil, his ympreze, a Faulcon, the woord, *Pour temps*: Pol. attired in blacke, Pompe in rich roabes, and Pleaſure in collours.

Strowe the faire flowers and herbes that be greene,
To grace the gaieſt wedding that euer was ſeene.

If London liſt to looke, the ſtreetes were nere ſo cleene,
Except it was when beſt it might, in welcome of our Queene:
Three louely Lords of London ſhall three London Ladies wed,
Strowe ſweeteſt flowers vpon the ſtones, perfume the bridall bed.
Strowe the faire flowers, &c.

Enter firſt Diligence with a Truncheon, then a boy with Pollicies Launce and ſhield, then Pollicie and Loue hand in hand: then Fraud in a blew gowne, red cap and red ſleeues, with Ambitions Lance and ſhield, then a boy with Pomps Launce and ſhield, then Pompe and Lucre hand in hand: then Diſſimulation with Prides Launce and ſhield, then a boy with Pleaſures Lance and ſhield: then Pleaſure and Conſcience hand in hand: then Simplicitie with Tirannies Lance and ſhield; they al going out, Nemo ſtaies and ſpeakes.

82. R. JONES I Wilson, R. *Three lords . . . of London.* 1590
STC 25783 Malone 232(2) Sig. B1r, I2r

diſordered imagine you would he thinke you to be in your affections.

And were it not that ſo manie coaſtes had ſeuered him both
by land and ſeas, peraduenture wearied with your bitter outcries in the conceited image and ſhape of death, you might in
apparance heare him, in theſe like ſpeaches accuſing and rebu-
king ſuch your diſtẽperate actions. And with breathing ſpirit to Proſopopœia
crie out vnto you ſaying. What is it you goe about? what meen
you by teares to ſearch out for a thinge ſo irrecuperable? Whie correctio.
torment you your youthful yeares, with ſuch vnprofitable, or rather as I may call it, deſperate kind of mournings? whie with ſuch
vniuſt complaints accuſe you Fortune, and ſo often doe appeale
death and deſtinie of ſo hainous treſpaſſe? Is it for that you enuie my happie ſtate, ſo ſoone tranſported from this vntowarde
ſoile, to a more proſperous felicity? thus credit me, & in this ſort
(were it poſsible he could ſpeake to you) would hee accuſe you,
in which conſideration, were there not iuſt cauſe thinke you (of
ſuch intemperance) whie you ſhould be greatlie aſhamed? Beleeue me good coſin, there is neither profit or liking at all: of this
bitter continuance reaped, you haue alreadie waded ſufficiently
in your teares, you haue mourned for him in earneſt loue as be-
ſemed a wife, it is now high time you be after al this comforted.
Thinke that the greateſt ſtorme is by time at length ouerblown Allegoria.
ſuperfluitie of coales encreaſeth rather heate than flame, the ar-
dencie of affection, with vehemencie ſufficient may bee expreſſed, though not by extremitie enforced. What ſhould I ſay vnto
you? You may not as other fooliſh creatures, that are neither go- Similitudo.
uerned by wit, nor ordred by diſcretiō, make your ſelf a ſpecta-
cle to the world, but rather with ſuch tẽperance (for euen in this
extremitie of ſorrow, is alſo planted a rare pattern of modeſtie) Hyperbaton
ſeek in ſuch maner to demeane your ſelfe, as the lookers on may
rather pittie you, by inſight of your great diſcretion, then in this
ſort to torment your ſelfe by a needleſſe ſuppoſition. Much
more haue I conſidered with my ſelfe, whereby to ſatisfie my Peroratio.
grieued imaginations, in which being recomforted, and repoſed
in my ſecrete thoughtes, I haue deemed it neceſſarie hereby
to impart the ſame vnto you, beſeeching that as well in regarde
of your ſelfe, as the little pleaſure, your friendes haue to beholde

 you

83. R. JONES 2 Day, A. *The English secretory.* 1595
STC 6403 Douce D.200 Sig. R2r

The table.

The ſecond Part.

What

84. T. JUDSON Hill, T. *The schoole of skil.* 1599
STC 13502 4° D.30.Art Sig. S7v

hym. By whoſe example we may perceiue. It is euery mans part chiefly to take
heede, that vvhen they ouercome theyr ene
mies, they reioyce not ouer muche, nor
vvaxe proude for the matter, for vvho
knovveth vvhat ende they ſhall haue them
ſelues? Theſe thinges done, the Jewes
ſeyng the walles of the Temple and
the three walles that compaſſed the
towne to bee raſed and pulde downe,
Gg.v. knowing

Dani.8 as it is written. VVhiles he is yet alyue,
his kingdome ſhalbe broken, and deuyded
into foure coaſtes of the heauens. He left
behynde hym a ſonne of tender yeares
called Archelaus, whoſe tutour or gouernour perceiuing hym to be toward:
gaue him impoiſoned drinke, and made
hym awaye. Thoſe captaynes made
warre one vpon another: of whom one
that was named ptolomee, procured
Moſes law to be tranſlated into Greke,
to the entent he might finde ſome occaſion to picke a quarell againſt Iſraell.
For by theyr law he ſought meanes to
withdrawe them from their religion,
Pſa.129 according to the Pſalme. Many a tyme
haue they afflicted me fro my youth vppe
may Iſraell novve ſay. There were ſe-
uenty auncient men that tranſlated the
lawe,

85. R. JUGGE I Joseph ben Gorion *A compendious history.* 1561
STC 14796 Tanner 508 Sig. A1v, 2G5r

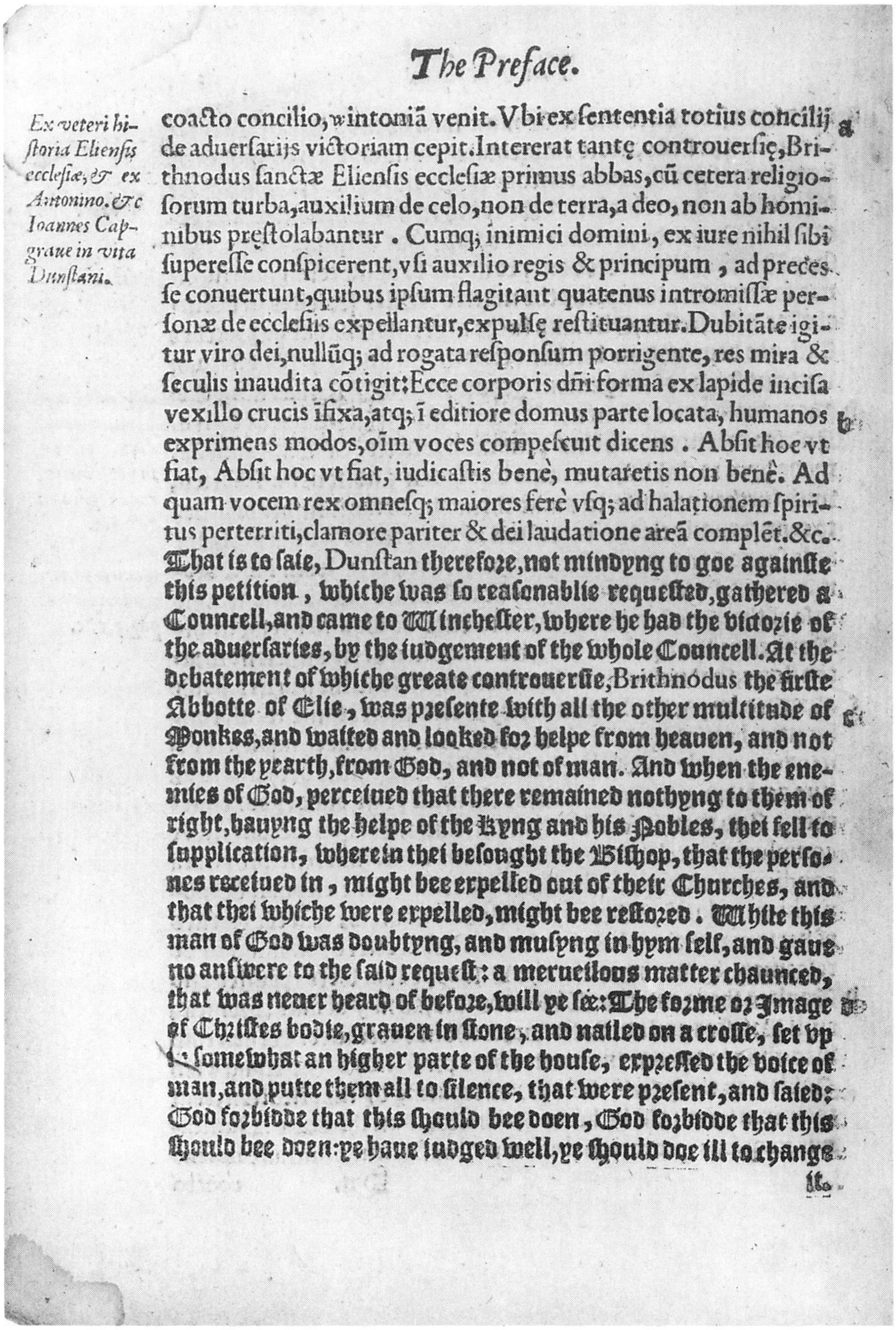

The Preface.

Ex veteri hiſtoria Elienſis eccleſiæ, & ex Antonino. &c Ioannes Capgraue in vita Dunſtani.

coacto concilio, wintoniã venit. Vbi ex ſententia totius concilij a
de aduerſarijs victoriam cepit. Intererat tantę controuerſię, Brithnodus ſanctæ Elienſis eccleſiæ primus abbas, cũ cetera religio-
ſorum turba, auxilium de celo, non de terra, a deo, non ab hominibus pręſtolabantur. Cumq; inimici domini, ex iure nihil ſibi
ſupereſſe conſpicerent, vſi auxilio regis & principum, ad preces
ſe conuertunt, quibus ipſum flagitant quatenus intromiſſæ per-
ſonæ de eccleſiis expellantur, expulſę reſtituantur. Dubitãte igi-
tur viro dei, nullũq; ad rogata reſponſum porrigente, res mira &
ſeculis inaudita cõtigit: Ecce corporis dñi forma ex lapide inciſa
vexillo crucis ĩfixa, atq; ĩ editiore domus parte locata, humanos b
exprimens modos, oĩm voces compeſcuit dicens. Abſit hoc vt
fiat, Abſit hoc vt fiat, iudicaſtis benè, mutaretis non benè. Ad
quam vocem rex omneſq; maiores ferè vſq; ad halationem ſpiri-
tus perterriti, clamore pariter & dei laudatione areã complẽt. &c.
That is to ſaie, Dunſtan therefore, not myndyng to goe againſte
this petition, whiche was ſo reaſonablie requeſted, gathered a
Councell, and came to Winchester, where he had the victorie of
the aduerſaries, by the iudgement of the whole Councell. At the
debatement of whiche greate controuerſie, Brithnodus the firſte
Abbotte of Elie, was preſente with all the other multitude of c
Monkes, and waited and looked for helpe from heauen, and not
from the yearth, from God, and not of man. And when the enemies of God, perceiued that there remained nothyng to them of
right, hauyng the helpe of the Kyng and his Nobles, thei fell to
ſupplication, wherein thei beſought the Biſhop, that the perſo-
nes receiued in, might bee expelled out of their Churches, and
that thei whiche were expelled, might bee reſtored. While this
man of God was doubtyng, and muſyng in hym ſelf, and gaue
no anſwere to the ſaid requeſt: a merueilous matter chaunced,
that was neuer heard of before, will ye ſee: The forme or Image d
of Chriſtes bodie, grauen in ſtone, and nailed on a croſſe, ſet vp
somewhat an higher parte of the houſe, expreſſed the voice of
man, and putte them all to ſilence, that were preſent, and ſaied:
God forbidde that this ſhould bee doen, God forbidde that this
ſhould bee doen: ye haue iudged well, ye ſhould doe ill to change
it.

86. R. JUGGE 2 Martin, T. *A defense of priestes marriages.* 1567
STC 17519 Tanner 948 Sig. D2v

ſcantly wil that be made vp which might make the reſt vnder Greekes and Romanes three hundred and ſixtie to agree with Gabriels foure hundred and ninetie yeeres. Therefore Plutarch to fill vp the common ſumme giueth him ſixtie and two yeeres of reigne and ninetie foure of life. not knowing Daniels viſion againſt the Perſians at ſharpe ſwift Tigris: nor bookes opened before the firie throne iudging the Perſian beare: nor comparing Leuites a ſcore Neh. 12. with the Perſians: nor yet Amyntas king in Macedon the thirde of the Peloponneſian warres: whoſe ſonne Philip reigned but twentie yeeres. Athen. and Alexander but ſix before his monarchie. Thucid.bok.2.

Moreouer Amyntas him ſelfe reigned but few yeeres, two of his elder ſonnes not long: Philip died at ſeauen and fortie, who was brought vp in Epaminondas fathers houſe. Thus the Perſians by Greekes will not exceede.

Againſt Eratoſthenes account.

This ſtanding thus: howe can Eratoſthenes ſay true, whom in Clemens pag.126. (though Clemens reiecteth him as deceaued) yet ſome great men greatly follow? He hath theſe diſtances. From Xerxes voiage to Archidamus warres eight and fortie yeeres. That ended at ſeauen and twentie. There Athens loſt the ſuperiority of Grecia and Lacedemon, by Lyſander gate it. which they loſt at Leuctra, where Epaminondas the Theban victor died after 34. yeeres. And thence to Philips death, who died 47. yeeres old, he reckoneth yeres 35. But how could he be a fit companion for Epaminondas: or yet ſonne to Amyntas: reigning young and but a little while. Polybius granteth the Lacedemonians but twelue yeeres of quiet ſuperioritie pag.1. & Iuſtine abridging Trogus Pompeius maketh Amyntas ſon to Menelaus brother to Alexander

who

87. W. KEARNEY I Broughton, H. *An apologie.* 1592
STC 3845 4° B.27.Th Sig. D4r

Ezra, who liued aboue 400. yeeres ago: a great Astronomer in Sebastian Munsters iudgement, whereby he coulde not be ignoraunt of Ptolomyes Chaldeans. A deadly enemy he was to Christ, and therefore deserueth better credite, speakyng for vs agaynst his owne purpose, then Chaldeans, more wicked and perpetuall haters of Daniel.

The one speche of seuen seuens Dan. 9. graunted commonly the tyme seperated for buylding Ierusalem (which must be the fyrst part in the partition) forceth an yeelding to a plaine declaration of Gabriels Chronicle for our redemption.

5 All they who make 49. yeeres for the buylding of Ierusalem, who are full many, wyl be founde as well damners of these Chaldeans: whereof amongst Romistes in Spayne Hector Pintus gaue the same reuerence to Daniels playnnes as dyd Iohn Caluin in Geneuah, and careth not for humane credite, where Greekes thought them selues strongest. And the Diuines in the last Frenche edition, haue despised this Chaldy dreame. Genebrard for the French, Romistes is no small man (honored now as I heard at Rome) whom Adricomius folowed in the Chronicle ioyned to his Mappes. Henry VVolphius is a learned, godly, and zelous reuerencer of the Scriptures playnnes, who friendly controlleth M. Scaliger, and confirmeth Beroaldus, departyng euen from his owne Fathers iudgement for the holy trueth. Agaynst all this must it be my particuler lot, in so many of myne opinion, to be onely counted new?

6 Learned men by them haue gon too farre. For I. Sc. condemneth all the thousandes of Diuines, who do thinke that Darius the Mede. *Dan. 5.* gate Babylon by conquest. A strange thing. Such wryters shoulde be hated, who deceyue so learned men, as M. Scaliger is knowen to be of all Learned men.

Two more deceites from these Chaldeans, deceyuing him and an other Scholer wel deseruing of learnyng, should make vs thinke no better of these stale Chaldy forgery, then Priamus shoulde

 haue

88. W. KEARNEY 2 Broughton, H. *An apologie.* 1592
STC 3845 4° B.27.Th Sig. E3r

sodainelie at one time or other be coloured with their good things: so the godlie abiding in the „ *Note.*
meetings of the wicked, vnlesse they be very circumspect, and suspect their owne weakenes, will „ *Note well*
sodainlie be taken. We know that *Ioseph* being in *Pharaohes* Court, began to be coloured with „ *the society*
the Egyptians corruptions. If then we haue any iust cause of meeting with the wicked, wee must „ *of the wicked.*
not auoide their companie; but we must mislike their manners, wee must rebuke, reproue, and „
cry against their sinnes; we must feare our selues, and in euery thing suspect them. But let vs see „
how dangerous a thing it is to be with the wicked, and what meanes there be with them for our „
destruction: Whether we be friendes, and in league with them, or foes and at defiance with them, „
all is one. For if we be at defiance with them, how will they bring our persons in contempt, and „
raise many calumnious speeches against vs, and afray vs with iniuries? If we be in friendship with „
them, in what danger are we least they should inueagle vs, allure vs, & take vs slilie away from a „
good conscience. If we be at defiance with them, they will dismay vs with threatnings: if wee „ *Note.*
be in friendship with them, we cannot deale so roughlie against their sinnes, we can hardly gaine-„
say them in their wickednes, wee are drawne away by them, and wax cold by little and little in „
those thinges wherein we haue bin zealous. Oh here then appeareth the wonderfull and vnspeakeable mercie of God to his children in this world to keepe them as sheepe among wolues, and to saue them from the infection of sinne, in the middest of a wicked and sinfull generation.

It followeth in this verse, *that I may keepe the Commaundements of my God.* As if he should haue said, he is not your God, because you put not your trust in him, but follow your owne inuentions: he is my God, I loue him, I feare him, I put my trust in him; I loue his word, because his promises are sweet to me; I feare to sinne, because his threatnings proue true; I trust in him, because of his word: he is none of your God, neyther can you assure your selues of him. For as port. 20.31 *Saluation is farre from the wicked, because they seeke not thy statutes.* No, no, God is grieued, and displeased with you, though for a while he spare you, he shall one day punish you, hee is my protectour and defender.

This is a notable thing, and worthy to be obserued. The man of God recouereth himselfe, because God hath promised in his word, that hee will defend his as with a shield, but hee will put to flight the armies of their aduersaries. Hee reasoneth therefore thus with himselfe. The Lorde hath promised to be a tower and buckler for them, that put their trust in him, and beleeue his word: I beleeue this to be true, I see it shall come to passe according to his word: therefore hee is my God, my shield, and my refuge.

Let vs learne in time of trouble, thus to recouer our selues. For doe wee not see, how now a dayes some take this way, and some take that way, some vse this shift, and some haue that policy, doe their dealings shew, that God is on their side, or that hee will take their part? nay rather that he is farre from them. We must euery one frame this reason, which the Prophet vseth, that euerie man may say, I trust in Gods word, I hate the vaine shifts of the wicked, God is my God. *My God*: we must here marke, that we giue not God sufficient honour, vntill wee cleaue whole vnto „ *To loue God*
him, as he requireth of vs in his first commandement. For we then haue him to be our onlie God, „ *onely as we*
when we onlie feare him, when we onlie loue him, when we onlie obey him, when wee put our „ *be taught in*
trust in him alone. So that we denie him his honour, vntill we leauing all other fetches and deuises „ *his word.*
of louing, fearing, obeying and trusting in him; and loue, feare, obey, and trust in him, as wee are onlie and wholie taught in his word. Excellent is that place of the Prophet Psal. 73. where the man of God, seeing the euill men in number many, in power great; and good men in number few, and abilitie weake, began to be in a dangerous estate, in thinking almost wickedly of Gods prouidence, and began to be moued, and to dispute as it were with God about the prosperitie of the wicked, and pouertie of the godlie, vntill hee came to looke into the glasse of Gods word, where he found, that though the wicked seemed to haue an happie time for a while, yet through Gods secret curse, they had a fearefull end, and though Gods children were tryed with many troubles, yet through Gods secret blessings they had happie issues.

Thus saith hee, *was I so foolish and ignorant, and as a beast before thee,* whiles by mine owne wit and reason I would goe about to search out thy secret iudgements. Yet saith he, *I was alway with thee, thou haste holden me by my right hand,* and howsoeuer it went with the wicked, my faith in thy prouidence did assure me, that thou diddest watch ouer mee, and wouldest not finallie forsake me. *Whom haue I in heauen but thee, and I haue desired none in the earth but*

from the darts of our enemie. So that, if we haue the Lord for our tower against Sathan, if we be in pouertie, we shall see the Lord our shield and wealth; if wee be in sicknes, he shall be our castle and health. The Israelites had proofe hereof, who, so long as they made the Lord their shield and refuge, were not once touched of their enemies. If this faith be in vs, then shall wee be perswaded, that the hearing of the word, and time which wee spend in prayer to the Lord, will not hinder our calling, nor hurt our profit: but so long as wee walke in our waies, ioyning with our calling the hearing of Gods word, and prayer, hee will be our defence and tower, and either saue vs from domage, or turne all our euils to our good. We must see all this out of the word of God. For our Sauiour Christ (as we sayd before) did not rest in the omnipotencie of God, or put away Sathan being an euill spirit, and therefore hauing nothing to doe with him, but withstood him with this, *It is written*, still alleaging the word of God: shewing, that whilest he had bread, he should vse it as an ordinarie meane, and when he had none, he should not make bread of stones, but stay vpon the blessing of God, which is aboue all meanes. Thus we see how the promises of God in his word did stay him.

How the faith of Gods children differeth from the vaine imaginations of vnbeleeuers. *Simile.*

And here see how the faith of Gods children differeth from the loose imaginations of the wicked, who, though they giue great titles to the Lord of his mercie, iustice, loue, and prouidence, neuer looke for this in his word. But if we will obey the Lord, and waite vpon his promises, we must doe it by the word, which is as a pipe, through which doe flow Gods graces towards vs, and as a chariot to bring his will vnto vs. We are not then to looke into the ayre, or elsewhere for Gods will, than in his word; but trusting still on God, wee must looke for helpe in his promises.

That the man of God might doe this the better, hee seuered himselfe from the wicked, giuing vs to vnderstand, that he could not goe forward, in that he saw so few examples of good, and so many examples of euill, whereby so many by-paths are ministred vnto him to step out of the right way, in seeing the corruptions of that generation. When wee see then out of the word how we should beleeue, what we should doe, what we should eschue, and looke into the world, wee shall finde so many wicked ones, that which way soeuer a man would turne himselfe, although hee would search the world with a candle, hee shall finde many euill to corrupt him, but few good to guide him. And seeing our times are worse, than the times wherein the Prophet liued, and wee are easier and readier to take harme by euill examples, than he was; we must know, that whosoeuer will be truly taught to hate vaine inuentions, and loue the word of God, he must learne that which is written in the first Psalme, that is, *that we walke not in the counsell of the wicked, nor stand in the way of sinners.* Away then with them that say, the Preacher indeede speaketh well, and teacheth the truth aright, but who doth it? and rather let vs bid the euill away from vs, let vs followe them that doe well, so farre as they follow Christ and his word, let vs be heedfull to looke to our waies, and be the more carefull, because in former ages the Lord hath set before vs so many examples of falling. Wee may communicate with them in one calling, we may be knit to them by consanguinitie, wee may be ioyned with them in affinitie, and as neighbours dwell together, we cannot in these things be well free from them: yet we must not deale with them as they be wicked, we must not draw in the yoke with them, we must not be giuen to the like studies, to the like endeuours, and enterprises with them. Concerning their calling in the world, wee may vse them, but not according to their corrupt dealing with the world. We see the Prophet his meaning is, Away from me ye wicked, ye weaken my faith in Gods promises by your inuentions, you inkindle mistrust in me, I will not yeeld to you, I will not consent to you, nor take part in any of your inuentions: for I trust in my God, he is my shield, and my refuge.

Difference betweene persons, and callings, & liues.

Here wee may also learne, how to discerne betweene their persons, wherein they beare the Image of God and their callings, which are the ordinance of God, & betweene their liues, which are full of corruptions. If wee looke but into the first commandement, wee shall see how hard a thing it is, to keepe Gods law, vnlesse wee sequester our selues from the societie of sinne. How shall we beleeue among vnbeleeuers, or pray to the Lord among prophane persons, or trust in the Lord among such shifters? For as euill men continuing in the companie of godlie men, shall sodainelie

Quadragesimus,a,um.
Quinquagesimus,a,um.
Sexagesimus,a,um.
Septuagesimus,a,um.
Octogesimus,a,um.
Nonagesimus,a,um.
Nongentesimus,a,um.
Millesimus,a,um.&c.

Adiectiues of numbre.

Adiectiua numeralia.

¶ Vnus,vna,vnum.
In plu duo,duę,duo.
In plu. Tres & tria.
Quatuor, quinq; , sex, septem, octo,nouem,decem,vndecim, duodecim,tredecim, quatuordecim,qnindecim,sedecim,vel sesdecim, Decem & septem : decem & octo , vel duodeuiginti. Decem & nouem, vel vndeuiginti.
Viginti.
Viginti vnum.
Vinginti duo.&c.
Triginta.
Triginta vnus.
Triginta duo.&c.
Quadraginta , quinquaginta, Sexaginta,Septuaginta,octoginta,Nonaginta.
Centum.
Centum vnum. &c. vnde centeni : vt centeni pedes latitudinis.
Ducenti; tæ,ta.
Trecenti,tę,ta.
Quadringenti,tę,ta.
Quingenti,tæ,ta.
Sexcenti,tę,ta,vel Sescenti,tæ,ta.
Septingenti,tæ,ta.
Octingenti,tæ,ta.
Nongenti,tæ,ta.
Mille.
Sed hic notandum est , quôd mille adiectiuum , nunquàm declinatur.
Duo millia,vel bis mille.
Tria millia,vel ter mille , & sic deinceps.
Mille vnum. mille. duo . & sic vsq; ad duo milia.

Aduerbes of numbre.

Aduerbia numeralia.

¶ Onse,semel. Twise,bis.
Thrise,ter.&c.
Quater.
Quinquies.
Sexies.
Septies.
Octies.
Nonies.

 Decies.

91. J. KINGSTON 1a Withals, J. *A shorte dictionarie.* 1556
STC 25875 Huntington Library Sig. Z3r

124.

So far as eies of man coud them pursue, or marke coud make.
Than whan against Auerna mouth they came, (that stinking lake,)
They lift them selfes aloft, and through the tender aier they slyde.
And falling down at last, they toke their tree, & there did byde,
Where glistring braunches shewes of sondry glossyd shining gold.
None otherwyse, than mysteltewe on woodes in wynter cold
Renewes his busshes grene, whome tronck of tree did neuer breede,
But saffronfrutyd bows the stubbes therof doth ouerspreeds.
So from the tree that golden branche did shewe, soche was ẏ kynd,
So wauering soft it wagde, and tyncling sweete it made in wynd.
Eneas at it straight, and caught a crop with moch ado.
And glad with comfort great, dame Siblies house he brought it to.

Mysteltew callyd of some mysteldén growyng on trees in wynter with a yelowe slymy bery clamy lyke byrd lyme, it cometh by donging of byrdes on the trees.

Nor nothing lesse this whyle, the Troians al in solempne gyse
Did wayle Misenus corps, and gaue to him their last outcries.
Furst, cut in culpons great and fat of sappe with pytche among
A stately pile they bylde, with tymber trees, and cipers strong
(That dead mens treasour is) his gorgeous armes also they set.
Some brought the water warme, & caudrons boylyng out they fet.
The body cold they washe, & precious ointments on they powre.
Lamenting loude is made, than close his lymmes in bed on floore
Thei couch wᵗ weeping teares, & purple weedes on him they throw:
His robes, his harneis bright, & enseignes al that men may know.
In mourning sort, some heaue on shulders hie the mighty beere,
(A dolefull seruice sad) as childern do their father deere,
Behind thē holding brondes, than flame vprising, broad doth spreede
And oyles and deinties cast, and frankynsens the fier doth feede.
Whan falne his synders were, and longer blase did not endure:
His reliques and remain of dust with wynes they washyd pure.
Than Choryney his bones in brasen coffyn bright did close.
And sprincling water pure, about his mates thre tymes he goes,
And dropps of sacryd dewe wᵗ Olyue palmes on them did shake.
And compas blest them all, & sentence last he sadly spake.
To feldes of ioye thy soule, and endles rest we do betake.
But good Eneas than, right huge in height his tombe did rere,
And gaue the lord his armes, his ore and trompet firyd there.
On mountain nere the skies, that of Misenus beares the name:
And euerlasting shall from world to world retayne the same.

The funeral seruice of Misen⁹ maruelously expressyd of Virgill.

Warme water and cryengs, for manye seme dead and be yet alive.

Nouissima verba.

This

92. J. KINGSTON 1b Virgilius Maro, P. *The seven first bookes of the Eneidos.* 1558
STC 24799 Malone 322 Sig. P4v

¶ *Gualterus Haddonus D. Iuris Ciuilis,*
ET REGINAE MAIE-
ſtatis, à Libellis ſupplicibus.

Retoricen Logice ſoror, eſt affata ſororem:
Quem didicit nuper, ſermo Britannus erat.
Retorice tacuit, magno perculſa dolore:
Nam nondum noſtro nouerat ore loqui.
Audijt hæc, Logices, Vuilſonus forte, magiſter:
Qui fuerat, noſtros addideratq; ſonos.
Retoricen mutam, verbis ſolatus amicis:
Seuocat, & rogitat num eſſe Britanna velit?
Deijciens oculos reſpondit velle libenter:
Sed ſe, qua poſsit, non reperire, via.
Ipſe vias [inquit] tradam, legeſq; loquendi:
Quomodo perfectè verba Britanna loces.
Liberat ille fidem, noſtro ſermone politur:
Retorice, noſtra eſt vtraque facta ſoror.
Anglia nobilium ſi charus ſermo ſororum:
Eſt tibi, ſermonis charus & author erit.

¶ *Thomas Wilſonus in Angli-*
cam Rhetoricen ſuam.

Anglia ſi doceat, quod Græcia docta: quid obſtat
Quo minus ex Anglis Anglia, vera ſciat.
Non (quia Greca potes, vel calles verba Latina)
Doctus es, aut ſapiens: ſed quia vera vides.
Aurea ſecreto tegitur ſapientia ſenſu.
Abdita ſenſa tenes Anglus? es ergo ſciens.
Sed mea Rhetoricen nequeat cùm lingua polire:
Cui vacat, hoc vnum quod valet, oro velit.

93. J. KINGSTON 1c Wilson, T. *The arte of rhetorique.* 1562
STC 25801 Tanner 248 Sig. A8v

To the right honourable, the Lord Fride-rike of Nachod, Lorde of Danouiz and of Beſke, &c. his verie good Lorde and Patrone.

AVncient and noble is the queſtion concernyng the originall of the worlde, and firſte beeginning of all things, Right honorable Baron, which hath not only long tyme and much troubled the wittes of the Philoſophers, but alſo of Chriſtians, & in the end by reaſon of the diuerſe iudgements of men hath reſted ſo doubtfull, that many graue writers coulde not tell what to determine therin. For amõg the Chriſtiãs, *Origen*, in his bookes of the beginnings (which bookes aboue the reſidue moſt men do iudge to bee his woorthy woork) and they which after him wrote the *Examera*, are ſo diuided in opinions, that nothing may ſeeme certeinly to bee gathered out of their writinges. But among the Philoſophers, men ignorant of God and his trueth, there is farre more diuerſitie of opinions, ſo that concernyng this matter a man may better gheaſſe than vnderſtand by their doctrine what hee hath to follow. Now touchyng theſe Philoſophers, perhaps there is no ſuch cauſe to wonder at their blindnes in ſo great a matter, and that thei were ſo deepely drowned in darknes, foraſmuch as they were deſtitute of Gods woord, that is to ſay, the true light of knowledge. But among Chriſtians ſuche diſcorde and diſagreement cannot with like vprightnes bee excuſed, for that there is but one way of the trueth, wherof they might haue found moſt aſſured groundes in the woord of God, if they had had regard therto. What was thã the cauſe of ſo greate diſagreement among the Chriſtians concernyng this matter? Forſooth it was the Heathen Philoſophie, with the preceptes whereof they were not onely then inſtructed and infected, but many alſo of them beeing ſtuffed, beewitched and deceiued therwith, (in reſpect that they aſcribed moſt vnto this art) would graunt and admit nothyng whiche they ſuppoſed to bee repugnant to the principles thereof. And this miſcheif did not onely continue in the tyme of our forefathers, and the firſte

A.iij. age

94. J. KINGSTON 2 Daneau, L. *The wonderfull woorkmanship.* 1578
STC 6231 4° N.28.Th BS Sig. A3r

my good will ſhall want no fauourers,in that I haue firſt laboured , to bring ſo noble a maiſtreſſe , both of reaſon and iudgement,acquainted with ſo noble a Countrey, and here to bee made of a ſtraunger,a free Deniſon. Wherein I take not vpon me ſo cunningly,and perfectly to haue written of the ſayd Arte,as though none could doe it better : But becauſe no Engliſhman vntill now , hath gone through with this enterpriſe,I haue thought meete to declare,that it may be done. And yet herein I profeſſe it to be but a Spurre,or a Whetſtone,to ſharpe the Pens of ſome other,that they may poliſh,and perfect, that I haue rudely and groſſely entered. And albeit,I doe herein take vpon me no more,but to be as a poore meane man, or a ſimple perſon, whoſe charge were to bee a Lodeſman , to conueigh ſome noble Princes,into a ſtraunge lande,where ſhe was neuer before, leauing the entertayning,the enriching , & decking of her,to ſuch as were of ſubſtance,and furniture according:yet if this worke may not at the firſt enteraunce, haue the ſaufe conduct and protection,of your moſt noble royall Maieſtie, I truſt it ſhall in proceſſe appeare , and proue , that I haue not altogether in vaine,taken vpon me this ſtraunge labour,but rather to very good purpoſe and effect , attempted the ſame . I knowe your Grace , for your owne ſtudie,little needeth any helpe, of ſuch an Engliſh enterpriſe , being ſo well trauailed , both in the Greeke,and in the Latine, for the ſame purpoſe,thorowe the helpe of thoſe right worthie men , *Sir Iohn Cheke*, and *Sir Anthonie Cooke*,your Maieſties teachers, & Scholemaſters in all good literature . But to feede and ſatiſfie the thirſt and deſire of ſuch Engliſh-men , as for default of the ſayd tongues, could otherwiſe not come to the knowledge of *Logike* : I haue iudged it labour worth , to giue the precepts and rules thereof in Engliſh , that all men, according to the gift,that to euery one is meaſured,may bee the more prouoked,to followe the examples of your Maieſtie , aſwell in ſtudiouſnes , and deſire of knowledge, as alſo in the exerciſe of all vertue , and Princely worthineſſe , wherein your Grace hath made a goodly entrie . In which moſt godly

95. J. KINGSTON 3 Wilson, T. *The rule of reason.* 1567
STC 25814 Cambridge U.L. Sig. A3r

ſtill be called wiſe men, to win credit to there deluſions: & then he addeth, *eſt horribile exemplum laxat as magis habenas:* this is a horrible example, that magitians ſhould haue this libertie. Againe, he ſaith, *Deum c arti ſuæ hoſtem opponunt:* they oppoſe God as an enemie to their arte: by theſe few words, it may ſoone be vnderſtood, what magitiās theſe were, in this learned mans iudgement. Brentius *d* ſaith, *Miracula Egiptiorum erant ludibria Sathanæ:* The Egiptians miracles were the deluſions of Sathan. Gellaſius *e* writeth on this manner: *Iſti aſtrologiæ & phyſicæ, magiam ac divinationem, inuocationem demonum, &c. adiunxerat.* Theſe Egiptians added to their aſtrologie and natural philoſophie, magicke and divination, inuocation of deuils, &c. Muſculus, Com. in Geneſ. 41. 8. ſaith plainely, theſe had their artes of Sathan. All theſe (as thou ſeeſt Myſodæmon) teſtifie, that the magitians of Egipt, wrought by the deuill.

c Com. in e. 8. 15.

d Com. in Exod. 7.

e Com. in Exod. 7. 11.

Myſodæmon. Now let me heare what is the ſecond kinde of witches, mentioned in Scripture.

Theoph. The witches of the ſecond kinde, are called in the originall tongue, *Aob, Aoboth:* by this word, the holy Ghoſt vnderſtandeth certaine familiar ſpirites, which whiſper with their witches, at it were, out of a tubbe or bottle, ſaieth Danæus, Heming. Calv. Luth. Bodin, and others: for the worde properly ſignifieth a bottle; as Iob. 32. 19. *Ceoboth cadaſhim,* as new bottles. But whatſoeuer is the cauſe of that borrowed name, for this witches deuill, this muſt be obſerued diligently, that this witch & her ſpirit, are alwaies clearely diſtinguiſhed. For the witch, 1. Sam. 28. v. 6, 7. is not called *Aob,* but *Bagnalath,* maried to *Aob,* for ſo the word ſignifieth, *Aob,* or poſſeſſing *Aob. Predita pythone,* ſaith Tremel. & *Shoel Aob,* Deu. 18. 10. one which enquireth, or ſaluteth, praieth, & intreateth *Aob,* if therfore here be but cooſenage, there muſt be two cooſeners at the leſt, ſo there are, & the witch is one, the deuil an other. Againe, Lev. 20. 27. *Ciyhieh bahem Aob,* if *Aob,* that is, the deuill, be in them.

Myſodæmon. If this *Aob,* was but a pythoniſt, as Tremel. and others ſay, then I prooue it to be but cooſenage, on this manner. Apollo the pythoniſt, and the oracles at Delphos were of this kind, & were moſt famous indeede, yet but meere cooſenage, & therfore this was the like. I prooue mine Antecedent. a *Gregori Neocæſarienſis,* ſoiouruing with Apollos prieſt one night, after his departure

a Diſ. p. 137. 138.

96. J. LEGATE I Holland, H. *A treatise against witchcraft.* 1590
STC 13590 Douce H.H.266 Sig. C1r

that is conuerted; with his death he is not delighted, nor wills his death. Therefore it is not truly cited of the destruction of the reprobate, who neuer turne, and of whome the holy Ghost pronounceth the cleane contrarie, Pro. 1.24. *I will laugh at your destruction, &c.* 4. The place out of the Psalme is impertinent: for is eternall reprobation, vanitie, or iniquitie? 5. To the place out of Wisdome, the answer to Ezekiel will serue.

The mouing cause for which eternall reprobation was made, is not sinne: for the better vnderstanding whereof, I will explane this position.

Whomsoeuer God condemneth and punisheth with eternall death, those he decreed to condemne euerlastingly & punish with death, so that the immediat cause of damnation and punishment is sinne. But this is not now the question, but onely what is the cause of the decree, why God when he foresaw that all men would be sinners alike in Adam, and by nature the children of wrath, determined to shew his mercie in the one, & to leaue the other in their sinnes and condemne them for the same? there can be no other cause rendred of it, but Gods pleasure only. Yet more plainly. Why did God choose the one, and refuse the other, that is, decreed to cast off them, to leaue them in their sinnes, and for their sinnes to condemne them, when as the Elect should haue bin no lesse the children of wrath by nature then all other? I

they are said to be *vnanimi*, knit together in one minde as the Ap ostle phraiseth it. 1. Cor. 1. 10. according to that which is sai dof the beleeuing companie in the Acts. 4. 32. *they were of one heart and of one soule.*

Equalitie is sometime taken for à paritie or likenes: when the Apostle would haue vs to be equally affected, he willeth vs to be like minded one to another. Rom. 15. 5. & not to beare the proud mind of the insulting Pharise to saie, I am not like others, or the ambitious mind of Pompey to admit none to be his equall, but as we are taught to make our selues equall to them of the lower sort, Rom. 12. 16. (not in titles and degrees as some vrge equalitie, or in possessions or goodes as many pretend community where God hath put à difference) but in lowlines of mind, as one commentes vpon that place, by imitating him which saith, *learne of me I am meeke and lowly*: Math. 11. 29.

Equabilitie is so called of *æquali habilitate*, of equall abilitie; because it doth most properly extend to *Abilities* by the naturall etymologie of the word.

What Ability & *Non-abilitie* is in our common lawes, I will omit, but in the scriptures it is most commonly takē for à temporall state of liuing, to signifie that as there ought to be an vnity in profession, an vnanimitie in affection, à sympathy in affliction, so there ought to be an equalitie in outward affaires, that where mē are of equabilitie or equall value in abilitie, they should be equiualent in all good actions; both by the prescript rule of God. *Let euery one minister accordingto his abilitie.* 1. Pet 4. 11. and by president in the godly, *we according to our abilities* doe. Neh. 5. 8.

Thus in some transparent sort I haue giuen some light and introduction to the matter: for by the sundry acceptions of the word you may see that to be euen, all one, equall, & like, are but synonomies or wordes of like sense and signification, and by the deriuation of the word you may perceiue the signification of the subiect: for as in the beginning Adam gaue names agreeable to the nature of euery creature, so in the first inuention of wordes Etymologicians gaue denomination according to the significatiō of euery word, which might be deriued from some language by exquisite linguistes, although now where we want

reason

98. J. LEGATE 3 Gibbon, C. *The order of equalitie.* 1604
STC 11817 4° E.1.Jur Sig. A4v

iudgemēt:at the left, it becam not him so to brag: It might haue better beseemed the other, if any such thing were, to haue acknowledged it: As *August.* thus modestly writeth to *Petrus*, a Bishop to a Presbyter: *Vellem rescriptis tuis, quid te docuerit me docere: absit enim vt erubescam à presbytero discere, si tu non erubuisti à laico:* I would haue thee by thy rescript to teach me, what taught you: farre be it, that I should be ashamed to learne of a Presbyter, if you were not ashamed to learne of a lay man. De orig.anim. lib 2.tom.7.

Further he chargeth the great English Bible, which is authorised to be read in our Curches, with error in the translation, and with blasphemie in the annotations. Imput.8.recrim.6.

7. Concerning the allegation of the Fathers, I haue shewed partly his ignorance, in mistaking and misquoting them, partly his vnfaithfulnes in vntrue alleadging them, in 30. seuerall places: as namely his ignorance in [a] *Cyril*, [b] *Hierome*, [c] *Augustine*: [d] *Tertullian* also is strangely produced, contrarie to his owne iudgement: thus he dealeth also with the new writers, as with *Calvine, Beza.*

a Imput.12. iustif.2.2.
b ibid.iustif 3. and recrim. 1.4.
c recrim.7.3. and 4.
d ibid.recr. 8.3

8. Neither can the Scripture escape his vncleane fingers: as instance is giuen in 26. places: as *loc.* 17. the Scripture saith, *He shall not preserue the vngodly*, Iob 36. 5. he readeth, *thou wilt not preserue*: *loc.* 19. S. *Iames* saith, *which hath conuerted, &c. and shall saue a soule*, Iam. 5. 20. he readeth, *which conuerteth*, in the present: and shall *saue his soule*: adding (his:) and he maketh as bolde with many places beside.

This it is for one to deale out of his element, and to meddle beyond his skill, for a professor of Grammer, to take vpon him to teach Diuinitie. He must needes stumble that walketh in darkenes, and he can not be without error, that is corrupt in iudgement. Now is verified that saying of the wise man, εἰσὶν οἱ πλουτίζοντες ἑαυτοὺς, μηδὲν ἔχοντες, *There is that maketh himselfe rich, and hath nothing*: As this man maketh himselfe skilfull in the tongues, in the Scriptures, in the Fathers, and in what not, in all these proclayming his ignorance: *Hierome* spake it mo- Prov.13.7.

99. C. LEGGE Willet, A. *Liodoromastix.* 1607
STC 25693 4° A.61.Th Sig. ¶¶1r

macie in all causes; all these we hold changeable according to times, and places, whereas those (who will needes be our aduersaries in this cause) will haue all such as concerne the substance of discipline to be appointed by God, and to be alwaies firme, and immutable, and the Eldership to haue the execution of them; and to this end in euery parish or precinct, there must be a presbyterie of doctors, pastors, elders, and deacons; and of diuers presbiteries, conferences and synodes; all which (say they) are precisely required in Gods word. But seeing remonstrance hath been made both of the errors of them all, and the infinit dissentions amongst themselues, we can be content to let that discipline fall, which stronger then they (if they were willing) could hardly haue strength for to hold vp. This discipline of the Church ought to see the execution of those lawes, and ordinances, which God by his Apostles in their time, and daily since by the Church maketh; neither doe we thinke that any in the bosome of the Church, after so long a time of knowledge, can now doubt, but that God hath left vnto his Church, an authoritie to make lawes, the execution whereof in reason is committed to those, who succeed in place and authoritie, the Apostles of Christ, that did plant the Church; whose dominion (notwithstanding) we make not so absolute, that like tyrants at their pleasure, they may rule ouer Christs flocke; yet the power that the rulers of the Church haue, in matters of a lower nature, are lesse limited by farre (hauing warrant to ordaine and appoint things indifferent) which serue for order, comlines, and the edification of Christs Church. By this authoritie the Apostles ordained many things in the Church, whereof from Christ they had no expresse mention; by this power S. *Paul* ordained that gatherings should be made at Corinth, vpon the Lords day; that the man should pray bare headed, and the woman couered. Such authoritie at this day a particular Church hath (as of *England France* end *Scotland*, or any other) that the clergie with the allowance of the prince and the rest, whom it may concerne for to make lawes, may ordaine, and appoint, such ordinances, as seruing for edification,

D.Sutcliff.

1.Pet. 5.

Zanch. in decal pag. 671.

Omnia decenter.

1.Cor. 14.

O order,

Sixe of the nine were not his equall peeres,
Full thirty kingdomes he to his did bring,
Yet was his life not many moe in yeares.
Braue *Britaine* then take place among the best,
And midst our worthie *Henries* take thy rest.
Next *Charlemaine* of *France*, a Monarch great, *Charle-maine.*
So called great, and Emperour he was.
French Chronicles his actions all do treat,
He for a Christian Worthy wel may passe.
Yet *Henry* ours the eight as good as he,
Shall for a Christian King compared be.
Godfrey de Bulleigne was a Prince of fame,
He wore vpon his helme a crowne of thorne, *Godfrey*
He freed all Christian captiues where he came:
And not forsooke them, till in peeces torne
He left their foes laid groueling on the ground,
That durst attempt a Christian to confound.
See then nine Worthies in their ranke and place,
Three of which number gouerned the Iewes,
Great *Iosua* is formost of that race:
But, for king *Dauid* brought vs better newes,
I place him first, and do withall compare
Henry the eight a worthie King most rare.
Henry the eight gaue vs our primier taste
Of milke which is most meete for infants foode:
Edw. and *Eliza.* stronger meates imbrac't,
And fed vs till we better vnderstood
The word of God, which *Rome* had vs bereft:
This grace to *England* gracious *Henry* left.
Three more of Worthies by their names to call,
Great *Alexander* was the *Græcians* ioye:
And *Iulius Cæsar* mighty Romane shall
Be second here, then *Hector* stout of *Troy*:
Threee mighty Princes, peerelesse in their dayes,
Whose worthy valour won them endlesse praise.
Three Worthies more of Christians beare the name,

Arthur

THus haue you receyued of mee (moste renoumed Prince) a present, not truely with wit and learninge polished, in either of which because I knowe my defect, I am right hartely sory: but yet meete and conueniente bothe for that trade of life which you apply your selfe vnto, and also for your noble and haughty courage. For beinge as you are wõderfully furnished with the vertues of courtesie, liberality, constancie, and fortitude, that is surely amonge the rest of youre morall qualities worthy singular commendation, that you frame and measure all your deuises conformably to the rule of Godlines and Christian religion. For the nobility of your house and familie, comminge as you do, of the race of noble kinges by lineall descent, doth not so puffe vppe your mind with pride and insolencie, but that you suppose mutch more glory and worthines reposed in the worthye callinge of a Christian, then in those glorious titles. Neyther so tooke you in hande noble actes, as thoughe you should respecte therein the laude and prayse of the vulgar people. Neyther with that mynde and intent dyd you expose your life to many perillous daungers, that you might thereby purchase a rewarde of mortall men. But beinge as you are of haughty mynde, in all thinges which you bringe to passe both with singular forsyghte and prouidence, and also with wonderfull courage and stoutnes, whether they appertaine to ciuill gouernment in time of peace, or to martiall prowesse in time of warre, you geue most manifest notice and significatiõ, that you set no store by humaine thinges, but do with moste earnest endeuour and intention of minde affect those thinges that be Heauenly and euerlastinge. Therefore not without iust desarte of yours, all good men loue you, all nobility with reuerence beholde you, all Spaine with all maner of praise and cõmendation extolleth your name.

E.2. So

102. T. MARSH I Osoria da Fonseca, J. *The five bookes of . . . nobilitie.* 1576
STC 18886 C.17.27.Linc Sig. 2E1v (mis-signed E2)

honour which ſeeme to haue a certayne affinity and reſem-blance with ſuch as were the very vertues and cauſes of commendatiō in any that euer deſerued the title of moſt perfect or iuſtly renowmed: for if euer the Queene of *Carya* was meritorious for her magnanimity and bountiful diſpoſition the Queene of *Saba* which ſome wryters call *Nycaula*, & other *Manqueda*, was had in honour for her wiſedome, which was ſuch, that both the old & new teſtament affirm, that ſhe trauelled frō the end of the world & extreme cōfines therof to the lād of *Iuda*, to come & heare the doctrine of *Salomon*, with whō ſhe diſputed no leſſe learnedly thē with profoūd iudgement, or if the cōſtant Lady *Plaudina* a Chriſtiā borne in the heart of *Europe*, hath purchaſed a Crown of eternity, in keeping her fayth and vow to God and the worlde euē to the laſt ſeperatiō of her ſowle & body, or if any other, eyther of antiquity or familiar experience, of what degree and cōdition ſo euer haue bene noted of renowme for the gifte of nobility in any ſort, your Ladiſhip may chalenge place with the beſt, eyther for moderate gouernemente whoſe effectes in al thinges you attempt, argue your worthy participation with the excellent giftes of temperance and wonderful modeſty in the ij moſt famous Earles of Leiceſter & Warwike your Brethren, & moſt vertuous & renowmed Ladye the Cōuteſſe of Huntington your ſiſter, to whoſe glory and general loue amongeſt al ſorts of people in this land, I nede not adde further circumſtance or increaſe of prayſe, conſideryng the whole ſtate, fixing their eyes vpon them with an vnfayned zeale and admiration of their wyſdome and vertues, do aduouch in more ample ſort their good will that way, then I am ether worthy or able to declare: and for your clemency to the caſe of the afflicted, vpright dealing, without exaction or cauſe of grudge to any, wōderful reſpect to the honour of your callyng, with dutiful awe and feare of God, and obedience to my Lord your huſband, for other arguments or effectes, wherein conſiſtes the prayſe of a vertuous mynde, or

oughe

103. T. MARSH 2 Fenton, G. *Certaine tragicall discourses*. 1579
STC 1356.3 Douce F.193 Sig. ¶5v

or a colde and careleſſe newter (which God forbid) the harme could not be expreſſed which you should do to your natiue Cuntrie. For (as *Cicero* no leſſe truely than wiſely affirmeth, and as the ſorowfull dooings of our preſent dayes do too certeinly auouch) greate men hurt not the cō-mon weale ſo much by beeing euil in reſpect of themſelues, as by drawing others vnto euil by their euil example. I aſſure your Lordshippe I write not theſe things as though I ſuſpected you to be digreſſed frō that ſoundnes and ſinceritie, wherein you were continually trayned and traded vnder that vigilant *Vliſſes* of our common welth, ſometyme your Lordships careful *Chyron* or *Phoenix*, and nowe your faithful *Patroclus*, or as though I miſtruſted your Lordship to be degenerated frō the excellent towardnes, which by foreward proof hath giuen glad foretokens and (I truſt alſo) luckye hanſels of an honorable age too enſue: but bycauſe the loue that I owe to God and his religion, the care that I haue of the church and my natiue cuntrie, the dutie wherin Nature hath bound mee to your Lordship, and (which is an occaſion too make all good and honeſt men look about them) the perilouſnes of this preſent time wher in all meanes poſſible are practized to ouerthrowe Chriſtes kingdome, and to abolishe all faithfulnes from among men, make mee to feare and forecaſt, not ſo much what is true, as what may bee noyſome and hurtful: and therfore I ſeek rather too profite by wholeſome admonition, than to delight by pleaſant ſpeeches. Theſe be no dayes of daliance: for Sathan the workmaſter of all miſcheef being greued that his own king dome draweth to an end, not onely goeth about like a roring Lyon too deuoure folke by open force: but alſo like a ſlie Serpent ſetteth ſnares and pitfalles innumerable, to intrap men and bring them to deſtructiō by policie: laying wayt for all men, but ſpecially for ſuch as are of high eſtate, as who alwayes carye greateſt nombers with them which waye ſo euer they incline. Hee turneth himſelfe intoo mo shapes than euer did *Proteus*: and ſuche as himſelfe is, ſuche are his miniſters. Firſt and formoſt the obſtinate and ſtubborneharted *Papiſtes*, the ſworne enemies of God, the peſtilent poyſon of mankinde, and the verye welſprings of all error, hipocriſie and vngraciouſnes, (who while they beare ſway bee more cruel than Beares, VVolues, and Tigres: and when they bee kept vnder, more deceitfull than *Ceraſtes* and *Crocodyles*: & at all times more miſcheuouſe than the Diuel himſelfe) labour with tooth and nayle too winde their owne trash into credit with all men, and to bring the heauenly doctrine of the Goſpel in hatred. Ageine the *Atheiſtes* which ſay in their hartes there is no God: and the *Epicures* which depriue GOD of his prouidence in gouerning the world, as though hee eyther vnder-

*.iii. ſtode

104. H. MIDDLETON 1a Calvin, J. *The psalmes of David and others.* 1571
STC 4395 LL.44.Th Sig. *3r

taile after it, for ſuch women ſeeing themſelues noted of infamie, vtterly renounced their chriſtendome, as it were vppon a ſpite. And therefore S. Paule will not haue any widowes taken in, vnder the age of three ſcore yeares at the leaſt. Trueth it is that mariage is not to be found fault with all of it ſelfe, neither hath it any euill blemiſh in it, ſo that euerie of the parties conſider well the ſtate whereunto he is called. And becauſe the women might be yet ſubiect to mariage, if they were not paſt theſe yeares, therefore S. Paul flatly ſhouteth out all them that are vnder three ſcore yeares. This is a thing well worth the noting: for we ſee howe the ſpirite of God hath prouided for all inconueniences, & to the end ẏ if there were any widowe taken in, ſhe ſhould not forſake the church by renouncing ẏ promiſe, which ſhe had giuen. And how hath he prouided for it? By meanes that mariage hath alwayes had his courſe, & was neuer condemned. Therefore ſeeing mariage is a ſtate allowed of God, & ſo holy, S. Paul woulde not giue occaſion to turne them away from it that were yet of age to be maried, but woulde keepe and reſerue them ẏ had no occaſion to be maried euer after: and yet he is not content with the age, but addeth: *That hath beene the wife of one husband,* as if hee had ſaide a woman that hath had two or three huſbands, may yet take the fourth rather then a widowe that hath gouerned her houſhoulde quietly after the death of her husband, if ſhee abide a widow, & we ſee by long cõtinuance of time, ẏ ſhe hath no deſire to take a new ſtat: this cauſeth vs to be better aſſured. Thus we ſee ẏ meanes that S. Paul kept here, to the end that the widowes that had giuen themſelues to the church, might continue to doe their duetie, and yet might not mariage be blamed, and libertie alſo to marie might not be taken from any, but that they might vſe it as God had ſuffred. And it is a point that wee muſt marke well: for we ſee, howe vnder a clooke of chaſtitie there is ſo much filthineſſe and ſo much ſtinch ingendered, that all the world hath ben infected, & that ſince this diuelliſh imagination hath ben forged, that they ẏ abſtained from mariage, led an Angels life, a ſtate of perfection. There vpon, needs muſt their church men (as they call them) be cut off from this libertie, that they may not marie. Then were monkeries founded more ouer, to vowe virginitie. And it is true, that the Prieſtes, & Monkes, and Nonns, did abſteine from mariage, but what chaſtitie was there in a number of them, yea almoſt in al of them? Do wee not ſee at this day ẏ theſe prieſts & al the popes cleargy are a cauſe that mariages are broken & marred, and that there is not one iot of faith nor honeſtie?

Do we not ſee that the prieſts, which

105. H. MIDDLETON 1b Calvin, J. *Sermons on . . . Timothie and Titus.* 1579
STC 4441 Mason F.117 Sig. 2G3v

durst spewe out this blasphemie which they haue drawen out of this pit of hell, that marriage is a filthie thing, and therefore wee must vtterly abstaine from it, if we will lead an Angels life, and a perfect and blessed state. GOD therfore to reuenge such a beastly vngodlinesse, let Satan the bridle loose, so that there came that horrible confusion wee see. And therefore we must note this place of S.Paul so much the more, wher wee see, that though the seruice whiche the widowes did to the Church was good, yet God wold not haue it let ẏ ordinarie course of marriage. And moreouer, hee woulde not haue such widowes receiued, as were put yet in state to be maried, not bicause it might hinder marriage, but to shewe, ẏ that libertie which God hath set in the world, must be reserued to euery one, and no man be depriued of it, and that marriage bee maintained in that honor it ought to be. Wherby wesee, that he is not against him selfe in his commaundements, but all of them agree together very well, so that wee can submit our selues wholy to him. As for that that Saint Paul addeth, that *Widowes must be well reported of, for all good workes.* Hee sheweth hereby, that they that are called to a publique charge, must not bee placed in it, vnlesse there bee good hope of them, to say, we know such an one can do it: but thē must we haue had some experience of him. As if we take a man to be a Minister of the word of God, and some would say, It is like he will vse him selfe well, hee was neuer an vnthrift, no man did euer see any hurt in him. If wee should thus lightly cast it on him, God wold punish this rashnesse. And why so ? Bicause he must be wel reported of before, he that is to bee chosen to so hard and so honourable an office, must first be proued, and we must know what he can do. So fareth it with all other offices : they must bee knowen first, that must bee chosen. And, I pray you, if you goe but to the market to buy peares or apples, yet you will haue a taste of them, and knowe where they grewe.

And when wee should chose men to serue GOD, and that in most excellent offices, shall wee take them, as if wee should make a King of cloutes, the first that commeth, the veriest harebraine, or foole ? should such an one occupy the place? what a reckoning were this ? And therefore let vs marke, that when there is any question of choosing men to a publique office, thei must be proued before, and bee such as men may boldly trust in, and haue ben well reported of before time, that they will doe their dutie as they ought: and if we goe otherwise to worke, woe bee vnto vs that goe on in such sort. For if wee compare the office that Saint Paule speaketh of here in this place, with offices that are more high,

and

106. H. MIDDLETON 2 Calvin, J. *Sermons on . . . Timothie and Titus.* 1579
STC 4441 Mason F.117 Sig. 2H1v

ning and blemiſhing the honour and glorie of god, that it is rather a confirmation of it. For if the men that bring vs the doctrine of ſaluation for our ſoules are our fathers, what is hee that ſendeth them to vs, and is the verie authour, & vſeth the labour of men as he thinketh good? when he giueth the abilitie and means, when he giueth vertue to the doctrine that it may profite vs, when (I ſay) God worketh in ſuch ſort, that it is he that beginneth and perfiteth all, ought not the glorie to bee giuen him, and hee haue all the praiſe? As when it is ſaid that the miniſters of the worde forgiue ſinnes, that they vnbinde ſoules, it is not becauſe God hath reſigned this office to them, and put it of from himſelfe: but when hee committed his worde to them, he ſhewed them alſo to what ende it muſt be preched, and what this office is. For they that receiue the promiſes which we offer in Gods name, muſt be aſſured that whatſoeuer we haue preached is confirmed in the kingdom of heauen: for wee haue ſent them to God, who gaue vs this charg. And therfore they that haue this charge to preache the Goſpell, vnbinde ſoules, forgiue ſins in Gods name: but yet that remaineth alwayes true, ẏ is ſaid to vs by the prophet

Eſai.43.25.

Eſai. This is he that forgiueth thy ſinnes, O Iſrael, and putteth them forth: ſo that God will haue no creature mixed with him, ſhewing that it is his office onely, to put out ſinnes: but yet his wordſ which he hath committed to mortall men, is the means, and inſtrument, as it were, to doe it: So then we ſee nowe, that S. Paule did exalt himſelfe beyond meaſure, but onely ment to ſhew what the office of the doctrine of the goſpel is, to wit, that by it wee are made new creatures. And why ſo? for it is an incorruptible ſeede. As wee are begottē in this preſent & flitting life by the corruptible ſeede, ſo the worde of God quickeneth vs, to the ende wee may come to this immortall inheritance which is prepared for vs. Hereby we are aduertiſed when it pleaſeth God to ſend vs his worde, to receiue it with ſuch an affection, as though it brought vs life: for in deede ſo it doeth. We feele it not, nor perceiue it in our fantaſie, but ſo the matter ſtandeth. And therefore let vs conſider what a bleſſing god maketh vs partakers of, when hee ſendeth vs his worde. And for this cauſe alſo the Church is called our mother: as S. Paule ſaith, that the truth of God is committed to it to be kept.

Gal 4.26. 1.Tim.3.15.

Therfore ſeeing God beſtoweth his worde vpon vs, by the meanes of men, and hee hath ſetled this order in his church, that euen as God is our Father, ſo is the Churche our mother, ſhe conceiueth vs, and giueth vs milk and nouriſheth vs. As the huſband agreeth with the wife to nouriſhe their children, and the wife hath the care for her part, ſo God hath committed this charge to

107. H. MIDDLETON 3 Calvin, J. *Sermons on . . . Timothie and Titus.* 1579
STC 4441 Mason F.117 Sig. 3V5r

professe publikely that wee thinke otherwise, vnlesse wee doe most certaynely know the contrary, yet may wee in the secret of our hearts remaine in some doubt, carefully seeking by the Scripture and Monuments of antiquity to find out the Truth. Neither is it necessary for vs expresly to beleeue whatsoeuer the Councell hath concluded, though it be true; vnlesse by some other meanes it appeare vnto vs to bee true, and wee bee conuinced of it, in some other sort then by the bare determination of the Councell onely. But it sufficeth that we beleeue it, *implicitè*, and, *in præparatione animi*, that out of the due respect wee beare to the Councells Decree, wee dare not resolue otherwise, and bee ready expresly to beleeue it, if it shall bee made to appeare vnto vs.

But, concerning the Generall Councells of this sort, that hetherto haue beene holden, wee confesse that in respect of the matter about which they were called, so neerely, and essentially concerning the life and soule of the Christian Faith, and in respect of the manner and forme of their proceeding, & the euidence of proofe brought in them, they are, and euer were expresly to bee beleeued by all such as perfectly vnderstand the meaning of their determination. And that therefore it is not to bee maruayled at, if[x] *Gregory* professe, that hee honoureth the first foure Councells as the foure Gospells; and that whosoeuer admitteth them not, though hee seeme to be a Stone elect and precious, yet hee lyeth beside the foundation and out of the building.

[x] *Gregorius. li. 1. Epist.* 24.

Of this sort there are onely sixe; the first, defining the Sonne of GOD to be co-essentiall, co-eternall, and co-equal with the Father. The second, defining that the holy Ghost is truely God, co-essentiall, co-eternall, and co-equall with the Father and the Sonne. The third, the vnity of Christs person. The fourth, the distinction and diuersity of his natures, in, and after the personall vnion. The fifth, condemning some remaines of *Nestorianisme*, more fully explayning things stumbled at in the Councel of *Chalcedon*, and accursing the Heresie of Origen and his followers, touching the temporall punishments of Diuells and wicked Caste-awayes: and the Sixth, defining and clearing the distinction of operations, actions, powers and wills in Christ, according to the diuersity of his natures. These were all the lawfull Generall Councells (lawfull I say both in their beginning, and proceeding, and continuance) that euer were holden in the Christian Church, touching matters of Fayth. For the Seauenth, which is the second of *Nice*, was not called about any question of Faith, but of manners: In which our Aduersaries confesse there may be some-thing inconueniently prescribed, and so as to bee the occasion of great and greeuous euills: and surely that is our conceit of the Seauenth General Councel, the second of *Nice*: for how-soeuer it condemne the religious adoration and worshipping of Pictures and seeme

108. N. OKES I Field, R. *Of the church.* 1606
STC 10857.5 4° F.20(1)Th Sig. 2F3r

ſtence of that tree into which it is implanted : the ſecond, for that it hath no roote of it owne, and ſo wanteth one part pertaining to the integritie of the nature of each tree. But if a braunch of one tree ſhould by diuine power be created and made in the ſtocke of another, this compariſon would faile but onely in one circumſtance, and that not very important; ſeeing, though the humane nature want no part pertaining to the integritie and perfection of it, (as the implanted braunch doth of that pertaineth to the integritie of the nature of a tree, in that it hath no roote of it owne) yet the humane nature in Chriſt, hath no ſubſiſtence of it owne, but that of the Sonne of God communicated vnto it; and therefore in that reſpect it is, in ſome ſort, like to the braunch that hath no roote of it owne, but that of the tree, into which it is implanted, communicated vnto it.

This compariſon is vſed by *Alexander* of *Hales*, and diuers other of the Schoole-men, and, in my opinion, is the apteſt and fulleſt of all other. For as betweene the tree and the braunch there is a compoſition, not *Huius ex his*, but *huius ad hoc*, that is, not making a tree of a compound or middle nature, and qualitie, but cauſing the braunch, though retaining it owne nature, and bearing it owne fruite, to pertaine to the vnitie of the tree into which it is implanted, and to beare fruite in and for it, and not for it ſelfe: ſo the Perſon of Chriſt is ſaid to bee compounded of the nature of God and Man, not as if there were in him a mixt nature ariſing out of theſe, but as hauing the one of theſe added vnto the other in the vnitie of the ſame perſon. And as this tree is one, and yet hath two different natures in it, and beareth two kinds of fruite: ſo Chriſt is one, and yet hath two different natures, and in them performeth the diſtinct actions pertaining to either of them.

Laſtly, as a man may truly ſay, after ſuch implanting, this Vine is an Oliue tree, and this Oliue tree is a Vine; and conſequently, this Vine beareth Oliues, and this Oliue tree beareth Grapes: ſo a man may ſay, this Sonne of *Marie* is the Sonne of God: and on the other ſide, this Sonne of God, and firſt borne of euery creature, is the Sonne of *Marie*, borne in time: the Sonne of God, and Lord of life was crucified, and the Sonne of *Marie* laied the foundations of the earth, and ſtretched out the Heauens like a curtaine.

teacheth how to vse and well employ our weapons: It exhorteth euery one in his vocation to embrace pietie & to honor Iustice: It teacheth Princes, Lordes, and generally all gentrie the true path & high way to climbe to vertue, and to recouer the auncient honor of *France*, as also how to eschue the danger of shame and miserie. To be brief, whatsoeuer is most rare and excellent throughout all the most famous Philosophers and Historiographers, concerning the conduct and good ordering of a great estate, either the instruction of such as make profession of honor is founde to bee herein set downe in as pleasant a language and delectable varietie of matter, & withall so accōmodated to the humour of our nation, that I hope to get the goodwilles of al those that shal reade this discourse, as hauing bene the occasion that they are not frustrated of the fruite and pleasure herein to be reaped: And this will they accompt to be the greater, if they vouchsafe but to behould and consider of the horror of the place where so exquisite a matter was conceiued and brought into the world. For who is he that waying the miserable captiuitie wherein the Lord of *la Nouë* was deteined when he wrot these remembrances, being past hope, or at the leastwise voyd of all apparance that euer he should get foorth, oppressed with sicknesse of bodie and anguish of minde, & besides all this most straightly kept: who I say is he that viewing him in this miserable captiuitie will not admire his wonderfull constancie and valiant courage, which had bene rare euen in the most vertuous ages, that could in the middest of so many calamities and apparitions of most terrible things: yea as it were in the bottome of the gulph of death, thinke vpon the commoditie of his countrie, and in such bitter bondage maintaine his soule in such libertie, that to heare him in his discourses it might seeme his prison had no power but ouer his passions, and ouer all that might molest or empeach the tranquilitie of his mind: either, as *Plato* saith, that those that are in heauinesse and agonie of death beginning to put of their mortall bodies, haue the powers of their soules more excellent then in their perfect health; so the incōuenience of this prison hauing quailed and suppressed his bodie, did helpe him to purge his vnderstanding, by vnclothing him of the cares of this life & nourishing him with most beautifull and high meditations farre more

110. T. ORWIN I La Noue, F. de *The . . . discourses.* 1588
STC 15215 Douce N.260 Sig. A5r

Psalm.4.8.] *and be quiet from feare of euill* [i. not onely, no euill it selfe, but no suspition or feare of it shall go to his heart, he shall bee so strengthened through Gods promises, and defended by his almightie power.

Vers.1. Teacheth vs, that it is a great blessing, when God giueth to any countrie or common wealth, wise and godlie Princes. *Vers.2.* Teacheth vs, that Gods word is, and ought to bee the ground of all our knowledge. *Vers.3.* Teacheth vs, that it ought to bee the rule of all our actions, either publique or priuate. *Vers.4.* Proueth, that the knowledge of Gods worde belongeth euen to the simple, contrarie to the Popish assertion, which would haue none meddle with it, but great schollers and learned men. *Vers.5.6.* Shewe, that euen the wisest also may out of the same learne, for increase of iudgement and knowledge: so that wee may rightly say, that, the word are waters, wherein the great Elephant may swimme, and the little Lambe wade and goe. *Vers.7.* Teacheth vs, that wee can neuer come to sound knowledge of God and his truth, vnlesse there bee a right reuerence of his Maiestie in our hearts. *Vers.8.* Teacheth vs, first that it is parents dueties, to instruct those, whom God hath giuen them. Secondly, that children should reuerently hearken vnto the wholesome counsell of their friends and parents. *Vers.9.* Teacheth vs, that it is a notable grace to bee bowable to the good wordes of exhortation. *Vers.10.* Teacheth vs, at no hand to consent, to wicked perswasions and inticements. *Vers.11,12,13,14.* Teach vs, that the wicked will leaue no stone vnrolled, to the end they may drawe some to commit wickednesse with them, sometimes setting before them pleasure, sometimes profite, and sometimes one thing, and sometimes another. *Vers.15.* Teacheth vs two things: first to auoyd the companie of the wicked: secondly, not to bee like vnto them in outward conuersation. *Vers.16.* Sheweth, how egar and sharpe set, the wicked are vpon mischiefe. *Vers.17.* Teacheth vs, that the wicked are not so sure of the accōplishment of their practises, as they suppose. *Vers.18.* Teacheth vs, that through Gods iust iudgements, the vngodly are many times taken in the mischieuous imaginations of their owne hearts. *Vers.19.* Teacheth vs, that there is no wicked man, of what estate or condition so euer he be, which continueth in his sinne, that shall escape vnpunished. *Vers.20,21,22.* Teacheth vs, that the heauenlie wisedome vseth all meanes and opportunities, to bring men vnto it, which are stragling from it. *Vers.22.* Sheweth, that the wicked preferre vanitie and sinne, before all goodnesse whatsoeuer. *Vers.23.* Teacheth vs, that those which vnfeignedlie turne to the Lord, shall not only escape iudgements in this life, and in the life to come, but shall bee throughlie instructed in all the waies of God. *Vers.24,25.* Teacheth vs, that there can be no greater sinne committed against God, than rebellion, and the contempt of his maiestie. *Vers.26.* Teacheth, that the Lord will haue no care of them, that haue no care of him. *Vers.27.* Sheweth, that Do.

Leaue to be mournyng ſtil, let this moſt heauy departure
This death of *Phillis* bring wiſhed death to *Amyntas*,
Here did he pauſe for a while, and home at night he returned.

The eyghth day.

Now ſince fayre *Phillis* was cheſted duly, the eighth tyme
Night gaue place to the light, and eu'ning vnto the mornyng:
Whē to the woods ſo wilde, to the wilde beaſts dangerus harbors,
Forſaking hye ways, by the bye wayes paſſed *Amyntas*:
And there ſetts hym downe all wearyed vnder a Myrtle,
For grief ſtil groanyng, with deepe ſighs heauyly pantyng,
Stil *Phillis* namyng, ſtil *Phillis* fayntyly callyng.
And muſt one wench thus take all the delyte fro the contrey?
And muſt one wench thus make euery man to be mournyng,
Euery man whoſe flocks on theſe hills vſe to be feeding?
And muſt *Æglon* weepe? and muſt that fryendly *Menalcas*
Weare his mournyng roabe, for death of my bony *Phillis*?
And muſt good *Corydon* lament? muſt *Tityrus* alter
His pleaſant melodies, for death of my bony *Phillis*?
And muſt *Damatas* for grief leaue of to be louing?
Muſt *Amaryllis* leaue, for death of my bony *Phillis*?
And muſt drooping bull conſume as he goes by the meddow,
Muſt Sheepe look lowring for death of my bony *Phillis*?
And muſt ſighs ſeeme wyndes, muſt teares ſeeme watery fountayns?
And muſt each thing change for death of my bony *Phillis*?
O then what ſhal I doe for death of my bony *Phillis*?
Syth that I lou'd bonylaſſe *Phillis* more dearly than all theſe,
Syth that I lou'd her more than I loue theſe eyes of *Amyntas*,
O then what ſhal I dooe forlorne forſaken *Amyntas*,
What ſhal I doo but dy, for death of my bony *Phillis*?
Phillis whoe was woont with bowe and ſhafts to be ſhooting,

Phillis

112. T. ORWIN 2b Fraunce, A. *The Countess of Pembrokes Yuychurch*. 1591
STC 11340 Wood 482 Sig. I2v

Phillis whoe was woont my flock with care to be feeding,
Phillis whoe was woont my mylch ſhee-goates to be mylking,
Phillis whoe was woont (moſt handſome wench of a thouſand)
Either clowted creame,or cakes,or curds to be making,
Either fine baskets of bul-ruſh for to be framing,
Or by the greene meddowes gay dancing dames to be leading:
Phillis whoſe boſome filberds did loue to be filling,
Phillis for whoſe ſake greene lawrell lou'd to be bowing,
Phillis,alas,ſweete Laſſe *Phillis*,this braue bony *Phillis*,
Is dead,is buried,makes all good company parted.
  O how oft *Phillis* conferd in fields with *Amyntas?*
O how oft *Phillis* did ſing in caues with *Amyntas*,
Ioyning her ſweete voyce to the oaten pipe of *Amyntas?*
O how oft *Phillis* clypt and embraced *Amyntas?*
How many thouſand tymes hath *Phillis* kiſſed *Amyntas*,
Bitten *Amyntas* lips,and bitten againe of *Amyntas*,
Soe that *Amyntas* his eyes enuy'de theſe lipps of *Amyntas?*
  O ſweete ſoule *Phillis*,w'haue liu'd and lou'd for a great while,
(If that a man may keepe any mortall ioy for a great while)
Lyke louing turtles,and turtle-doues for a great while,
One loue,one lyking,one ſenſe,one ſoule for a great while,
Therefore one deaths-wound,one graue,one funeral only
Should haue ioyned in one both loue and louer *Amyntas*.
  O good God,what a grief is this that death to remember?
For,ſuch grace,geſture,face,feature,beauty,behauiour
Neuer afore was ſeene, is neuer againe to be lookt for.
O frowning fortune,ô death and deſteny diſmall;
Thus be the poplar trees that ſpread their tops to the heauens,
Of their flowring leaues deſpoyld in an howre,in a moment:
Thus be the ſweete violets,that gaue ſuch grace to the garden,
Of theyr purpled roabes deſpoyld in an howre,in a moment.
  O how oft did I cry,and roare with an horrible howling,
When for want of breath *Phillis* lay faintyly gaſping?
O how oft did I wiſh,that *Phœbus* would fro my *Phillis*
Driue that feauer away,or ſend his ſon from *Olympus*,
Whoe,when Lady *Venus* by a chaunce was prickt with a bramble,
Healed her hand with his oyles and fine knacks kept for a purpoſe?
Or that I could perceaue *Podalyrius* order in healing,
Or that I could obtaine *Medaaes* exquiſit oyntments,
And baths moſt precious,which ould men freſhly renued:

113. T. ORWIN 3a Fraunce, A. *The Countess of Pembrokes Yuychurch.* 1591
STC 11340 Wood 482 Sig. I3r

To the Reader.

THere were (good Chriſtian Reader) foure haynous accuſatiōs laid againſt the Church of England, for which the accuſers haue condemned her,& all her publique aſſemblies, as moſt wicked Antichriſtian Idolatrous ſynagogues of Sathan. I ſhewed how falſely they doo accuſe, and howe preſumptuouſly agaynſt God they doo condemne: And that indeede they are the very ſame with the auncient Donatiſts. They haue replyed and publiſhed in print their defence, but their bookes are intercepted: yet ſome few haue eſcaped, and are diſperſed among theyr fellowes. Wherefore I hold it needfull to publiſh ſome anſwere, not dealing with euery error and abſurditie,(for that would aske the trauaile of ſome yeares) but onely with the chiefe grounds of their Schiſme. In this, I truſt euery ſimple man that hath a Chriſtian heart, ſhall ſee the effectuall power of Sathan, when he turneth himſelfe into the likenes of an Angell of light, to ſeduce ignorant men, which are lifted vp in their mindes, with opinion of their knowledge: For being men vnlearned (onely ſome little froth excepted, I ſpeake thus becauſe they peruert that little which they haue read in other mens writings, in ſundry poynts) yet as if they were ſent from heauen with reuelations, or as great Apoſtles, they take vpon them to confute, and controll, and condemne all Churches, and all the moſt worthy Inſtruments which GOD hath rayſed vp in theſe laſt times. For knowe this (good Reader) that the foure accuſations which they haue brought agaynſt the Church of England, to condemne her,

114. T. ORWIN 3b Gifford, G. *A short reply*. 1591
STC 11868 Ashm.1243(7) Sig. A2r

seeme to be the complaint of a desperat man, not hauing so much as one sparke of faith: yet then he sayth: *my God, my God:* which wordes containe a confession proceeding from true faith: so that in Dauid it appeareth, that the faithfull when they feele themselues forlorne, and vtterly reiected of God, according to the sense and iudgement of the flesh, yet by faith they can apprehend his hidden mercie, and beholde it a farre off in the glasse of his promise. And so they doe often shewe contrarie affections in their prayers as Dauid doth. [t] Iacob when he wrastled with the Angell for life and death, neuer gaue ouer: and when he was foild, he would not cease before the Lord had blessed him. This his wrastling is a type of the conflicts which the faithfull are to haue with the Lord himselfe, who vseth to bring his owne children (as it were) to the field: and he assaileth them with the one hand, and with the other he holdeth them vp, that so he may prooue and exercise their faith. And for this cause the Church [u] is called Israel by the name of Iacob. An example may bee had in the woman of Canaan. [x] First, our Sauiour Christ gaue her faith, and by that faith she was mooued to seeke to him: But when she was once come to him, he gaue her three repulses. First, by saying nothing. Secondly, by denying her: Thirdly, by calling her dogge. Thus Christ in appearance made shewe, as though he would neuer haue graunted her request. But shee at euery repulse was more instant, crying more earnestly vnto him: and shee plainly opposed her selfe to him, and would take no deniall: for such is the nature of true faith. Wherefore, the faithfull when they feele themselues ouerwhelmed with sinne, turmoyled with conflicts of Sathan, when they feele the anger of God offended with them, yet they can euen then lift vp their eye lids, and giue a glimps at the brasen Serpent Iesus Christ, and can fling themselues into the armes of Gods mercie, and catch hold of the hand of God buffetting them, and kisse it.

t *Gen.* 32.28

u *Psal.* 130.

x *Matth.* 15 22.23.24. 25.26.27.

LX.

Dangerous falles of a Christian.

By these temptations it comes to passe, that a Christian though hee cannot fall finally from Christ, yet hee may fall very dangerously from his former estate. First, the graces of

115. T. ORWIN 4 Perkins, W. *A treatise . . . of damnation.* 1595
STC 19754 Antiq d.E.1595(5) Sig. I3r

hatefulnesse of the matter that enforced him. Now that we vnderstande the cause why he wrote this Epistle: let vs come to the order of the handling thereof. He contendeth in the two firste chapters about the authoritie of his Apostleship: sauing that by occasion, about the end of the second chapter, he entreth into the principall (state of the matter): that is to say into the question of the iustification of man: wherof neuerthelesse at the last in the thirde chapter he openlye frameth a full disputation. Although he seeme to intreate of many thinges in these two Chapters: yet this one thing he indeauoureth, to proue himselfe equall with the highest Apostles: and that he lacketh nothing but that he maye bee reckoned an Apostle in like degree of honour, as they. But it is worth the while to know why hee tooke so great pains about the triall of his estimation. for so that Christ raigne, and that the puritie of doctrine remaine sound, what skilleth it whether he be aboue Peter, or lesse then Peter, or whether they bee all equall among themselues? If all must decrease, that only Christ may encrease, vnfruitfull is the contention about the dignitie of men. Moreouer this maye bee demaunded, why he compareth himselfe to the other Apostles. for what controuersie had he with Peter and Iames, and Iohn? to what purpose then did it belong, that those who were of one mynde and good friendes among themselues, shoulde be at oddes against themselues? I aunswere, that the false Apostles, who had beguiled the Galathians, to the end they might the better aduaunce themselues, pretended the names of the Apostles, as though they had ben sent of them. This was a notable shouldring in of thēselues, for that they were beleeued to be the Apostles deputies, and spake as it vvere out of their mouth: and in the meane while did pluck away from Paule the name and right of an Apostle. For they did obiect that he was not chosen of the Lord, one of the twelue, that he was neuer acknowled to be such an one by the colledge of the Apostles: and that not only hee had his doctrine not from Christ, but not so muche as from the Apostles, so came it to passe that not onelye the authoritie

of

116. T. PURFOOT I Calvin, J. *A commentarie vpon . . . Galatians.* 1581
STC 4401 Mason AA.494 Sig. A4r

Mall No rudenesse Gentlemen: Ile go vndragd.
O wicked, wicked Diuell. *Exit.*

Sir Lyo. Sir, the daie of triall is this morn,
Lets prosecute the sharpest rigor, and seuerest end:
" Good men are cruell, when the'are vices friend.

Sir Hub. Woman we thanke thee, with no emptie hand,
Strumpets are fit, fit for som-thing. *Farewell.*

All saue Frevile departs.

Fre. I, for Hell: O thou vnrepriueable, beyond all
Measure of Grace dambd immediatlie:
That things of beautie created for sweet vse:
Soft comfort, and as the verie musicke of life,
Custome should make so vnutterablie hellish?
O heauen: what difference is in women, and their life?
What man, but worthie name of Man:
Would leaue the modest pleasures of a lawfull bed:
The holie vnion of two equall harts
Mutuallie holding either deere as health,
The vndoubted yssues, Ioyes of chast sheetes,
The vnfained imbrace of sober Ignorance:
To twine the vnhealthfull loynes of common Loues,
The prostituted impudence of things.
Senceless like those by Cataracks of Nyle,
" Their vse so vile, takes awaie sence how vile,
" To loue a creature, made of bloud and hell,
" Whose vse makes weake, whose companie doth shame,
" Whose bed doth begger: yssue doth defame.

Enter Francischina.

Fran. Metre *Frevile* liue: ha, ha, liue at mestre Shatewes:
Mush at metre Shatews. *Frevile* is dead. *Malherenx* sall hang,
And swete diuel, dat *Beatrice* would but run mad, dat
she would but run mad, den me would dance and sing,
Metre *Don Dubon*, me pre ye now go to Mestres
Beatrice, tel her *Frevile* is sure ded, and dat he
Curse hir selfe especiallie, for dat he was
Sticked in hir quarrell, swering in his last gaspe,
Dat if it had bin in mine quarrels,
Twould neuer haue greeued him.

117. T. PURFOOT 2 Marston, J. *The Dutch courtezan.* 1605
STC 17475 Malone 252(5) Sig. G4r

haue good education and to bee brought vp in a Tauerne, I doe keepe as gallant and as good companie, though *I* ſay it, as any ſhe in *London*, Squiers, Gentlemen, and Knightes diet at my table, and I doe lend ſome of them money, and full many fine men goe vpon my ſcore, as ſimple as *I* ſtand heere, and I truſt them, and truely they verie knightly and courtly promiſe faire, giue me verie good words, and a peece of fleſh when time of yere ſerues, nay, though my husband be a Citizen and's caps made of wooll, yet I ha wit, and can ſee my good aſſoone as another, for I haue all the thankes, my ſilly husband, alaſſe, hee knowes nothing of it, tis *I* that beare, tis *I* that muſt beare a braine for all.

Cocl. Faire hower to you Miſtreſſe.

Mrs. Mu: Faire hower, fine terme, faith ile ſcore it vp anone a beautifull thought to you ſir.

Cocl. Your Husband, and my Maiſter Mr. *Garniſh* has ſent you a *I*ole of freſh Salmon, and they both will come to dinner to ſeaſon your new cup with the beſt wine, which cup your husband intreats you to ſend backe by mee, that his armes may bee grau'd a the ſide, which he forgot before it was ſent.

Mr. Mul By what token, are you ſent by no token? nay, *I* haue wit.

Cocl. He ſent me by the ſame token, that he was dry ſhaued this morning.

Mrs. Mu. A ſad token, but true, here ſir, I pray you commend me to your Maſter, but eſpecially to your Miſtreſſe, tell them they ſhall be moſt ſincerely welcome. *Exit.*

Cocl. Shall be moſt ſincerely welcome, worſhipfull *Cocledemoy*, lurke cloſe, hang toaſts, be not aſhamed of thy qualitie, euerie mans turd ſmels well in's owne noſe, vaniſh Foyſt. *Exit.*

Enter Mrs. Mulligrub, with ſeruants and furniture for the Table.

Mrs. Mul. Come ſpread theſe Table Diaper Napkins, and doe you heare, perfume this Parlour do's ſo ſmell of prophane Tabacco, I could neuer endure this vngodly Tabacco, ſince one of our Elders, aſſured me vpon his knowledge *T*abacco was not vſed in the Congregation of the family of loue: ſpread, ſpread handſomely, Lord theſe boyes doe things arſie, varſie, you ſhew your bringing vp, *I* was a Gentlewoman by my ſiſters ſide, I can tell

118. T. PURFOOT 2 (mixed 'M') Marston, J. *The Dutch courtezan.* 1605
STC 17475 Malone 252(5) Sig. E3v

of substance, euery one will flie from thee, and reproach and sorrow accompanied with griefe, will pursue and follow thee, banished from all estimation, as a thing by thee, and vnto thee, worthily merited: for saith the Poet;

We cannot enough reproue
  him, that his goods so spends:
Or who in lust doth loue,
  his fame and credit ends.

Likewise it appeareth, that the worthy Poet and most famous Philosopher Hesiodas, went about carefully to aduertise and withdraw vs by these his verses:

Beware and take good heede,
  that thou so rul'st thy hart,
That it be not agreed
  to take an harlots part.
For when she fairest speakes,
  and sweetliest seemes to smile:
Then onely doth she breake
  her traines, thee to beguile.

Likewise where-vnto tendeth all the comicall Poets, or the end of their Comedies, for Comedie is nothing else after Cicero, alledged in the Aucolastus of Gnaseus, then the mirrour and representation of humane life, saue onely to reproue and blame this filthy, shamelesse, and abhominable loue: and from the same, as from a thing most vicious and infamous, to estrange & turne all wanton youthfull folke, as also to be an example and instruction to flye and abhorre the baits and allurements of these harlots; together their infinite cautels and deceptions, and as many dangers and euill haps as depend there-vpon: beheld in the Merchant of Plautus, how the father with sharpe threatnings and verball rebukes, with all the force hee hath, endeauoureth himselfe to reuoke and vnwrap his

119. R. RAWORTH Salter, T. *A contention betweene three brethren.* 1608
STC 1968.7 C40d33 (BL) Sig. B1r

Masse, & consecrated many Wafers to giue vnto the Communicants wherof sundry were left, whence returning to the Vestrie, one fell down, which he treading vpon, it claue to his wet feet, without being able any way to pull it off: but was mixed with the dirt which could not be wiped away. Foure *Augustin* Monkes were hanged in *Seuel*, for that they said Masse, and did not purpose to consecrate: such is their extraordinarie proceeding to cause the people to become idolaters to the bread and chalice. *Molon* an inquisitor at *Barselone*, after the consecration, did cut the host with cissers. Also Pope *Sixtus* the fourth in the towne of *Florence*, commaunded that when the Priest held vp the host, the people thẽ worshiping should be murdred: which bloudy choler was put in executiō. Pope *Gregory* the 7. hauing asked the Sacrament touching the reuealing of certaine things against the Emperor, & receiuing no answer, threw it into the fire. To be short, Pope *Victor* the 3. a Bishop of *Ebora* and also the Emperour *Henry* the 7. were poysoned in taking the host and chalice. Loe, these are the absurdities and prodigious actes wherunto transubstantiation would subiect the glorious body of our lord, if it could preuaile. Besides the *Concomitancie*, which is falsly pretended therein, is the occasion of the peoples priuation of the cupp against the ordinance of Christ, who hath commaunded, saying, *Drinke yee all Mat.* 26. and the practise of the Church, 1. *Cor.* 11. and so they are depriued of consolation in participating through a liuely faith really the benefits of the bloud of our Sauiour for the remission of sins, and confirmatiō of Gods couenant. Now the taste of the substance of bread, the sauour and odour of wine, the inseperable accidents of the essence, their true foundation, and wherin they subsist, do teach vs that the signes abide in their naturall and essentiall proprietie: not in their vsage, which represẽts vnto vs (as a liuely image and really present, and as an instrument of Gods grace) the spirituall food, the quickning refectiō, the pledge of immortality to the penitent & faithful soule; bread being the cõmunion of the body, & the chalice sanctifieng the comunion of the bloud of life, known, receiued, apprehended & applied, aswell throgh the secret operation of the minde in the elect, as through the efficacie

Sacraments vnder one kinde.

120. R. READ I B., W. *Ten learned personages*. 1601
STC 1074 Mason AA. 484 Sig. E2r

Peter was ordained of Christ the Monarch of the whole Church, that to him was committed the right both of the spirituall and temporall Monarchy: that in this Monarchy the Pope succeedeth *Peter*, as Christes vicar generall, as the vniuersall Bishoppe, as the Lorde of the whole earth. They haue fayned a donation of *Constantine* wherein hee should not onely giue the Citie of Rome to the Pope, but also resigne vnto him the whole Empire of the West. Vpon these groundes they haue obtained both of Princes and Prelates, what their greedy couetousnesse armed with such authoritie shamed not to demaund. England, Fraunce, Germany and other countreys haue beene exceedingly, or, as some speake, miserably impouerished by the intollerable exactions of the Pope and his Court. For first, the first fruites hee claimed of all spirituall promotions: which in these partes of Europe subiect to that See, did amount vnto two millions and foure hundred and three score thousand, eight hundred fourty and three Florenes. The first fruites of the spirituall liuings in Fraunce, and the charges of obtaining the same liuings, haue beene obserued in three yeares, to amount vnto nine hundred fourtie and sixe thousand, six hundred sixty and six french crownes. By the same title hee tooke vpon him to bestowe or rather to sell openly and without shame the liuings of the church: and not onely when they were void, but also before hand, and that to diuerse men. Insomuch that sometimes ten, sometimes twelue haue purchased aduousons or reuersions of the same preferments against the next auoidance. But which of all them, whē the liuing fell, was to haue the benefit of the Popes graunt, that was to bee decided at Rome: whither they were to their great charge, but to the enriching of the Romish Harpies, to repaire. This gainefull trade may well bee called making Merchandize of men: for together with the benefices the poore people were bought and solde. In respect hereof *Blondus* saith, *That all Europe almost sendeth tributes to Rome*, greater or at least equall to the reuenewes of the olde times, *Dum singulæ ciuitates à Romano pontifice beneficia sacerdotalia accipiunt*, *Whiles the spirituall promotions* in

Ludouic.9. cōstit. an. 1228. tit. de tallijs.

Iewel. ex legatione Hadrian. 6. excus. VVittembergæ. 1538

Fulm. brut. ex postulatis senatus Paris. Ludouico 11. delatis. art. 72. &c.

Ibid. art. 62.

Rom. instaur. lib. 3.

And what ſo poore a man as *Hamlet* is,
May doe t'expreſſe his loue and frending to you
God willing ſhall not lack, let vs goe in together,
And ſtill your fingers on your lips I pray,
The time is out of ioynt, ô curſed ſpight
That euer I was borne to ſet it right.
Nay come, lets goe together. *Exeunt.*

Enter old Polonius, with his man or two.

Pol. Giue him this money, and theſe notes *Reynaldo.*
Rey. I will my Lord.
Pol. You ſhall doe meruiles wiſely good *Reynaldo,*
Before you viſite him, to make inquire
Of his behauiour.
Rey. My Lord, I did intend it.
Pol. Mary well ſaid, very well ſaid; looke you ſir,
Enquire me firſt what Danskers are in Parris,
And how, and who, what meanes, and where they keepe,
What companie, at what expence, and finding
By this encompaſment, and drift of queſtion
That they doe know my ſonne, come you more neerer
Then your perticuler demaunds will tuch it,
Take you as t'were ſome diſtant knowledge of him,
As thus, I know his father, and his friends,
And in part him, doe you marke this *Reynaldo?*
Rey. I, very well my Lord.
Pol. And in part him, but you may ſay, not well,
But y'ft be he I meane, hee's very wilde,
Adicted ſo and ſo, and there put on him
What forgeries you pleaſe, marry none ſo ranck
As may diſhonour him, take heede of that,
But ſir, ſuch wanton, wild, and vſuall ſlips,
As are companions noted and moſt knowne
To youth and libertie.
Rey. As gaming my Lord.
Pol. I, or drinking, fencing, ſwearing,
Quarrelling, drabbing, you may goe ſo far.
Rey. My Lord, that would diſhonour him.
Pol. Fayth as you may ſeaſon it in the charge,

E. You

VVherein I am not vnlike vnto the vnskilfull Painter, who hauing drawne the Twinnes of Hippocrates (who were as like as one peaſe is to another) and being tolde of his friends, that they were no more like then Saturne and Apollo, hee had no other ſhift to manifeſt what his worke was, then ouer theyr heads to write: The Twinnes of Hippocrates. So may it be, that had I not named Euphues, fewe would haue thought it had been Euphues, not that in goodneſſe the one ſo farre excelleth the other, but that both beeing ſo bad, it is hard to iudge which is the worſt. Thys vnskilfulnes is no waies to bee couered, but as Accius did his ſhortneſſe, who beeing a little Poet, framed for himſelfe a great Picture, and I being a naughtie Painter, haue gotten a moſt noble Patron; being of Vliſſes mind, who though himſelfe ſafe vnder the ſhield of Aiax.

I haue now finiſhed both my labours, the one beeing hatched in the hard VVinter with the Alcion, the other not daring to bud till the cold were paſt, like the Mulberry; in eyther of the which, or in both, if I ſeeme to gleane after anothers Cart, for a few eares of Corne, or of the Taylors ſhreds to make mee a liuery, I will not deny but that I am one of thoſe Poets, which the Painters faine to come vnto Homers baſon, there to lap vp that he doth caſt vp.

In that I haue written, I deſire no praiſe of others, but patience; altogether vnwilling, becauſe euery way vnwoorthy to bee accounted a worke-man. It ſuffiſeth me to be a water bough, no bud, ſo I may be of the ſame roote; to be the yron, no ſteele, ſo I be in the ſame blade: to be Vinegar, not VVine, ſo it be in the ſame caske: to grind colours for Appelles, though I cannot garniſh, ſo I be of the ſame ſhoppe. VVhat I haue done, was onely to keepe my ſelfe from ſleepe, as the Crane doth the ſtone in her foote, and I would alſo with the ſame Crane I had been ſilent, holding a ſtone in my mouth.

But it falleth out with mee as with the young wraſtler that came to the games of Olympus, who hauing taken a foyle, thought ſcorne to leaue, till he had receiued a fall: or him that being pricked in the finger with a bramble, thruſteth his whole hande amongſt the thornes for anger. For I ſeeing my ſelfe not able to ſtand on the Iſe, did neuertheleſſe aduenture to runne, and beeing with my firſt booke brought into diſgrace, could not ceaſe vntil I was brought into contempt by the ſecond, wherein I reſemble thoſe that hauing once wet theyr feete, care not how deepe they wade.

In the which my wading (right Honorable) if the enuious ſhall clap Leade to my heeles to make mee ſinke, yet if your Lordſhip with your

123. J. ROBERTS 2 Lyly, J. *Euphues and his England.* 1597
STC 17075 Antiq e.E.1597/1(2) Sig. A3r

Hem nosti'n.

Or els (alas) his wits can haue no vent,
To broch conceits industrious intent.
Another yet dares tremblingly come out:
But first he must invoke good *Colin Clout.*
Yon's one hath yean'd a fearefull prodigy,
Some monstrous misshapen Balladry,
His guts are in his braines, huge Iobbernoule,
Right Gurnets-head, the rest without all soule.
Another walkes, is lazie, lies him downe, (crowne
Thinkes, reades, at length some wonted slepe doth
His new falne lids, dreames, straight, ten pound to
Out steps some Fayery with quick motion, (one,
And tels him wonders of some flowry vale,
Awakes, straight rubs his eyes, and prints his tale.
Yon's one, whose straines haue flowne so high a
That straight he flags, & tumbles in a ditch. (pitch,
His sprightly hote high-soring poesie,
Is like that dreamed of Imagery,
Whose

124. J. ROBERTS 3 Marston, J. *The scourge of villanie.* 1599
STC 17486 C39b43 (BL) Sig. E5r

Ham. Vppon my ſword.
Mar. We haue ſworne my Lord already.
Ham. Indeede vppon my ſword, indeed.

Ghoſt cries vnder the Stage.

Ghoſt. Sweare.
Ham. Ha, ha, boy, ſay'ſt thou ſo, art thou there trupenny?
Come on, you heare this fellowe in the Sellerige,
Conſent to ſweare.
Hora. Propoſe the oath my Lord.
Ham. Neuer to ſpeake of this that you haue ſeene
Sweare by my ſword.
Ghoſt. Sweare.
Ham. *Hic, & vbique,* then weele ſhift our ground:
Come hether Gentlemen
And lay your hands againe vpon my ſword,
Sweare by my ſword
Neuer to ſpeake of this that you haue heard.
Ghoſt. Sweare by his ſword.
Ham. Well ſayd olde Mole, can'ſt worke it'h earth ſo faſt,
A worthy Pioner, once more remooue good friends.
Hora. O day and night, but this is wondrous ſtrange.
Ham. And therefore as a ſtranger giue it welcome,
There are more things in heauen and earth *Horatio*
Then are dream't of in your philoſophie, but come
Heere as before, neuer ſo helpe you mercy,
(How ſtrange or odde ſo mere I beare my ſelfe,
As I perchance heereafter ſhall thinke meet,
To put an Anticke diſpoſition on
That you at ſuch times ſeeing me, neuer ſhall
With armes incombred thus, or this head ſhake,
Or by pronouncing of ſome doubtfull phraſe,
As well, well, we knowe, or we could and if we would,
Or if we liſt to ſpeake, or there be and if they might,
Or ſuch ambiguous giuing out, to note)
That you knowe ought of me, this doe ſweare,
So grace and mercy at your moſt neede helpe you.
Ghoſt. Sweare.
Ham. Reſt, reſt, perturbed ſpirit: ſo Gentlemen,
Withall my loue I doe commend me to you,

And

125. J. ROBERTS 4 Shakespeare, W. *Hamlet*. 1604
STC 22276 Dep.e.4 Sig. D4v

giuen, should afterwards be layd to a mans charge in *Roome*. But what cannot malice doe? Or what will not the wilfull deuise, to satisfie their mindes, for vndoing of others? God be my Iudge, I had then as little feare (although death was present, and the torment at hand, wherof I felt some smart) as euer I had in all my life before. For, when I saw those that did seeke my death, to bee so maliciously set, to make such poore shifts for my readier dispatch, and to burden me with those backe reckeninges: I tooke such courage, and was so bolde, that the Iudges then did much maruaile at my stoutnesse, and thinking to bring doune my great heart, told me plainly, that I was in farther perill, then wherof I was aware, and sought therupon to take aduauntage of my words, and to bring me in daunger by all meanes possible. And after long debating with me, they willed me at any hand to submit my selfe to the holy Father, and the deuout Colledge of Cardinalles. For otherwise there was no remedie. With that beeing fully purposed, not to yeeld to any submission, as one that little trusted their colourable deceipt: I was as ware as I could bee, not to vtter any thing for mine owne harme, for feare I shoulde come in their daunger. For then either should I haue dyed, or els haue denyed both openly and shamefully, the knowne trueth of Christ and his Gospell. In the ende by Gods grace, I was wonderfully deliuered, through plain force of the worthie *Romaines* (an enterprise heretofore in that sort neuer attempted) being then without hope of life, and much lesse of libertie. And now that I am come home, this booke is shewed me, and I desired to looke vpon it, to amend it where I thought meet. Amend it, quoth I? Nay, let the booke first amende it selfe, and make mee amendes. For surely I haue no cause to acknowledge it for my booke, because I haue so smarted for it. For where I haue beene euill handled, I haue much a doe to shewe my self friendly. If the Sonne were the occasion of the Fathers imprisonment, would not the Father bee offended with him thinke you? Or at the least, would he not take heede how hereafter he had to doe with him? If others neuer get more by bookes then I haue done: it were better be

126. G. ROBINSON Wilson, T. *The arte of rhetorique.* 1585
STC 25806 Tanner 786 Sig. A5r

Gelasius a learned man was chosen Bisshopp of Roome the yeare after Christ 493. And therfore it is easely to be seene that their transubstantiation was not inuẽted in his time, neither yet receiued into the Church of God, as may manifestly appere in his wrytinges.

transubstantiated into the naturall bodie of Iesus Christ.

I Gelasius Pope of Rome do in no wise allowe of your transubstantiation: for I will neuer goe frõ that which I haue written against Eutiches and Nestorius the Hereticks in this sorte. The Sacraments of the body and blood of Iesus Christ which wee receiue, are diuine things. Wherfore, we are by them, made partakers of the diuine nature, and yet the substaunce of bread and wine remayning still. And surely, the similitude and likenesse of the bodie and blood of Christ are celebrated in the action of the misteries. Wherefore wee euidently vnderstand what it is that we are to feele and taste in Iesus Christ our Lord.

This venerable Bede is not altogether popish, because he beleeueth not their transubstantiation.

I venerable Bede, will not receiue your transubstantiation, for I wil not go from that which I haue written vppon the 22. Chapter of Sainct Luke, in this sorte. It was the will of Iesus Christ to put the Sacrament of his flesh and blood, vnder rhe figure of bread & wine, in stead of the flesh and blood of the Lambe, because he would shewe himself to be the self same to whom the Lorde had sworne that he would not repent him, Thou art an hie Priest for euer.

How euer the matter is, this Frier hath written well in this point,

I Durhumarus a Frier of Sainct Benets order, doth no whit allow your transubstantiation: For I wil not go from that which I haue commented vppon S. Mathewe, saying thus.

Wine

127. R. ROBINSON I Bèze, T. de *The popes canons*. 1585
STC 2029 Syn 8.58.118 (CUL) Sig. B4v

beautifull,comly nor heauenly, then vertue her selfe. And therefore employ your selfe alwaies to the ayding and relieuing of such as be vertuous. It is no wonder therefore, that I haue here attempted to offer both my selfe and my labours to your highnes. For where could I finde in all Italy any one Patron beside, that delighteth in learning? And that can either vnderstand and Iudge of a verse when it is brought vnto him? O most corrupt and lamentable times. What speake you of a Prince whose discretion consists all in deputie? and hath neither eye nor tongue of his owne? Giue me such a one as is able of himselfe to discerne right from wrong to whom no flattering merchant dares say that the Crowe is white, or the Swanne blacke. Sith such a one doth all men account your grace (most mightie and renoumed Prince) I haue boldely presumed to come vnto you and so much the more, because Antonius Musa Brasauolus, a man of singular learning and wisedome, and one that faithfully honoreth your highnes, perswaded me thereunto, in wonderfull commending your graces learning and wisedome, clemencie and bounty, whose wordes I credit aboue all others. By his persuasion therefore, this labor of mine called the Zodiake of life digested in twelue bookes, and many yeares in framing, I present, giue and offer to your excellencie, to the end your name may be the more famous and renoumed hereafter. And though your worthines deserue, to be presented with a farre more precious Iewel: I trust your grace will not disdaine this simple and slender gift, esteeming more the minde of the giuer, then the value of the thing, nor doubting but if this boke may, vnder your graces protection passe abroade, it shall easily finde fauour at the handes of Godly and learned men, especially of such as shall succeede our age. For the

Iudgement

128. R. ROBINSON 2 Palingenius, M. *The zodiake of life*. 1588
STC 19152 Douce P.P.249 Sig. ¶3v

This thou ſeeſt,and ſure I do know,it grieues thee to ſee this,
Though they cal thee tyrant,though ſo thou iuſtly be called,
Though thy nature paſſe *Buſiris* beaſtly behauiour:
For what makes me to mourne, may cauſe thee to yeelde to my mour-
One rude rock,one wind,& one tempeſtuous outrage (ning:
Batters,breaks,and beats my ſhip to the quickſands.
Our harms are equal,thy ſhipwrack like to my ſhipwrack,
Loue did loue *Phillis*,*Phillis* was lou'd of *Amintas*,
Phillis loues dearling,*Phillis* dearling of *Amintas*,
Dearling,crowne,garland,hope,ioy,wealth,health of *Amintas*,
And what more ſhal I ſay?for I want words fit for *Amintas*.
  And thou churliſh ground,now ceaſe any more to be fruitful,
Ceaſe to be deckt with flowres,and al in greene to be mantled,
Thy flowre is withered,my garland latelie decaied,
Phillis thine and mine with death vntimelie departed,
Whoſe ſweet corps thou bar'ſt,whoſe footſteps in thee be printed,
And whoſe face thou didſt admire for beautie renowmed.
Belch out roaring blaſts with gaping iawes to the heauens,
That thoſe roaring blaſts may ſcoure by the skies,by the heauens,
And foule ſtrugling ſtorms caſt downe fro the cloudes,fro the heauens,
For ſuch foule weather wil beſt agree with a mourner.
Howle and mourne thou earth,and roare with an horrible outcrie,
Howle as then thou didſt,when mountains were to the mountains
Put,by thy curſed brood,to be climing vp to *Olympus*,
When great flakes of fire came flaſhing downe fro the heauens,
When thy crawling ſons came tumbling downe from *Olympus*.
  Howle as Ladie *Ceres* did then,when prince of *Auernus*
Stole her daughter away from fields that ioined on *Ætna*,
Vnto the dungeons dark,and dens of his helliſh abiding.
Thou ground,forgetful what was by duetie required,
Should'ſt ſend vnbidden,with *Phillis*,teares to *Auernus*.
Her bleſſed burden thou waſt vnworthie to carie,
Therefore tender girle in flowring age ſhe departed.
O frowning fortune,ô ſtars vnluckilie ſhining,
O curſed birth daie of quite forſaken *Amintas*.
Phillis,alas,is changd,*Phillis* conuerted in aſhes,
Whoſe pretie lips,necke,eies,and haire ſo ſweetlie beſeeming,
Purple,ſnow,and fire,and gold wire ſeemd to reſemble.

129. R. ROBINSON 3 Tasso, T. *The lamentations of Amyntas*. 1589
STC 25118.6 Bliss A.84 Sig. B4r

people. This hath bene answered pag.45. Also *they are made in nubibus* (say they) but if these factioners had not made their owne ministers in *tenebris*, they might with lesse impudencie haue blamed the making of ours. *Besides* they say, that *at her maiesties entrance vnto the crowne our ministers were set ouer the people without an outvvard calling.* Wherein I will not oppose the ministerie of Luther and Caluin, whose ministerie they cannot deny to be warrantable, pag. 53. of their booke, and yet they had not a better calling then our men had; but I dare auouch the calling of our men vnto the ministerie at the entring in of her maiestie vnto the crowne, to be the selfe same that euen our aduersaries haue warranted, pag. 59. of the aforesaid treatise, viz. the magistrate did send them to instruct the vnbeleeuers: but (say they) *they vvere no ministers vnto them.* Then let them tell vs what other ministerie this might be, and what warrant they haue for it in the word, or else they giue vs iust cause to complaine that they are filled with conceites.

Confer.with Spering.

Now the gouernement vnder the which they execute their ministerie is such, that master Caluin acknowledgeth the antiquitie thereof to be great, and saith that it was in vse before the time of Papacie, and the vse thereof to be good, viz. *ad disciplinæ conseruationem,* for the vpholding of discipline, and for the auoyding of confusion. *But* master *Barrow* saith, that *the Queene and Parliament do vvickedly in giuing this authoritie vnto the Bishops, vvhich they haue committed vnto them:* the same is published by his owne procurement vnto the view of all men, who reading it, and considering of it, may see the dealings of master *Barrow*, I say no more. *But* to make an end with this Argument, notwithstanding all the exceptions afore said, the Church of England

Instit.lib.4. sect.4.

Conf.with Sper.pag.10.

To the moſt Noble Erle of Leyceſter.

Nowynge youre Honor amongſt other your good delyghtes, to delyght moſte in reading of Hyſtories, the true Image and portrature of Mans lyfe, and that not as many doe , to paſſe away the tyme, but to gather thereof ſuch iudgement and knowledge as you may therby be the more able, as well to direct your priuate actions, as to giue Counſell lyke a moſt prudent Counſeller in publyke cauſes, be it matters of warre, or peace: I that haue no other meane to ſhewe my thankfull mynde towardes your Honor from tyme to tyme,but with yncke and Paper: thought I coulde not wryte of anye thing more pleaſing, or more gratefull,than of thoſe preceptes that belong to the order

A.ij. of

131. W. SERES 1a Blundville, T. *The true order and methode.* 1574
STC 3161 55.C.223 Sig. A2r

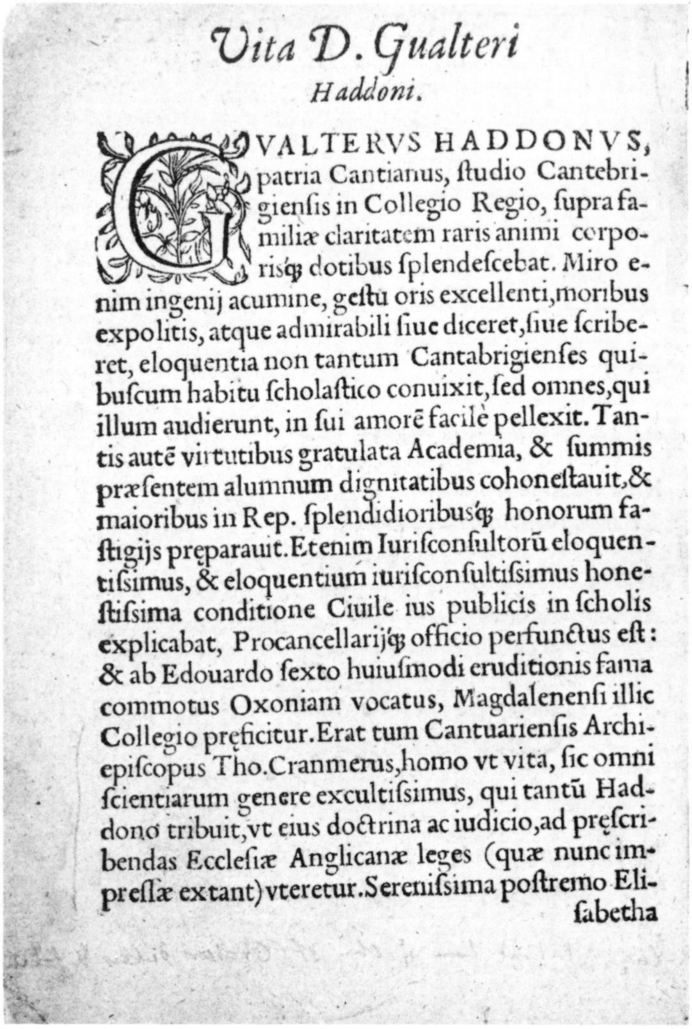

Vita D. Gualteri
Haddoni.

GVALTERVS HADDONVS, patria Cantianus, ſtudio Cantebrigienſis in Collegio Regio, ſupra familiæ claritatem raris animi corporisq; dotibus ſplendeſcebat. Miro enim ingenij acumine, geſtu oris excellenti, moribus expolitis, atque admirabili ſiue diceret, ſiue ſcriberet, eloquentia non tantum Cantabrigienſes quibuſcum habitu ſcholaſtico conuixit, ſed omnes, qui illum audierunt, in ſui amorē facilè pellexit. Tantis autē virtutibus gratulata Academia, & ſummis præſentem alumnum dignitatibus cohoneſtauit, & maioribus in Rep. ſplendidioribusq; honorum faſtigijs preparauit. Etenim Iuriſconſultorū eloquentiſsimus, & eloquentium iuriſconſultiſsimus honeſtiſsima conditione Ciuile ius publicis in ſcholis explicabat, Procancellarijq; officio perfunctus eſt: & ab Edouardo ſexto huiuſmodi eruditionis fama commotus Oxoniam vocatus, Magdalenenſi illic Collegio pręficitur. Erat tum Cantuarienſis Archiepiſcopus Tho. Cranmerus, homo vt vita, ſic omni ſcientiarum genere excultiſsimus, qui tantū Haddono tribuit, vt eius doctrina ac iudicio, ad pręſcribendas Eccleſiæ Anglicanæ leges (quæ nunc impreſſæ extant) vteretur. Sereniſsima poſtremo Eliſabetha

132. W. SERES 1b Haddon, W. *Poematum . . . libri duo.* 1576
STC 12597 11409a28 (BL) Sig. A2v

When hollie and deuout religious men,
Are at their beads,tis hard to draw them thence,
So ſweet is zealous contemplation.

Enter Rich.with two biſhops a loſte.

Maior. See where he ſtands between two clergie men.
Buck. Two props of vertue for a chriſtian Prince,
To ſtaie him from the fall of vanitie,
Famous Plantaganet,moſt gracious prince,
Lend fauorable eares to our requeſt,
And pardon vs the interruption
Of thy deuotion and right Chriſtian zeale,
Glo. My Lord,there needs no ſuch apologie,
I rather do beſeech you pardon me,
Who earneſt in the ſeruice of my God,
Neglect the viſitation of my friends,
But leauing this,what is your graces pleaſure?
Buck. Euen that I hope which pleaſeth God aboue,
And all good men of this vngouerned ile.
Glo. I do ſuſpect I haue done ſome offence,
That ſeemes diſgracious in the Citties eies,
And that you come to reprehend my ignorance,
Buck. You haue my Lord,would it pleaſe your grace
At our entreaties to amend that fault.
Glo. Elſe wherefore breath I in a Chriſtian land?
Buck. Then know it is your fault that you reſigne
The ſupreame ſeat,the throne maieſticall,
The ſceptred office of your aunceſtors,
The lineall glorie of your roiall houſe,
To the corruption of a blemiſht ſtocke;
Whilſt in the mildneſſe of your ſleepie thoughts,
Which here we waken to our countries good,
This noble Ile doth want her proper limbes,
Her face defac't with ſcars of infamie,
And almoſt ſhouldred in the ſwallowing gulph,
Of blind forgetfulneſſe and darke obliuion,
Which to recure we hartily ſolicit,
Your gratious ſelfe to take on you the ſoueraingtie thereof,
Not as Protector ſteward ſubſtitute,

Or

133. P. SHORT Shakespeare, W. *King Richard the third.* 1597
STC 22314 Malone 37 Sig. H1v

So long a growing,and ſo leiſurely,
That if this were a true rule, he ſhould be gratious.
Car. Why Madame, ſo no doubt he is.
Dut. I hope ſo too, but yet let mothers doubt.
Yor. Now by my troth if I had beene remembred,
I could haue giuen my Vnckles grace a flout,
That ſhould haue neerer toucht his growth then he did mine.
Dut. How my prety Yorke? I pray thee let me heare it.
Yor. Mary they ſay,my Vnckle grew ſo faſt,
That he could gnaw a cruſt at two houres olde:
Twas full two yeares ere I could get a tooth.
Granam this would haue beene a biting ieſt.
Dut. I pray thee prety Yorke who tolde thee ſo.
Yor. Granam his nurſe.
Dut. His nurſe: why ſhe was dead ere thou wert borne.
Yor. If twere not ſhe, I cannot tell who tolde me.
Qu. A perilous boy, go to, you are too ſhrewde.
Car. Good Madame be not angry with the childe.
Qu. Pitchers haue eares. *Enter Dorſet.*
Car. Here comes your ſonne, Lo: M. Dorſet.
What newes Lo: Marques?
Dor. Such newes my Lo: as grieues me to vnfolde.
Qu. How fares the Prince?
Dor. Well Madame, and in health.
Dut. What is thy newes then?
Dor. Lo: Riuers and Lo: Gray are ſent to Pomfret,
With them, Sir Thomas Vaughan, priſoners.
Dut. Who hath committed them?
Dor. The mighty Dukes, Glocester and Buckingham.
Car. For what offence.
Dor. The ſumme of all I can, I haue diſcloſed:
Why, or for what, theſe nobles were committed,
Is all vnknowen to me my gratious Lady.
Qu. Ay me I ſee the downfall of our houſe,
The tyger now hath ceazd the gentle hinde:
Inſulting tyranny beginnes to iet,
Vpon the innocent and lawleſſe throane:
Welcome deſtruction, death and maſſacre,

I ſee

to ioyne hands with you in friendship, which now willingly breaketh forth into a flame, and displaieth it selfe vnto your sight; and if it shall please you to accept the same, you shal henceforth find me as forward to shew my selfe gratefull, as at this time, I am desirous you should gratifie mee in this action. To these *Lucilla* bowed hir selfe, and *Eliosto* proceeded. Since thē matter is to be vnfolded between friends, I need not vse any glozing phrase, flowers of Rhetoricke, or colours of eloquence; thou knowest, gentle *Lucilla*, how difficult it is to loue, and how much difficult not to loue: Is the iron faulty, because it cleaueth to the forcible Adamant? the needle because it is drawne by the vertue of the Loadstone? gold, in that it cannot withstand the hidden strength of the Chrysocol? or the rush, because it moueth to the jeate or Amber? or is flesh and blood to be blamed, because subiect to Beautie? No, no, gentle *Lucilla*: It is the attractiue " force of flowering beautie, which bewitcheth the wisest, " enchanteth the seuerest, curseth Sobriety from her Court, " & dislodgeth Vertue from her castle. The conquerd must " obey by constraint: for me to striue against the streame, is " furie; to beare a saile against the wind, frenzie. Wherefore exiling all mistrust, from the bottome of mine heart, I wil briefly display vnto thee the whole shrine of my secrets; then will I vnfolde both our ensuing profits, and also the meanes of eschewing our perill. I loue my mother *Cleodora*, neither is the fault (if any fault be) to be fathered by me, but by Fortune, who holdeth the helme or stearne of al humane life. I was not earst acquainted with mothers manners, nor initiated in the elements of her country curtesies. I thought that womens eies had euer beene true embassadours of their hearts, I tooke their lookes for their sutors, and their glaunces to be tokens of their speciall good-wil: alas, herein I failed in my physiognomie; for noting *Cleodora* often sweetely to smile on me, and gathering thereby (as I thought) infallible signes of her fauour towards my selfe: and on the other side, supposing that I should shewe my selfe to be but of a very cold constitution, in that I could not loue, or prooue

H my

135. V. SIMMES 1b Hind, J. *Eliosto libidinoso.* 1606
STC 13509 Malone 674 Sig. H1r

most monstrous lying,may pay the one with the other. In sound learning and religion, that must stand in summe which best agreeth with scripture for the same times: otherwise Greekes disagree for ech kings yeeres.

The Nobles of Iuda, that touch principally the booke of Daniel.

IN sundrie partes and sundrie maners spake God of Redemption to the fathers, before the dayes of *David*: and to him he promised that his seed should sit vpon a throne for euer. That speech was fit to allure all men vnto searching of the spirituall kingdome. But the carnall still vnderstood that carnally. The ten tribes despised it, and went to Ohelehem, and Elohehem, to their owne tents and Gods. *Salomons* house hoped to hold still that outward kingdome, and would not beleeue otherwise, the most of them, till the Chaldean tooke away, and ouerthrew all their state. VVhen the visible kingdome fell, all Iuda was to be resolued what should become of *Davids* throne. The whole booke of *Daniel* is a satisfaction for that perplexitie, and cleare, being considered for that point, how *Salomons* house being extinct in *Iechoniah*, the house of *Nathan*, from *Salathiel*, *Pedaiah*, and * *Zorobabel*, come to be heires of the kingdome. But as the kingdome of Christ first suffers and hath glorie after; so they and their faithfull shall be conformed. Babel, the Medes with Elam, and Greekes, whole and parted, shall rob them: but they shall possesse a kingdome for euer and euer. And when the seuentie yeeres of Babels rage giue a taste of Gods defence and reuenge, they are tolde of that celestiall speech, how at seuen times that space, the most holy will bring an eternall kingdome opened for all.

*For Zorobabels house, the onely then true and right princes, of all the world, Daniel hath his reuelations, and his 490. yeares are to be compared with their liues in two families.

There-

136. G. SIMSON Broughton, H. *Daniel his Chaldie visions.* 1597
STC 3853 (=2786) 4° B.27.Th Sig. B4r

theſe I cannot juſtly ſay, therefore I forbeare to ſet it downe. When we were come to Theobalds, wee vnderſtood his Mageſtie to bee within the compaſſe of three quarters of a mile of the houſe, at which tidings wee deuided our ſelues into three parts, each one taking a place of ſpeciall note, to ſee what memorable accidents might happen within his compaſſe, one ſtanding at the vpper end of the walke, the ſecond at the vpper end of the firſt court, the third at the ſecond court dores and we had made choice of a gentleman of good ſort, to ſtand in the court that leads into the hall, to take notice what was done or ſaid by his highneſſe to the Nobilitie of our land, or ſaide or done by them to his Mageſtie, and to let vs vnderſtand of it, all which accidents as they hapned in their ſeuerall places, you ſhall heare in as few words as may be. Thus then for his Mageſties comming vp the walke, ther came before his Mageſtie ſome of the Nobilitie, ſome Barons, Knights, Eſquires, Gentlemen and others, amongſt whom was the Shriefe of Eſſex, and the moſt of his men, the trumpets ſounding next before his highneſſe, ſometimes one ſometimes another, his Mageſtie riding not continually betwixt the ſame two; but ſometimes one ſometimes another, as ſeemed beſt to his highneſſe, the whole Nobilitie of our land and Scotland round about him, obſeruing no place of ſuperiotie, all bare-headed, all whom alighted from their horſes, at their entrance into the firſt court, ſaue onely his Mageſtie alone, who rid along ſtill, foure Noble men laying their hands vpon his ſteed, two before and two behind, in this manner hee came, till hee was come to the court dore where my ſelfe ſtoode, where hee alighted from his horſe, from whom hee had not gone ten princely paces, but there was deliuered him a petition by a yong gentleman, his Mageſtie returning him this gracious anſwere, that he ſhould bee heard and haue juſtice.

At the entrance into that court ſtood many noble men, amongſt whom was Sir *Robert Cecil*, who there meeting his Mageſtie conducted him into his houſe, all which was practiſed with as great applauſe of the people as could bee, hartie

137. T. SNODHAM I Savile, T. *King James his entertainment*. 1603
STC 21784 8° T.27.Art Seld Sig. B1r

Reply vnto Mr. Ainſworths *Anſwer to this ſixt Likelihood.*

Page 159.

Reply.

THis Likelihood, which I haue propounded and confirmed in my former Booke, from Page 32. to 42. and haue preuented many obiections, alledged ſome teſtimonies of it, and eſpecially *George Iohnſons* Booke, he wholly (in a manner) paſſeth ouer with ſilence, onely vnder pretence of his Anſwere made alreadie vnto Mr. *Sprint*, vrging more prudently, as he ſaith, this ſame Likelihood; to which he putteth ouer his Reader, who muſt goe ſeeke an Anſwere to what I ſay, and as I doe affirme it, where it is not to be found: a prettie euaſion if he could ſo eſcape.

Mr. *Ainſworth* paſſeth by the inſtances giuen of Gods iudgement againſt them, for that he can not anſwere them.

The truth is my Likihood, and Reaſons, are not ſo ſet downe in Mr. *Sprints* Conſiderations, as I here vrge it. So although Mr. *Ainſworth* anſwere him, which is queſtionable, yet he hath not made anſwere to what I ſay. But he is wiſe to paſſe that by, which he wel knew (being ſo laid open, as it is in my Booke) he could neuer make particular anſwer vnto, but with great and publike ſhame in the particulars.

I deſire the Reader to peruſe my former Booke, and conſider, whether it be not very likely, that God hath been offended greatly with their courſe: and with the chiefe of them from the very beginning of the firſt knowne man, to the laſt principall Ring-leader of the lateſt out-road of ſuch Separatours.

Obiection.

If he ſhould ſay vnto me, as hee doth vnto another in Page of his Booke 38. that we doe bring in mens perſons againſt the Cauſe of Chriſt, I would anſwere him, that I bring not man againſt Chriſt, but Gods fearefull hand, that is, euen God himſelfe againſt men running in a By-path, which by his iudgements he diſclaimeth to be his: Gods puniſhments are not mans work or word, but Gods witneſſe and teſtimonie againſt them.

Anſwer.

138. T. SNODHAM 2 Bernard, R. *Plaine evidence.* 1610
STC 1958 4135a14 (BL) Sig. M2r

the burdens, reproches and punishments of our nature, did humble himselfe to the death of the crosse; the Diuinitie in the meane while (according to *Irenæus*) resting or hiding it selfe, that he might be crucified, and die.

The other, of exaltation, whereby after his death, his humane nature did lay aside all the infirmities of his humane nature (but not the essentiall properties) and was wonderfully exalted aboue all creatures vnto most great honor, yet not in any case matched, and equalled to the diuine nature of Christ[a]. *a Phil. 2. 7. 9.*

What are the doctrines contrary to this?

The 1. heresie of *Macedonius* and *Valentinus*, who affirmed that Christ brought with him a celestiall body from heauen: as also of *Apelles*, who said his bodie was ayrie, his flesh starlike, and that he passed from the virgin as water from a pipe.

2. Of the Manichees, who fained vnto him an imaginarie bodie.

3. Of *Apollinaris*, who denied that Christ did assume a reasonable soule, but that his Diuinitie was vnto him in stead of his mind.

4. Of *Eunomius*, who affirmed Christ to be a meere man, and that he was called the sonne of God by adoption: and of *Ebion*, who said that Christ was borne by humane generation.

5. Of *Nestorius*, who taught, that as there be two natures in Christ, so there are two persons; and that the Diuinitie is present with the humanitie by *circumstance and combination, but not by personall vnion. Therfore he denied that *Marie* was *the mother of God, or brought forth God: and affirmed that man, not God, was crucified of the Iewes. *παράστασις. *θεοτόκος.

6. *Eutyches* heresie contrary to the former: for he taught, that the humane nature after the vnion, was endued with the proprieties of the Diuinitie.

7. Of the Manichees, who auouched that Christ had but one onely will, not two, a diuine and humane will.

8. Of the Vbiquitaries, who attribute to the humanitie of Christ the essentiall properties of the Diuinitie, altogether forgetting that saying, *He that taketh away the proprieties, taketh away the nature:* and on the contrary, *He that attributeth the proprieties, attributeth the*

139. G. & L. SNOWDEN Bucanus, G. *Institutions of Christian religion.* 1606
STC 3961 Vet.A.2.133 Sig. C4r

Summer. I muſt giue credit vnto what I heare;
For other then I heare, attract I nought.

Harueſt. I, I, nought ſeeke, nought haue: an ill huſband is the firſt ſteppe to a knaue. You obiect I feede none at my boord. I am ſure, if you were a hogge, you would neuer ſay ſo: for, ſurreuerence of their worſhips, they feed at my ſtable, table, euery day. I keepe good hoſpitality for hennes & geeſe; Gleaners are oppreſſed with heauy burdens of my bounty. They rake me, and eate me to the very bones, till there be nothing left but grauell and ſtones, and yet I giue no almes, but deuoure all. They ſay when a man cannot heare well, you heare with your harueſt eares: but if you heard with your harueſt eares, that is, with the eares of corne, which my almes-cart ſcatters, they would tell you, that I am the very poore mans boxe of pitie, that there are more holes of liberality open in harueſts heart, then in a ſiue, or a duſt-boxe. Suppoſe you were a craftsman, or an Artificer, and ſhould come to buy corne of mee, you ſhould haue buſhels of mee, not like the Bakers loafe, that ſhould waygh but ſixe ounces, but vſury for your mony, thouſands for one: what would you haue more? Eate mee out of my apparell, if you will, if you ſuſpect mee for a miſer.

Summer. I credit thee, and thinke thou wert beliede.
But tell mee, hadſt thou a good crop this yeare?

Harueſt. Hay, Gods plenty, which was ſo ſweete and ſo good, that when I ierted my whip, and ſaid to my horſes but Hay, they would goe as they were mad.

Summer. But hay alone thou ſaiſt not; but hay-ree.

Harueſt. I ſing hay-ree, that is, hay and rye: meaning, that they ſhall haue hay and rye their belly-fulls, if they will draw hard; So wee ſay, wa, hay, when they goe out of the way: meaning, that they ſhall want hay, if they will not doe as they ſhould doe.

Summer. How thriue thy oates, thy barley, and thy wheate?

Harueſt. My oates grew like a cup of beere that makes the brewer rich: my rye like a Caualier, that weares a huge feather

in

140. S. STAFFORD Nash, T. *Summers last will and testament.* 1600
STC 18376 Malone 212(5) Sig. E3v

our Repentance, Cries and Prayers, shall cause that lamentable Schisme to cease, being one of the greatest Plagues that euer happned or could happen among Christians. Your Highnesse shal see by marking that which I haue here compiled out of them and their writings, how the difficultie of reconciliation for a great part of our controuersies, whether it be with the East or South Churches, or between our selues of the Westerne Churches, lies not so much in the things themselues which fall in question, as in the peruerse opinion of the disputants: and that those things wherein we agree, are a thousand times of more importance, to the glorie of God, and our saluation, then those things wherein we varie and disagree; and shall haue farre more reason to loue vs for those things wherein we agree, then for to hate and persecute vs cruelly for those things, which remaine as yet to be auoided from among vs: yea seeing the greater part of our disputations, happen for want of vnderstanding the state of the controuersies in question; or els by reason of our termes and fashion of speaking: but farre more for want of conceiuing the true sense of the holy Scripture; which also some great men of our time haue shewed manifestly, in certain points of doctrine, which were iudged irreconcileable: wherein was manifested Gods iustice against our sinnes of presumption, curiosity, vaine-glory, enuie, auarice and ambition. I say the more, because Princes and Soueraigne Magistrates should beare sole authority, and by their absolute commaundement should testifie their good will therein, and employ the prudent aduise of their Ecclesiasticall subiects, not the wisest onely, but the best and godliest also, not so much to dispute and winne the victory, as to conferre, and amiably to agree: The God of peace will giue the fruit of peace, to his glory and our good. But I know not by what Inchantment or destinie, Kings for the most part know not their forces, and willingly do dispoyle themselues of a greate part of their owne Authoritie, and many times perceiue it too late. As for the particulars, many doe know and see the euill, but doe perswade themselues, that the remedie is most dangerous of all: or else

for

141. W. STANSBY Eudes, M. *Catholique traditions.* 1609
STC 10561 A.6.1.Linc Sig. A3r

CLARISSIMO VIRO D. GERARDO MERCATORI, RVPELMVNDANO, PHILOSOPHO ET MATHEMATICO illustri: ac amico suo longè charissimo IOANNES DEE LONDINENSIS. S. D. P.

VNDECIMVS iam agitur annus (humanissime, doctissimeq;, mi GERARDE) ab illo, quo nostris ego relictis Academijs, omnibusq; nostrarū scholarum, in artium septem (liberaliū dictarū) professione, percursis ordinibus: sine subere (vt in prouerbio est) nare: & in Regiones transmarinas cœperam peregrinari: ad ipsos inuestigandos fontes, à quibus hac nostra ætate, plurimi ad nos optimarum quarumq; Artium deducebātur canaliculi: & cum illis vitam ducere familiarem, quorum vel leuissimus quisq; vnius diei in scribendo, labor, nobis antea domi desidentibus, per anni ferè vnius spatium, satis (ad intelligendum) faceret negotii. Atq; in isto primæ meæ peregrinationis inchoato cursu, quoniam in te, primum omnium, Louanii tum agentem, incidere, maximo mihi summi Numinis obtigit fauore: & ex tuis mecū disceptationibus, tum primas tū altissimas vt radices ageret tota mea peregrina philosophādi ratio: Nūc proinde Ego esse æquū censeo, rationiq; maximè consentaneū, vt iam primò peregrinantes, laborū etiam tu meorum primitias, iure tibi vendices meritissimo. Et maximè, cum mutuæ nostræ amicitiæ, familiaritatisq; cōsuetudo ea erat, toto vt triennio, vix totos tres simul dies, alter alterius lubens careret aspectu: & ea vtriusque nostrûm discendi, philosophandiq; auiditas, vt postquā conuenniremus, tribus vix horę minutis, ab arduarum & vtilissimarum rerum indagatione abstineremus, An non huius nostrę tam sinceræ amicitiæ, & tam suauiter continuatę philosophandi rationis, gratia, aliquod saltem συνταγμα, vel monumentum, sempiternæ hominum memoriæ commendare debuimus: vt inde

✠i uauissi-

142. H. SUTTON Dee, J. *De praestantioribus*. . . . 1558
STC 6463 Ashm. 153(2) Sig. *1r

ledge disclosed in this pamphlet, then with rash & preiudiciall iudgment nothing hurtfull to the Author but redownding to his own reproch, to condemn it. All knoledge and arts rising first in the East amongst the Children of God, as by his secreat meanes reuealed vnto thē were by the painful toile of man diriued from cuntrie to cuntrie, from Nat ion to Nation. For Greece it selfe, whoshortly after became the storehouse of the highest misteries, attributelh the first receiued grounds to the hard trauail iuto Egipt of that diuine Plato. Rome eke was not smally inriched by her Orator, who seemed to spoil that famous Athens of her peculier eloquence, as witnessed the outcrie of Appolonius rapt in admiratiō, astonied, & sory, saiyng: O Tulli, as with wonder I praise thee, so lament I the fortune of the Greeks, sith that lerniug and eloquence which only was left vs, is now to Rome transported by thee. Herein as Nations began to grow, so began they to cōceiue a stately opinion of them selues ioyned with a maner contempt of others that lacked the knowledg they had. The Iewes called all other Gentils: The Grecians & Romans vsing a more reprochfull terme scorned the rest as Barbarous. The Italians euen at this day (a people in whom as yet lie raked the old sparks of the Romayn glory) call vs on this side the Alps, Tramontani: noting therby in vs the lack of ciuilitie & of their cuntry curtesy, thinking that nurture hath not yet crept ouer those wast huge hills. Thus see we by little & litle how knowledg crept to places erst vnkown: Yet for we are (as pretely noteth the Poet) seuered from the world, It is thought that common knowledges came later to vs then to others our neighbors, for our farther distance from the places where arts first sprang. But for the feats of chilualry and proper aduancements thereof, It is well knownthat this our Cuntry may compare with those who therin think themselues most victorious. For perdy their growing fame first grew by him out of whose loines the English Nation sprang. The sonns of Ebrancus the fift King from Brute sailyng into Germany, vnder

der

143. R. TOTTEL Legh, G. *The accedens of armory.* 1591
STC 15391 Douce C.215 Sig. A5r

Pſal.19.b.8. aut ſapientes inſtruunt, ſed rudem & integrum diſcipulum, cum excipiant, ex puero ſapientem reddũt:
a.Tim.3.d.15. Hinc illa Pauli ad Timotheum cum gratulatione coniuncta commonefactio, Permane (inquit) in his
quæ didiciſti & quæ tibi cõcredita ſunt ſciens à quo didiſceris, téque à puero ſacras literas nouiſſe quæ
a.Pet.1.d.21. te poſſunt ſapientem reddere in ſalute. En ſapientiæ conſequendæ expedita ratio, & via, ſapientiæ in-
quam, non ſeculi huius, nec à principibus huius mundi ingenijs nec ab opibus aut potentia præſtanti-
bus viris inuentæ & allatæ, ſed quam acti à Spiritu ſancto loquuti ſunt ſancti Dei homines : eámque
eiuſmodi quæ non ſit ſine aliqua acceſsione manca, ſed omnibus ſuis numeris abſoluta atque perfecta.
2.Tim.1.d.26. Quod vtrúmque mirabili compendio complexus Paulus, Tota inquit ſcriptura diuinitus inſpirata &
vtilis ad doctrinam, ad redargutionem, ad correctionem, ad inſtitutionem quæ eſt in Iuſtitia, vt perfe-
ctus ſit homo Dei ad omne opus bonum perfectè inſtructus. Hoc de ſcripturę & veritate, & perfectione
Apoſtolico teſtimonio quid illuſtrius eſſe poteſt? Vis non hominibus, qui fallere poſſunt ſed Deo qui
ipſe veritas eſt, in veritate perſcrutanda, & edicenda operam dare? Sacris literis operam dato: Vis vt
Eccleſiam Dei paſcas, omnes tanti muneris partes perfectè aſſequi? in Sacris literis totus acquieſcens
ex illis ſolis ſapito. Multa de Dei omnipotentia, ſumma ſapientia, bonitate, iuſtitia & miſericordia:
multa de eius cultu & veneratione docenda erunt: multa quæ ab hominibus impijs & ignorantibus cõ-
tra veritatis regulam adferuntur refellenda: multa quę ad prauos & ingenitos mores corrigendos, multa
quæ ad bonos inſtituendos pertineant, monenda & inculcanda: ſed Sacras literas omnia hæc abundè
ſuppeditare homini Dei res fideliter agenti, hoc de Dei verbo eiuſque præſtantia ac vbertate Paulinum
iudicium luculenter teſtatur. Vnde colligere eſt ſcripturam illam Sanctam, Theſaurum quendam lo-
cupletiſsimum eſſe, qui omnes diuinæ ſapientiæ diuitias contineat, quoque nobis aperto ad ſummum
bonum vitámque beatam, omnia ſuppetere certum ſit.

Sed quia alia eſt ratio Theſauri expoſiti, exponendi verò alia, factum eſt vt in Eccleſia, id eſt Dei
domo, cui fruendus totus conceditur, non vno tantum ordine diſpoſitus appareat. Loculis multis con-
ſtat: hic vitæ piæ & ſanctæ doctrinæ ſummam aliquam conditã conſeruat: Ille adulterinæ erroneæque
refutationem continet: ex alio vitæ impurioris emendationem, ex alio ſanctitatis & pietatis inſtitutionem depromere poteris: Denique vt vitæ beatæ partes & officia diſtincta vides, ſic eo Theſauro di-
ſtinctum latet, quod eorum cuique conuenit. Sed hæc diſtinctio in ſacris Biblijs minus aperte conſpi-
cua eſt, vbi iſte Theſaurus non diſponitur, ſed exponitur: & perinde ac in telonio cum aliqua pecunia
ſoluenda eſt, permiſcetur. Ea enim œconomia & Prophetis & Apoſtolis ferè perpetua eſt vt tanquam
gregi Domini debitores, has diuitias illi liberaliter numerent, nulla diuerſorum generum temeraria
confuſione, ſed doctrinæ, exhortationis, admonitionis, & reprehenſionis opportuna cõiunctione. Talis
huius ſacri Theſauri in ſacris Biblijs expoſiti ratio eſt.

At verò vt in ærario congerendo, tum ad ornatum ſplendoris, tum ad oportunitatem collocatio-

144. T. VAUTROLLIER 1a Marlorat, A. *Propheticae, et apostolicae*. 1574
STC 17409 A.9.a.8Th Sig. *2v(top)

OF those six reasons, whereby I take the great vse of this Elementarie to be vnfalliblie confirmed, the first is, bycause it doth season the tender, & vntrained minde with the best & sweetest liquor. Which that it doth, who will deny, whē he shal euidentlie se, nothing to be propoūded therein, but that, which is most pure & picked? *Plato Aristotle* & *Quintiliā* tho not theie alone, in those places of their fortrain, wheretheie wish a childe, that is to be brought vp well, neither to hear, nor to read, nor to se anie thing at all in his teaching kinde, & of set purpos, but onelie that which is most agreable in opinion with truth, in behauiour with vertew: by that their so saing declare vnto vs the qualitie of those things, which ar best for childern to deall withall at first. And our own relligiō, which best knoweth of what importance it is, to haue youth embrewed with the best at the first, is meruellous carefull, both to win them to it by precept, and to work it in them by practis. For the necessitie of beginning at the best, in euerie argument, which hath a beginning, and is to procede by order, I shall not nede to saie much either for the good which it bringeth, or for the ill which it blemisheth. One *Theodorus* a plaier of Tragedies, belike such a one, as *Roscius* was at Rome both excellent men in that kinde of action, wold neuer let anie mean or vnskilfull actor enter the stage before him, as *Aristotle* reporteth, bycause he himself wold work the first delite, euen with the verie best, for that he knew the force of the first impressiō, which being laid with pleasur in the beholders minde wold cause them procede on with cōtinewāce in like pleasur, wheras sō vnswetenesse at the first might cause harshnes thoroughout. Wherein I note also (tho the first planting of best sciences be our gardning here) that by his so doing, he either enforced his fellowplaiers to be like to him, & so partakers of the praise: or else he alone bare awaie all the praise, as deseruing it alone. Could one *Theodorus* a Tragedie plaier espy that in the stage, which was somtime allowed as tolerable, outlawed somtime, as vnlawfull, & maie not a scholer spy the like in the course of learnīg, which is still vpō the stage, as most profitable still? When the childe shall haue the matter of his *Reading*, which is his first principle so well proined and so pikked, as it shall catechise him in relli-

Plato.2.3.Pol
Arist.7.8.Pol.
Quint.1 Inst.

Reading.

145. T. VAUTROLLIER 1b Mulcaster, R. *The first part of the Elementarie.* 1582
STC 18250 4° M.35.Art Sig. C3r

The Printer to the Reader.

ALthough it be well known, that neither the first writer of these Letters nowe by me printed, nor yet the Spaniard *Don Bernardin* to whome they are directed, had any desire to heare of any good successe to the state of England: as may appeare in the writer, by shewing him selfe grieued, to make any good report of England, other then of meere necessitie he was vrged: and in *Don Bernardin*, who was so impudent, or at the least, so blindly rash, as to disperse in print, both in French, Italian, and Spanish, most false reports of a victorie had by the Spaniards, euen when the victorie was notable on the part of England, and the Spanish vanquished: yet whilest I was occupied in the printing hereof, a good time after the letters were sent into Fraunce, there came to this Citie certaine knowledge, to all our great comfort, of sundrie happie Accidents, to the diminution of our mortall enemies in their famous Fleete, that was driuen out of our seas about the last of Iuly, towards the farthermost North partes of Scotland. Wherfore I haue thought it not amisse to ioine the same to this Lettre of *Don Bernardin*, that he may beware, not to be so hastie of himselfe, nor yet to permit one *Capella*, who is his common sower of reports, to write these false things for truthes.

The particularities wherofare these. The Fleete was by tempest driuen beyond the Isles of Orknay, about the first of August, which is now more then sixe weekes past, the place being aboue three score degrees from the North Pole: an vnaccustomed place for the yong Gallants of Spaine, that neuer had felt stormes on the sea, or cold weather in August. And about those North Islands, their mariners and souldiers died daily by multitudes: as by their bodies cast on land, did appeare. And after twentie dayes or more, hauing spent their time in miseries, they being desirous to returne home to Spaine, sayled very farre Southwestward into the Ocean to recouer Spaine. But the Almightie God, who alwayes auengeth the cause of his afflicted people which put their confidence in him, and bringeth downe his enemies that exalt them selues with pride to the heauens, or-

146. T. VAUTROLLIER 2 Leigh, R. *The copie of a letter*. 1588
STC 15412 Douce A.272 Sig. F1r

Matthewes hebrew Euangell, for that it was first written. So Sainct *Iohn*, a Græcian Prophete, writing to the Græcians, spake of *Matthewes* greek Euangel, and setteth it in the third order, for that it came after both *Markes* and *Lukes*. Sixtlie, the precise time of their firste writing, and occasion why they did write these foure Euangelles, agreeth with the history and time of the foure first Seales, where their first comming is mentioned. For first, when the word of God passed out on the white horse in the first seale, betwixt the yeare of Christ 29. and 36. then (saith the text) one of the four beasts said, *come and see, &c.* that is, *Matthew* the Apostle, who came that time, and wrote his first Euangel in hebrew, exhibiting the same to be seen of the *Iewes* expresly, for conuerting thē, that Gods word of his new couenant might victoriouslie go out among them, to conquer & ouercome (as saith the text) Then, in the second seale, when S. *Steuen* and S. *Iames* were martyred, and greate persecution rose against the Church of God, *viz.* betwixt the 36. and 43. year of Christ, then (saith the text) the second Beast saith, *Come and see*: that is, the second Euangel was at that time set forth by *Mark*, to be seen & read, in comfort of the afflicted Church. Afterward, in the third seale, when hunger and dearth arose, betwixt the 43. and 50. year of Christ, the third Beast saith, *Come and see*, and this is *Luke*, whose Euangell came to light at that time, and was set forth to be seen, and also writeth of the same dearth, in his booke of the Acts of the Apostles. Act. 11. 28 Lastly, in the fourth seale, when deadlie heresies arose against the Diuinitie of Christ, betwixt the 50. and 57. yeare of Christ. Then (saith the text) came the fourth Beast: and so indeed at that time did *Iohn* write the fourth Euangell, beginning at the description of Christs Diuinitie, expreslie against the said Heretiks. Seuenthly, these foure Beasts wings, eies, and all their other tokens and circumstances, contained both in *Ezechiels* Prophecie, and here in the *Reuelation*, doeth so properlie agree with the foure Euangelists, that they cannot be so conuenientlie attributed to anie other, as shal be shewed at length in the principall Treatise. Eightlie, it appeareth by *Hierome* and others learned, that these indices and tokens, so aptlie

agree-

147. R. WALDEGRAVE I Napier, J. *A plaine discouery of . . . Reuelation.* 1593
STC 18354 Mar. 182 Sig. C7r

To the ſixt reaſon.

Further then it hath bene corrupt by popiſhe Monkes, which were(for ſome yeares) th'ordinary Iaylers to keepe it within the priſon of their cloiſters:we accuſe it not of *partiality* to popery,wherevnto it could hardly be partiall,when popery was not,But ſure we are , that the Greek is leſſe *partiall*.Secondly they might tranſlate with purpoſe not to hurt the truth,and yet fail of the purpoſe : as appeareth manifeſtly in th'example of *promeriting of God*,not only barbarouſly , but falſly tranſlated . As touching the *ſinceritie*,*grauitie*, and *maieſtie* of it , compared with other tranſlations of later yeares: the matter is before the Iudg, where our no , is as good as your yea. but if it were,as you ſay:yet your trãſlating it , in paſſing by th'originall of the Greek,can by no meanes bee excuſed:but only by this , that not able to clime vp into the Scriptures in the Greeke and Hebrevv tongues ; you vvere compelled to ſeaze vppon the

148. R. WALDEGRAVE 2 Cartwright, T. *The answere to the preface.* 1602
STC 4716 Mason A.A.74 Sig. G1r

THE EPISTLE.

Then *Hector* fearce the *Phrigian* Prince,and *Alexander* great,
And *Iulius Cæſar* painyms all, their God they did forgeat:
For which,amid their moſt eſtate,when they were higheſt of all,
Ambicion, Pride, and Auarice, gaue each of them a fall.
Then *Arthur,Charle-mayne* and *Guy*, were chriſtians as I geſſe,
The one was plagde in his moſt pompe, for his laſciuiouſneſſe:
The other two were godly men,wherfore they dyed well,
As in their ſeuerall Hiſtories the Sequell plaine doth tell.
A briefe of all whoſe liues,I haue in meeter with my pen
Compiled out of ſundry bookes of famous learned men.
And as I read of them alſo,according to my skill,
I haue all their proportions depainted with my quill:
And drawne the armes and cogniſaunce in euery ſeuerall ſhield,
Which when they liued vpon the earth they bare vnto the field:
The yeare & time where they did raigne,and when & where they died,
And what they were enclined too, I haue herein diſcried:
Beſeeching that your honour wil accept in gentle part
This litle booke which I preſent,to ſhew my faithfull hart.
And when your leaſure ſo ſhall ſerue, vouchſafe I humbly craue,
To read it ouer once or twiſe,and where I erred haue,
That crime or fault committed ſo,let ignorance excuſe,
Blame not the man that meaneth well,but blame his ſimple Muſe.
Record the matter in your minde,although this ſtyle be baſe,
Then ſhall your Lordſhip plainly ſee before your preſent face,
A myrror of mans mortall life, by them compared right,
Which well may be a looking glaſſe,to euery liuing wight:
And chiefly to the higher ſort, whom God ſhall pleaſe t'aduaunce,
In any wiſe here vpon earth to rule or gouernaunce:
To learne therby to know the Lord, who liues eternally,
Not to forget their owne eſtates,through pride nor ſurquedry:
To abandon wicked vice away,and vertue to embrace,
That to their latter end they may run out a happy race.
Thus humbly I do take my leaue,and hartily do pray,
That God will graunt you *Neſtors* yeares, in vertues honour ay.

Your humble Seruant,
Richard Lloyd.

149. R. WARD I Lloyd, R. *A . . . discourse of . . . the nine worthies.* 1584
STC 16634 Malone 649 Sig. A3r

paſſes of treaſons came to be propounded, to the ende to be renewed and ſworne vnto in full aſſembly of our Eſtats, to aunſwere vs moſt impudently that he would not doe any thing, neither would ſweare thereto: but that if he tranſgreſſed we ſhould cauſe him to be puniſhed: and yet all this notwithſtanding, together with diuers others warninges of his driftes and dealinges, dayly giuen vs by our good, faithfull and loyall ſubiects and ſeruaunts, we paſſed ouer all theſe thinges quietly, as perſwading our ſelues that our great patience and benefites, wherein we ſpared not any one gratification that lay in our power, to them and theirs, would mollifie the hardneſſe of their hartes, and reduce them to their iuſt obedience due vnto vs, conſidering the fierceneſſe of Lyons, and other the moſt wild beaſtes is commonly tamed by benefites: but as the ambitious deſire to raigne is inſatiable and infinite, and that he that offendeth doth neuer forgiue: ſo theſe mens inſolencies daily increaſed, and by an expreſſe meſſenger whō the ſaid D. of Aumalle ſent vs vve were aduertiſed that himſelfe had bene preſent in perſon, but not in will (ſaid he) in a counſell holden at Paris, wherein it was reſolued that the Duke of Guiſe ſhould ſeaſe vpon our perſon and bring vs to Paris, which notwithſtanding, we would not vpon our firſt conſiderations haue ſuch reſpect to this aduice as we ōught: howbeit vpon the view of him whom ſince the aforeſaid D. of Mayenne ſent vnto vs, ſeeing alſo the terme ſo ſhort as there was no ſafetie for vs, but in the preuention of the liues of thoſe who ſought to take away ours, and to vſurpe our eſtate and Crowne: we were forced to vſe and practiſe vpon their perſons, not what through their treacherous felonie they deſerued, but according as the ſeaſon would beare that which we ought, yet would not haue done.

This was the recompence that they had prepared for our gratifications and benefites, and is at this day proſe-

150. R. WARD 2 Henry III (of France) *The French kinges declaration.* 1589
STC 13098.5 4° L.90.Art Sig. B3r

A prologue.

knowen from errour and falſhed, that
God thereby may be glorified, and the
godly reader hereof, be edified. And as
for thoſe men agaynſte whoſe folly and
errour this worke is attempted, I hartely deſyre of GOD the father of oure
Lorde Jeſus Chryſte, that it woulde
pleaſe hym of his infinite goodnes, to
haue mercy vppon them, and once to o-
pen the eyes of their vnderſtandynge,
ſo that they maye ſee theyr errour and
faute, and acknowledge the ſame: and
that they may nowe at the laſte be won
vnto the pure and ſincere trueth, wher-
vnto they ſo longe time haue bene vtter enemyes, that we altogether maye
be gathered into one ſhepefolde, vnder
one onely ſheepeheard Jeſus Chryſte,
whoſe holy ſpirite bee thy leader and
guyde (gentle reader) in the readynge
hereof. Amen.

Marueyle not gentle reader I deſyre thee,
that I haue put dovvne their articles, and
haue not aunſvvered the ſame. For the
vvorke it ſelfe folovvinge doth ſufficiently
aunſvvere them, or the moſt part of them,
as thou ſhalt vvell perceiue in the
readinge of the ſame.

FINIS.

151. R. WATKINS I Ambrose, Saint *Twoo bookes*. 1561
STC 549 Tanner 75 Sig. A8v

fore tellyng the matter playnely: and ceasſing further particulers beyonde that age, that men ſhoulde reſt in the playnnes of his worde, as his holy Prophetes then taught of Redemption.

Holy writynges touching theſe poyntes, I haue ioyned togeather. The playnnes whereof, yf any ſtryue to ouerthrow, I wyll no more yeelde to him, then *Iob* woulde to *Eliphaz, Zophar*, and *Bildad*. Although many differ in their Chronicles, yet theſe places onely being noted, all ſtrife ceaſſeth. One, that after *Terahs* death, *Abraham* at ſeuentie and fiue yeeres olde, receyued the Promiſe: whereof I haue diſputed at large in the treatiſe of *Melchiſedek*. An other, that three hundreth and ninetie yeeres. *Ezek*.4. are from *Ieroboams* drawyng *Iſrael* away to the burnyng of the Temple, with the third captiuitie: which time, both in particulers, many haue caſt aright: and for the general ſumme theſe agree: *Iohn Caluin* vpon *Ezek*.4. *Gerard Mercator, Clement Schubert, Math. Beroald, Ioſeph Scaliger, Henry Bunting*. An other is, that *Nebuchad-nezars* houſe reigned but ſeuentie yeres: which the *Talmud*, wherin lieth all Countrey-Iewes conſent, expreſſely holdeth: alſo olde *Tatianus* in *Euſebius*, and old *Grecians* commonly, no leſſe of antiquity then the Apoſtles age: in hym, and in *Clemens*, with late writers very many, from *Dan*.1. and *Ier*.25. and the common rate of ages, in ſuch as were caried captiue: and ſaw both the fyrſt Temple, and the ſeconde buylded. The fourth knot is, the Seauens of *Daniel*: wherein the proprietie, as *Daniel* vnderſtoode it, and penned it, ſhoulde ſuffiſe.

Theſe foure places ryghtly holden, ende the endles controuerſies. Reade the textes, and vnderſtand them. The Lord teach vs ſo to number our dayes, that we may bring the hart to wyſedome.

H. B.

152. R. WATKINS 2 Broughton, H. *Textes of scripture*. 1591
STC 3888 Malone 655* Sig. A3r

that ſilence is farre to bee preferred before ſpeech: but ſpecially a man ought to keepe his owne ſecrets. For as Seneca ſaith, If thou art not able to keepe thyne owne ſecrets, how canſt thou require an other man to doe it? And therefore the Prouerb ſaith, Thou ſhalt be counted diſcrete and wiſe, if thou kepeſt thy ſecrets to thy ſelf, and that a man bringeth him ſelfe in ſubiection by ſpeech, but ſhall neuer bee harmed by ſilence.

88.

But yet I would not haue thee heere,
to be ſo ſtraightly tyed:
That from thy deere & ſpeciall friend
thou ſhouldſt thy doings hide.
For why? it were to great offence,
t'abuſe his friendſhip ſo:
And euen the redyeſt way it were,
to make thy friend thy foe.

The Paraphraſe.

SEneca in his third epiſtle ſetteth downe, the way and meane how to get freends, and being gotten, how to kepe them, ſaying

to

153. R. WATKINS 3 Lopez de Mendoza, I. *The proverbes of.* 1579
STC 16809 Crynes 886 Sig. N6v

That by our Nephew was in triumph led?
Gen. It was my Liege, the Prince of Portingale.
King But what was he that on the other side,
Helde him by th'arme as partner of the prize?
Hiero. That was my Sonne my gracious Soueraigne,
Of whom, though from his tender infancie,
My louing thoughtes did neuer hope but well:
He neuer pleasd his fathers eyes till now,
Nor fild my hart with ouer cloying ioyes.
King. Goe let them march once more about these walles,
That staying them, we may conferre and talke
With our braue prisoner, and his double Guard.
Hieronimo, it greatly pleaseth vs,
That in our victorie thou haue a share,
By vertue of thy worthy Sonnes exployt. *Enter againe.*
Bring hither the young Prince of Portingale,
The rest march on: but ere they be dismist,
We will bestow on euery Souldier two Duckets,
And on euery Leader ten, that they may know
Our larges welcomes them.
Exeunt all but Bal. Lor. Hor.
Welcome *Don Balthazar*, welcome Nephew,
And thou *Horatio* thou art welcome too:
Yong prince, althought thy fathers hard misdeedes,
In keeping backe the tribute that he owes,
Deserue but euill measure at our hands:
Yet shalt thou know that Spaine is honourable.
Balt. The trespasse that my father made in peace,
Is now contrould by fortune of the warres:
And cardes once dealt, it boots not aske why so,
His men are slaine, a weakening to his Realme,
His colours ceazd, a blot vnto his name,
His sonne distrest, a corsiue to his heart,
These punishments may cleare his late offence.
King. I *Balthazar*, if he obserues this truce,
Our peace will grow the stronger for these warres:
Meane while liue thou as though not in libertie,

154. W. WHITE I Kyd, T. *The Spanish tragedie.* 1602
STC 15089 Malone 234(1) Sig. B1r

to the poore. There need no ſuch wiſedome and learning for that. And when it is further remembred (as afore) that ſome of the 70. Diſciples were choſen to this Deaconſhip, and they being all of them Preachers, it can neuer enter into the heart of a reaſonable man, to thinke that they ſhould be pulled downe from an higher Chaire to a lower. *Nam qui prouehitur, prouehitur a Minorj ad Majus.* Doubtleſſe then, they (as their name ſignifieth) did *ſeruice*, not onely to the people in caſe of Meate and Money; but alſo, to the Biſhops in the caſe of Doctrine and Sacrament. And hereof we are further aſſured, in that all Antiquitie puts no other kind of Deacons into our hands, and for ſuch reſpect doth diuers times call them *Leuites*. And thus the old and new Teſtament, is ſtill more harmonious.

If ſince the Ten grieuous Perſecutions, the Miniſters of the one and other Order, haue come in the world to greater eſtate in outward thinges (a grieuous thing to ſoare eyes) what wonder is it, when for 300. yeares after Chriſt, the Church was vnder the gouernment of Heathen Tyrants, enemies to Chriſtianitie? Soone after 300. yeares, *Conſtantine* the Great, became Chriſtian; by whoſe example and motiue, many inferiour Kinges became Chriſtians alſo. Whereupon followed, freedome of the Fayth, and peace and plentie in all Churches. Then our Fathers counted it an holy duetie, to builde materiall Churches, and to endowe the Spirituall with euery good thing wanting. True it is, that ſuch temporarie bleſsinges haue ſince that time, been foulely prophaned. What then? So hath Heauen and Earth, and all their continentes; ſhall we therefore ſpurne at the creature? Indeed, while ſome ſo ſpurne, others ſacrilegiouſly ſnatch to themſelues all. To the Miniſter it ſhould be but an Idolathite; but to my Church-robber, it is a

155. W. WHITE 2 Clapham, H. *A chronological discourse*. 1609
STC 5336 4° C.87Th Sig. F3r

the Walnut, the Almond, the Cherie, the Figge, the Abricock, the Muske Rose, and a great sort of others, both Trees and Plants, beeing some Persians, some Scythians some Armenians, some Italians, some French, all strangers and aliantes, were brought in as noueltiesamongst vs, that doe now most of them as well, yea, and some of them better, beeing planted amongst vs in England, then if they were at home. I haue also been carefull about the planting and ordering of the Vine, (though some of my friendes would haue had it omitted, as altogether impertinent to our countrey: because I am fully perswaded if diligence, and good husbandrie might be vsed) we might haue a reasonable good Wine growing in many places of this Realme: as vndoubtedly we had immediatly after the Conquest, till partly by slothfulnesse, not liking any thing long that is painfull, partly by Ciuill discord long continuing it was left, and so with time lost, as appeareth by a number of places in this Realme, that keepes still the name of Vineyardes: and vppon many Cliffes and Hilles, are yet to be seene the rootes, and olde remaines of Vines. There is besides Notingham, an auncient house called Chilwell, in which house remaineth yet as an auncient monument in a great windowe of glasse, the whole order of planting, proyning, stamping, and pressing of Vines. Besides, there is yet also growing an old Vine, that yeeldes a Grape sufficient to make a right good Wine, as was lately proued by a Gentlewoman in the said house. There hath moreouer good experience of late yeeres been made, by two Noble and honorable Barons of this Realme, the Lord Cobham, and the Lord Villiams of Tame, who both had growing about their houses as good Vines, as are in many places of Fraunce. And if they answere not in all pointes euery mans expectation, the fault is rather to be imputed to the malice and disdaine peraduenture of the Frenchmen that kept them, then to any ill disposition, or fault of the soyle. For where haue you in any place better, or pleasanter Wines, then about Backrach, Colin, Andernach, and diuers other places of Germany, that haue in maner the selfe same latitude and disposition of the Heauens that we haue? Beside, that the nearenesse to the South, is not altogether the causer of good Wines, appeareth in that you haue about Orleans, great store of

good

156. T. WIGHT I Heresbach, C. *Foure bookes of husbandry.* 1601
STC 13200 Douce H.H.255 Sig. A3v

holy Apostles published to all the world, and taught all nations by Christes commandement. For I thought my duetie first vnto God, and then to my gracious prince, to shew some token of my thankefull mind, and secondly to acknowledge my bounden duetie to Christes Church here among vs, my deare mother, in whose wombe I freely confesse my selfe to be bgotten and borne one of Gods children, and though of thousands the most vnworthie yet one of the seruants of Christ and of his congregation in the ministerie of his Gospell. And especially that I might call to remembrance and set before the eyes of my louing country men, my louing and faithfull brethren and sisters in Christ, the assurednesse of truth and the good treasure of God among vs: namely that wee are lighted vpon that heauenly pearle (blessed be God) for which a man would sell all that he hath: that this might bee some meanes to blow away the ashes from the cooling zeale of some: stirre vp and awake some that are now readie to sleepe, and bring backe againe some, (if it please God) which are readie to go out of the way: and that I might admonish others that they receiue not the grace of God in vaine. For when a man shall thinke with himselfe (and well way it in his heart) that we haue the true faith which is vnchaungeable, by which all Gods elect are saued: will it not moue him to bestir himselfe, that he neglect not so great saluation, and that he trie euerie spirit, before he beleeue, and that he be not caried away with the vaine shew of ostentation in men of schoole learning: but whomsoeuer he heare with the men of Berea to search the Scriptures whether those things be so? yea though it were Paule or an Angel from heauen should preach another doctrine then that wee haue receiued, we should hold him accursed. I pray God for Christes sake to bee mercifull vnto mee, that as he put into mine hart to take this worke in hand, &

thing being obſerued , as in the figured rayes aboue

Front.

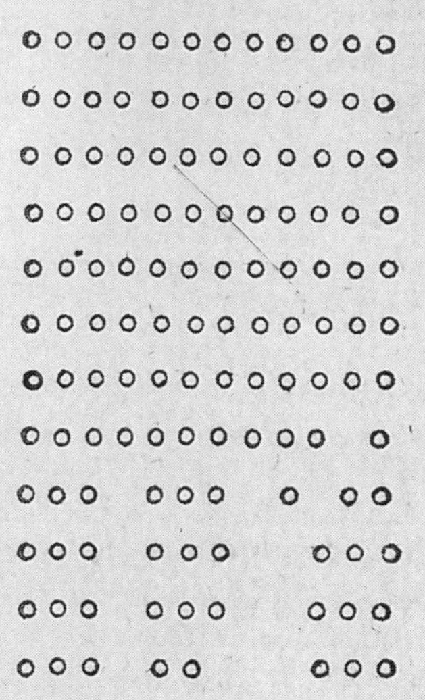

written, they ſame battales, ſhal be transformed in this other maner, like vnto the laſt figure , that is, thoſe 12. voide places ſhalbe tranſlated into the reward, as plainlye maye be ſeene.

¶ How to chaunge with ſpeede an Armie, that is, in battelray foureſquare, into a triangell fashiō, without diſordering the firſt ranckes, and without perill of confuſion. Cap. xix.

158. W. WILLIAMSON Machiavelli, N. *The arte of warre.* 1573
STC 17165 Antiq e.E.1573/4 Sig. D1r

¶ To the friendlie Readers,

Sailers and Mariners.

SEing by the positiue & diuine law of God, all men be generallie bound any way they are able, to be profitable and helpefull to their brethren, countrie & common welth, for whose sakes, as much as for their owne, they are borne and created, how can we but iudge verie hardly of their meanings and intentions, who publish and commit to the view of the world, their trauailes and labors to no other end, but to reape thereby, either priuate gaine, or popular applause and commendation, as though indeed they were not therevnto by dutie bound, with their whole studie, care, endeuour, and all faculties of their mind whatsoeuer. From which sort of ambitious persons, as my owne conscience doth cleerely exempt me: so yet neuerthelesse, I feare that I shall hardly scape the hard censures and cryticall doome of many *Lynces*, whose glancing penetrancie and quicke eisight, being able (as the fable reporteth) to looke through the stone wall, will (no doubt) be readie inough to encounter my honest meaning in simplicitie, & be a great deale forwarder to find faults, thā able to amend faults. Howsoeuer such seuere Stoickes shall daine to think of me, my owne conscience acquiteth me of all sinister pretence, and what peremptorie sentence soeuer shall be pronounced vpon me, I doubt not but the better moitie of the Marine sort (for whose vse this present worke is especially published) will accept in worth these my paines and trauailes.

Neither neede I to feare (as I hope) any sinister cōstruction at the hands of those, which with indifferencie will weigh my meaning, and without preiudicate opinions cōsider my laboures. For as the worke is the obseruations and collections of diuers and sundrie experimented trauailers: So

godlie aſſertion? And the auctors too,who are theie? Not nightbirds? Not light hedded,and fugitiue perſons? Not our profeſſed and knowen enimies?

It maie not be denied, but ſome do with-hold their pens from approuing that holie booke in euerie point by ſubſcription: yet are there none,I truſt,that proudlie contemne it, none that diſdainfulie deſpiſe it,none but in the feare of God,and in pub.Churches alwaies, and onely doe vſe it,and manie haue ſet their hands there-unto,and al,I doubt not but ſo would, were that which is offenſiue, reformed; and that which is crooked, made ſtreight; and that which is doubtful, made euident and plaine. Which things alſo are for number but verie fewe,and, therefore maie the more eaſilie be remoued: aud remaine,for the moſt part,in the directions and rubricks, and therefore with leſſe offence may be taken awaie.

Neither doth anie miniſter of the word,that I heare,denie by ſubſcription to allow the booke concerning the Articles,& ſumme of our faith,but what lawes do exact,or enioine moſt willinglie haue theie offered to performe. And no cauſe is there whie we ſhould not ſo doe: the auctors of the ſame do moue; the ſoueraigne authoritie,whereby it was eſtabliſhed,and is vpholden,doth moue; but the neceſſarie,and al Chriſtian doctrine there-in compriſed, doth moſt of al moue vs, not onlie in heart to like thereof, but with mouth alſo,and euerie waie to praiſe it, and to glorifie the goodnes of God for the ſame. Our fore-fathers manie of them deſired to ſee that, though it were but ſecretlie, and to the hazarding of their lands,goods,and liues, which in that booke we openlie and publiquelie to our vnſpeakable comfort,and profit do ſee maintained.

Beſides,it is the badge of Eng.Chriſtians whereby we are knowen to the vniuerſal worlde not onlie to agree with al the godlie that haue bine or do liue at this preſent in the material points of religion:but alſo to diſagree from the Iewes,Turks,Papiſts, Anabaptiſts, and al other prophane men. So that theie, or he which ſhal with-drawe his hand from allowing the ſame, maie vehementlie be ſuſpected to be a contemner of the ſacred auctoritie of this noble realme, and of the doctrine of Chriſt; a diſſenter not onlie from al the godlie in this land, and therfore not worthie to liue among vs:but alſo from the true Chriſtians who both haue liued heretofore,and remaine in anie reformed Church at this preſent time; and a fauorer either of the Iewiſh, or Turkiſh, or Popiſh,or Anabaptiſtical, or ſome vngodlie,and curſed opinion,or other.

Theis things(one of the weakeſt of my brethren knowne I confeſſe, yet through confidence iu our chiefe captaine Ieſus Chriſt,whoſe al power is *u*) I haue vndertaken to proue in two books or treatiſes: the former wherof is now before you,the other in good time, if ſo it pleaſe God,ſhal come abroad,In which aduiſedlie looke,and yee ſhal perceiue, that the Religion eſtabliſhed by the auctoritie,aud profeſſed of al degrees in this land,is neither a falſe religion, as the Papiſts do thinke,ſtil tearming it(how like Chriſtians iudge yee)*vngrateful hæreſie* x,*barbarous hæreſie* y, *brutiſh hæreſie* z, *cruel hæreſie* a, *wicked hæreſie* b, *wild condemned hæreſie* c, *diueliſh doctrine* d, but founded and built vpon the immouable fundations which the true Apoſtles of Ieſus Chriſt, and the Prophets haue laid,and therefore cannot deceiue; nor *a new religion* e, *a newe faith* f, *a newe and barbarous Goſpel* g, *a newe hæreſie* h, (as the Antichriſtians,and prieſtes of the breaden God woulde perſwade, and make their credulous companie to beleeue) *found-out by Zwinglius*, whom they cal, *The vnfortunate father of our Eng.faith* i, *and not extant in England aboue* 5. *or* 6. *yeres before the ſhort reigne of K. Edward the ſixt* k, but the moſt ancient,receiued euen from Chriſt himſelfe,and his written word; nor, *A wicked religion tending vnto Paganiſme,& Epicuriſme* l,but that the man of God maie be abſolute,being made perfect vnto al good workes *m*, nor at this preſent taught in a corner of the world by vs onlie,but with a ſweete harmonie and conſent of al the Churches proteſtant in Europe publiquelie embraced.

u. *Matth*.28,18.
x. *Anſwer to the Execut. of Iuſtice* c.6,p.128.
y. *Ibi*.c.1.p.4. c.4.p.71.
z. *Ibi*.c.6.p,126.
a. *Ibi*.c.1,p.11.
b. *Ibi*.c.6.p,132.
c *Ibi*.c.5.p,103.
d. *Ibi* c.8.p.166.
e. *Anſwere to the Execut. of Iuſtice in the præf.* & c.3,p.13.c.4.p.82. c.8.p,182.
f. *Ibi*.c.8.p,172.
g. *Anſwer to the Execut. of Iuſtice* c.4,p.83.
h *Ibi*.c.8.p.166.
i. *Ibi*.c.4,p.80.
k. *Ibi* c.3.
l. *Ibi* c.8,p.169.
m. 2.*Tim*,3.17.

Againe,beſides that al the enimies of name,which the truth hath had from time to time euen til this verie houre be here diſcouered,yee ſhal ſo cleerlie and plainlie beholde, as anie thing yee maie when the Sunne gloriouſlie doth ſhow himſelf,that *Poperie is not the onlie true worſhip of God* n; that *Poperie is not conſonant to* (God) *his ſacred word and wil* o; but planted by weake & wicked men; that *Poperie is not the old Religion* p,but a new,or more trulie a loathſome Chaos of all condemned hereſies,and antichriſtian opinions;and that Poperie agreeth not with the church of God in this land,or in anie other countrie or citie,almoſt in no one ſubſtantial & material point of Chriſtianitie,

u. *Aunſwer to the Execut. of Iuſtice*, c,5,p.103.
o. *Ibi* c,8,p,180.
p. *Ibi* c.2,p,19. c.3,p,36. c,9,p,211

160. J. WINDET 2a Rogers, T. *The English creede*. 1585
STC 21226.5 N.2.7.Jur(R) Sig. *3r

phets of the Apostles, & other holy men of whom the word of God beareth witnesse: they will not allow that the writings of the Prophets and Apostles shall be the tents of these shepheards, of whome Christ speaketh: they hold not that to be the only holesome pasture, with which they feed Gods people. And they will haue men looke to the steps of certaine Popes, Cardinals, Monkes, Friers, and a deale of such vermine, which for the space of some fiue or sixe hundreth yeares hath crawled vpon the earth. They send vs to the decrees of Popes and popish Prelates, and to their owne constitutions, there wil they haue the tents of the shepheardes to be, and the wholesome pastures. What a blindnes is it in all those which cannot see that these bee very theeues and murtherers? For when Christ willeth vs to goe forth by the steppes of the sheepe, and to feede by the tentes of the shepheardes: what sheepe but those whome hee hath giuen testimonie vnto by his word, that they were his faithfull worshippers? Where shall wee seeke the Church but in the holy scriptures of the Apostles and prophets? When he speaketh of the tents of the shepheards which fed and guided those ancient flockes, whom shall we take then to be but onely those whom he hath declared to bee his seruantes? euen the holie Apostles and Prophets? Then marke these popish seducers. They teach many strange doctrines contrary to the doctrine of the Apostles and reproueth, and as it were condemneth vs for our ſinnes. For God taketh no pleaſure in dealing with vs after this maner, but becauſe he knoweth the neceſsitie thereof. So then looke how many threatenings, ſentences of condemnation, of reproofes, and ſuch like are in the holy ſcripture, they are euen ſo many Mallettes to knocke vs on the heads, to bring vs vnto that humilitie which wee are ſo farre from, vntill ſuch time as hee hath violently in ſuch ſorte mortified vs. And thus much for this ſtraine. Moreouer, we muſt come to a larger account and reckening of that which hath bin already ſpoken, which is, that vntill ſuch time as we haue beheld our miſeries in the word of God, wee ſhall be lulled in a dead ſleepe in our hypocriſie & become very careles: and this ſecuritie will cauſe vs to contemne the word of God, and ſo by little and little be quite and cleane excluded from it. Now God hath ſet before vs our condemation, namely in the lawe: and in verie deed all the ſcripture is full of them: and when it is ſaid, that it is profitable, amongſt other thinges, it layeth out the reproofes. And beſides, we knowe what the Ghoſpell teacheth, *Repent and amend, for the kingdome of God is at hand.* Thus wee ſee how God diſpoſeth his elect to receiue the free righteouſnes

2.Tim.3.16.
Mat.3.2. & 4.17.

162. J. WINDET 3 Calvin, J. *Sermons on Melchisedech.* 1592
STC 4440 Mason AA.234 Sig. K4r

Vincenti Maximo

De Rege nostro Serenissimo, eiusque pro

genie clarissima poema

ἐυχαριστικον.

AD: IACOBVM: MAGNAE: BRITANNIAE

A great red *Dragon*, with 7. heads & 10. hornd power,
Design'd of late a soveraign Queene quite to deuour:
Intending eke, that *Son* to strike, for whom she gron'd
Affright whereat, to her good *God*, she timely mon'd,
Conspecting then *Iehovah* this his handmaides greefe
Omitted not with readie hand, to grant reliefe.
But first, her sweet *Soule* he convaighd (as seem'd him
Vnto his princely pallace there in peace to rest. (best)
Moreover, then he *Michael* with army stout,
Maugre the foe, sent forth in field, & cast him out.
And so, that when the tragedie should be effected,
God it withstood, & those complots in time detected.
Now sith the *Dragon* saw his purpose thus prevented,
And quaild himselfe, he might have coucht & so repē
Expecting pardon: but no lesse he erst reviv'd, (ted.
Bruite stratagems, and quaint designes by him cōtriv'd
Recounting, that loud lowing *Buls* might pierce deep
In roiall Lyons heart, and princely Vnicorne (lorne
That so, the *seede* right soveraigne (amongst the rest)
And all the flowers of this field should bee supprest:
Not by the lore of sacred lawes, or iustice right:
Nor with the dinte of valiant sword, or open fight
In manly wise: but savadgely, with stygian flame
And hellish hounds, attempted how to forge the same
Enlarging so his beastly bent, God him there staid,

¶4 Restraining

163. J. WINDET 4 Carpenter, J. *Schelomonocham.* 1606
STC 4666 4° C.90Th Sig. ¶4r

To the Reader.

HE who euer hath ſeene rebellions diſcouered, he that hath knowne that Traitors liue like Moles, who worke vnſeene till they be thrown vp to their deaths, and liue abroad like Flyes who ſucke the ſweete of others, yet infect them, ſhall find by this diſcourſe that Religion is made the Target to defend Treaſon: Ambition, the Originall, and confuſion the end. Yet for thy further ſatisfaction (Reader) that this diſcourſe & euery particular relation therein, may haue credit in thy iudgement, know, that there is nothing therein mentioned, but is to be approued by diuers Merchants and men of credite, now reſident in this Citty, and that in reading thereof, thou maiſt witneſſe to thy ſelfe, that this wonder and ſtroke of heauen vpon them, is reuealed and ſent vnto thee as a warning peece ſhot off, to admoniſh thee that thou fall not into the preſumption into which theſe Ieſuits and their Deſciples run headlong. I haue as in a map or Dutch Lanskip, ſhewed thee a Module in half an howers reading, of what held them two dayes in action: as the maner of the place where they played, the forme of their repreſenting heauen and hell, the dignitie wherein the Actors ſat, the cauſes wherevpon they prepared this iudgement: namely, Ambition (whoſe end is alwaies as theirs was, deſtruction) In any part of which, if thou beeſt eyther ſatisfied or admoniſhed, my paines were a pleaſure vnto mee.

164. J. WINDET 5 S., R. *The Jesuits play at Lyons*. 1607
STC 21514 4632b23 (BL) Sig. A3r

ſpondent to the auncient purpoſe of their predeceſſors who made themſelues *Charlemagnes* heires, ſo to ground a pretence to this realme, and perceiuing that they could find no hope to come to their purpoſe ſo long as it cõtinued whole, endeuoured by the continuation of the troubles, to ſcatter and deſtroy it. And indeede theſe men a yeare or two before procured a booke to be printed purpoſely, which (though falſely) prooued them to be diſcended from thence, and ſo conſequently true heires, and our kinges vſurpers of the crowne, for the which the auctor made amendes honorable in the kinges full counſaile. But when they ſee the Duke of *Aniou* deceaſed, the king to haue no children, and the king of *Nauarre*, chiefe Prince of the bloud, through his religion (as they thought) eſtranged from the peoples fauour, they imagined the way to be then open to their extreemẽ ambition, and the ſeaſon to growe fitte for the hatching of their driftes. Then beganne they afreſh to kindle their practiſes and conuenticles to ſearch out all malcontentes, whether iuſtly or wrongfully, to treat with the king of *Spaine*, and ſuch other potentates as enuied our realme, wherof in ſhort ſpace ſprong vp this curſſed warre of the *League*, which ſince hath kindled and conſumed our poore eſtate. Then by their publike proteſtation they required the king to name his heire, and the ſame a catholike prince, namely, the Cardinall of *Bourbon*, ſo to exclude the king of *Nauarre*. This did they, becauſe that they knew that they could not climbe ſo high but by degrees, and they would either gouerne or rule in *France* vnder the wings of the ſaid Cardinall: and now imagine you what a preſuppoſition this was, had there beene no deceit, that the ſaid lord Cardinall a prince alreadie verie old, ſhould ſuruiue our king being in the flower of his age. The king of *Nauarre*, whither by his right or by his vertue ſtopped their paſſage: hereupon they declare him to be an heretike, and ſo do pretend him to bee depriued of all the rights belonging to the blood of *France*: but note that the king of *Nauarre* alwaies proteſted that he ſubmitted himſelfe to a free counſell, offering thereby to be inſtructed, and proteſting that vntill then he could not be deemed an heretike. They do ſo feare leaſt hee ſhoulde returne into the *Romiſh church*, and thereby

165. J. WOLFE 1a *A caueat for France*. 1588
STC 11259 4° L.90Art Sig. A3r

1 Cor. 15. John 12.24 The wheat and other seede, though it dye and rot in the ground: yet springeth vp more beautiful then before. Plinie. It is written how certain summer birds lye dead all winter, and reuiue in the Lactantius. spring. The Phenix being burnt vnto ashes, yet of the same ashes is bred to liue againe.

So though our bodies layd shall be,
to rot in lothsome graue:
Yet afterwards in glorious state,
more bewty they shall haue:
When death hath held them downe awhile.
Anon they shall arise,
Eternally in ioy to liue
With Christ aboue the skyes.

Chapter V.

The passage to Paradise is aptly compared to a warfare.

PLato calleth a Philosophers life, a meditation of death. But it may truly be said, that the whole race of a Christian mans life: is nothing else, but a continuall warfare. For as the Israelites Beginning and ending in the hart. by bodily resistance, did assaile, fyght against, and ouercome seuen Nations, before they could obtaine a temporall inheritance, in the land of Canaan: so must Gods children, by spirituall resistance, Deut. 7.1. assaile, fight against, and ouercome their lewd

& that is the cause why there is discord or accord in the figures of *Geomancy*, which obtaine and haue signification, as is largely shewed by al this Booke: which thing being thus, we must of necessity conclude & say, that those things that be vnder the order and gouernement of these Stars or Planets must by naturall inclination be friendes or foes vnto those that be vnder subiection of another Planet or Signe, or Constellation, according to the conformitie or enmitie which is between the Starres gouerning those things. And this enmity is greater & more stronger when betweene the natures and qualities of the Planets to whom they be subiect, there is a great repugnancie. And contrariwise, the amitie is the better, when the conformity is great amongest the Planets, all which thing extendeth aswell vnto man as beast. True it is, that men being of a francke and liberall wil, although they feele in themselues this repugnance and inclination, they may by grace withstand it. But beastes which be depriued & exempted out of this priuilege, they yeeld themselues to be gouerned by the naturall inclination, and put the same in effect as much as they can: and the like do herbs and plants. As touching the amitie and good will which is amongst men, the Astrologians doe say, yea *Ptolomy* their Prince, that those men, which in the time of their natiuitie haue one very signe for their ascendant, shall willingly loue together. And likewise those which haue ☉ and ☽ in one signe wil loue together. They further say, that those which haue one very signe for gouernour in their natiuitie, that ingendreth between them a naturall loue, and conformitie of nature. And although that this be one verie Planet; it is also sufficient if there were two, so that they were friends, & not foes, or els be in one good aspect, which thing you may knowe, in making the figure of the natiuitie of the one and of the other. And this also maketh much to their conformitie, that is, if in that parte Fortune be all in one Signe or House, and that the House or Signe where ☽ shalbe in the natiuity of the one, be in good aspect to the other: for according as they haue more or lesse of these conditions, are to bee readde onlye of masters in ſuche arte, that can iudge the chaffe from the corne. and Ptolemye that worthye writer and myracle in nature, is to harde for younge ſchollars, except they be fyrſte inſtructed not onlye in the principles of the Sphere, but alſo well traded in Euclides his Geometrye, and alſo well exerciſed in the Theorykes of the Planetes. But nowe let me ſee the table that you haue collected.

1 The ordre and mouinges of the nine Spheres.
2 The ſpaces of their reuolutions by their propre motions.
3 The forme of heauen is rounde, and his mouynges circulare.
4 The earthe is rounde in forme, and the water alſo.
5 The earthe is in the myddle and Centre of the worlde, and is but as a pointe in compariſon to the Firmamente, and doth not moue anye waies.
6 The compaſſe of the earthe, and the diameter of it, what they make in common myles.
7 Of the circles in heauen what is theyr iuſte quantityes, their numbre, their ordre, their diſtaunce, and their offices.
8 Whye the Zodiake hath that name, and whether anye ſuche formes bee in the ſkye.
9 The diuers ſignifications of a figure, and the declyninge of them.
There are two Horizontes, one ſenſible, and the other onlye iudged by reaſon, and what the quantities of them bothe are.
10 The Greekes and the Latines doo not agree in the deſcription of the circles Arctike and Antarctike, and what are theyr reaſons.
11 Whether there bee anye dwellers in the Vntemperate Zones.
12 What bee the circles Verticall and circles of Heighte, the circles of howers, and of the twelue houſes.
13 Of the ryſinge and ſettynge of the Signes and other Starres, bothe in the Ryghte ſphere, and alſo in the Bowing ſphere, after the Aſtronomers.
14 Of the Latitude of the Sonne and the twelue Signes from the eaſte and weſte.
15 Of the riſinge and ſetting of the ſtarres, after the mynd of the poetes.
16 Of the diuerſitie of Naturall daies, as well as of Artificiall daies in diuers partes of the earthe.
17 The diuerſities of howers, wherof ſome ar equall, and other vnequall

168. R. WOLFE 1a Record, R. *The castle of knowledge.* 1556
STC 20796 K.48Art Sig. I2r

peneth vnto it by occasiõ, as ỹ they be shaped in certain figures, fashioned & deuided into mẽbres, and ỹ thei are cold or warm, black or white, or grey, & such like, thei haue no place in god, who is not of body, but a spirit: wherfore the errour of ỹ Anthropomorphites, is to be condẽned, which attributeth vnto god a body framed & disposed into mẽbres, accordig vnto ỹ fashiõ of mã: Yet is it manifest, ỹ there be some thigs in God, in respect of ỹ which it may be knowẽ, though not perfectly, yet somdeale of what mãner sort he is. As of what mãner essence or being, what substãce & nature he is of. In very deede, these things of thẽselues are vnsearcheable in God, but yet some part there is of thẽ necessarie to know, & is expressed in scriptures by ỹ spirit of reuelatiõ, ỹ consideratiõ wherof, as I iudge, pertaineth to this place. There be no qualities of body in God. In what poin tes the qualis te of God is.

Of what manner sort God is in the consideration of his Essence.

Of the Essẽce or being of God, beside ỹ it is the fountain & beginning of all thinges ỹ be, first it may be said ỹ it is only one, hauing none like neither in heauen nether in the earth: & therfore maketh only one God, excluding altogether the nũbre of gods, wherby ỹ Gentiles wer deceiued. To this place belongeth ỹ which is read in holy scriptures of the vnite of God, as in the. 6. of Deuteronomie: Heare Israel, ỹ lord thy God is one God. And in the. 44. & .45. of Esay: Besides mee, he saith, there is no other God. And in the eyght of the first to the Corinthiãs: We know that there is no ydole in the world, and that there is no other God but one. And in the. 4. to the Ephe. One God and father of all, which is ouer all and by all. What is sayd of the Essence of God. Of the vnite of the essense of God. *Deut.6.* *1.Corinth.8.*

This vnite of God ỹ Philosophers of ỹ gẽtiles did acknowledge. Plato doth manifestly defend the Monarchie or sole gouernãce of God. Aristotle witnesseth, that one minde and vnderstanding gouerneth the worlde. And Cicero folowing Plato, in many places confesseth one God. Of the poets Vergil spake in this sort of God. *Ephesians.4.*

For God doth passe through all the landes,
The waues of sea and through the sandes.
The deapth of heauen both whote and colde, *Geor.4.*
Frõm him come beast both yong and olde:
Both wilde and tame, and man also
Hath strength and life, both frende and foe.

And Ouide in the first boke of his transformatiõ doth clerely attribute ỹ workmanship of the whole world to one God alone. Wise men saw ỹ the world could nether haue ben made, neither after ỹ it was made colde haue been gouerned by many, bicause of ỹ vnspeakable and most constant agremẽt of all thinges (which doth most certainely proue the vnite of the true God) and ỹ could not be wout dauger, if many gods had the gouernance therof: So ỹ the strife and battels of the gods of the gentiles are not wout purpose set forth by Homere. Wherefore it is a mockery to talk wt them, which bicause, of the hughnes of thinges created, supposeth this world cã not be gouerned of one, as though one were not able to susteine so great a waight of thinges, but that it neded many. The reason of wisemen. The folishnes of the which maketh many goddes.

1 First they faile in this, that they considre ỹ hughnes of the workmãship either alone either more than they do the maiesty & power of the worker, so ỹ they think the work passeth the strength of the worker: as though the maker were not greater & more puissãt than ỹ work which he hath made. The creatour is greater thã the worke which hee created.

2 Againe they be fond in this point, ỹ they suppose ỹ world may be better gouerned of many gods thã of one, like as it is in mẽs cases, ỹ two are

169. R. WOLFE 1b Musculus, W. *Commonplaces of Christian religion.* 1563
STC 18308 4° Δ 339 Sig. A5r

To the Reader.

enormities,in part alſo he renounceth his Canons,as in the 94.Cap.appeareth,he inueigheth againſt the foule abuſes of Biſhops,Abbotes, Monkes, and Freers, and other ſuche like,defending alſo the Royal preſence of Chriſt his body. It is likely,that if he had ben in as good a time as this is,he would haue don accordingly, but being in a corrupt time, he did as the time required:where darknes is, menne muſte needes fale,and where wickednes raigneth,menne of force become naught. Like as the poiſonous Cokatrice infecteth all thinges , ſo oftentimes the ſhadowe of naughty menne hurteth the good. One euill corrupteth an other,and euill put to euill, is cauſe of mutuall deſtruction : *Epictetus* the Stoicke Philoſopher ſaithe: Vnderſtande,if thy companiō ſhalbe defiled,that he alſo whom he ſhal touch muſt needes be defiled, notwithſtandinge he were cleane before:wherefore his faulte is to be aſcribed to the time wherin he liued, and to the parſons with whom he was conuerſaunt. I conferred an *Jtalian* tranſlation with the Latine Copie,in the whiche I founde more then was mencioned in the Latine, whiche I haue put into my tranſlation , the places where this is added,are in the *96.98.* 100.101. Cap.betweene twoo ſtarres with this forme ⋆ placed in the Margent. I coniecture that this booke in the *Jtalian* was tranſlated out of that Copie,whiche the Authoure firſt publiſhed,and ſince that time other bookes of the ſame ſort haue ben printed, and in printing ſome thinges haue ben either depraued by negligence, or lefte out of pourpoſe , becauſe they ſharply inueigh againſte the Popes folowers , whiche coniecture is likelieſt,for negligence of the Printer woulde haue appeared aſwell in other places,as in theſe, if he beinge rechleſſe, had don things without aduiſement. VVherfore(friendly Reader) wel conſtrue my doinges,take in good part my labours,amende the faultes that are ouerpaſſed in printinge, and defende this againſte the malitious detractions of enuious *Zoilus*, then ſhall I accompte thee my friende, thinke my time well ſpente,and my paines requited.

170. H. WYKES Agrippa, H. C. *Of the vanitie of artes and sciences*. 1569
STC 204 Douce A.278 Sig. *4r

within their owne, and told me, that before they would declare vnto me a certeine busines of great importance, Thou must giue vnto vs thy faith & homage to keepe it so secrete, that although thou happen to be taken there, of the English, thou shalt not discouer this secrete, because it importeth the quietnes of all Christendome. And after I had giuen them my worde and faith, with all fidelitie and seruice in such an affaire, They tolde mee, *Steuen Ferrera de Gama*, hath written to vs, how D. *Lopez* hath offred and bound himselfe to kill the Queene of England with poyson, with condition the King of Spaine should recompence his seruices according to the qualitie of them. All which passed in the citie of Bruxels in the house of the *Counte de Fuentes*, and as farre as I can remember, it was the 9. day of December past. All this I certifie to haue passed in great truth and certentie, and do affirme it vnder mine othe.

I *Manuell Lewis Tinoco*, a Portingale Gentleman, doe confesse that it is true, that being in Bruxels, in the house of the *Counte Fuentes*, hee caused me to bee called for, and demanded of mee of what qualitie and Countrey *Andrada* was: And after that I had tolde him all that I knew of him, he commanded his Secretarie to shew me all the letters that *Andrada* had written to him from Calice: He shewed me three letters, In the first he signified, that he was come from England, where he had beene prisoner a long time, and that he was sent by order of Doctor *Lopez*, who as a man very zealous and friendly to the seruice of the King of Castile, was determined to doe the King such a peece of seruice, as thereby hee might with great

Printed in Great Britain at the University Press, Cambridge